KV-575-303

Macromedia® Director™ Game Development

From Concept to Creation

BY:

THE ARTISTS, ANIMATORS, AND PROGRAMMERS OF THE EPIC SOFTWARE GROUP

W.I.T.

0 6 NOV 2001

LIBRARY

A DIVISION OF PRIMA PUBLISHING

© 2001 by Prima Publishing. All rights reserved. No part of this book may be reproduced or transmitted in any form or by any means, electronic or mechanical, including photocopying, recording, or by any information storage or retrieval system without written permission from Prima Publishing, except for the inclusion of brief quotations in a review.

A Division of Prima Publishing

Prima Publishing and colophon are registered trademarks of Prima Communications, Inc. PRIMA TECH is a trademark of Prima Communications, Inc., Roseville, California 95661.

Publisher: Stacy L. Hiquet

Associate Marketing Manager: Jennifer Breece

Managing Editor: Sandy Doell

Project Editor: Heather Talbot

Technical Reviewer: Keith A. Davenport

Copy Editor: Kate Welsh

Interior Layout: LJ Graphics: Susan Honeywell and Melissa Mercado

Cover Design: Prima Design Team

Indexer: Sharon Shock

Proofreader: robin grunzweig

Macromedia, Director, Shockwave, and Flash are trademarks or registered trademarks of Macromedia, Inc.

Tetris is a trademark of Nintendo Corporation of America.

Pac-Man is a trademark of Namco Ltd.

Important: Prima Publishing cannot provide software support. Please contact the appropriate software manufacturer's technical support line or Web site for assistance.

Prima Publishing and the author have attempted throughout this book to distinguish proprietary trademarks from descriptive terms by following the capitalization style used by the manufacturer.

Information contained in this book has been obtained by Prima Publishing from sources believed to be reliable. However, because of the possibility of human or mechanical error by our sources, Prima Publishing, or others, the Publisher does not guarantee the accuracy, adequacy, or completeness of any information and is not responsible for any errors or omissions or the results obtained from use of such information. Readers should be particularly aware of the fact that the Internet is an ever-changing entity. Some facts may have changed since this book went to press.

ISBN: 0-7615-3227-7

Library of Congress Catalog Card Number: 00-110734

Printed in the United States of America

01 02 03 04 GG 10 9 8 7 6 5 4 3 2 1

ACKNOWLEDGMENTS

Many people contributed to the ideas and games presented in this book, while others provided encouragement and support. When I founded the epic software group, inc. in 1990, I realized that the most successful projects would be group efforts where each person would contribute his or her best work. And that was indeed the case with *Macromedia Director Game Development: From Concept to Creation*. Without a doubt, it would have remained just another interesting idea had it not been for the combined efforts of our most talented team members. I would like to offer my heart-felt appreciation to the following people:

First and foremost I would like to thank our customers who have allowed us the creative freedom to suggest ideas "outside the box." We seem to learn the most when we attempt to push game development to the edge and come face-to-face with the harsh realities of budgets and deadlines.

Next, I have to say thanks to Kris Jamsa, Ph.D., who believed in this book and was encouraging at every step of the process. As an accomplished writer and editor with more than 80 titles to his credit, Kris helped us understand the importance of style and format.

Of course it was the artists, animators, programmers, and support staff at epic that were instrumental in driving this book to completion. This manuscript was actually written and rewritten a total of three times. The idea began in 1994 when we developed a simple, yet addictive game for a CD-ROM product catalog, which we created for a large corporate client. This game was based on the use of the client's product. The game was included on the CD almost as an afterthought.

Only after the project was completed and the CD was distributed did we realize the value of the game to the client's overall effort to promote its brand. In 1994, electronic catalogs were new. Everyone seemed to like having the product literature in a digital format, but it was the game they all talked about. The most often heard comment was... "How are you going to top that game in next year's electronic catalog?". It was not difficult to convince our client to justify a bigger and better game in the next version.

From that point forth, we began including a game with a corporate twist in the electronic catalogs we created. It gave us a real advantage in the bidding process for new work. One game led to another, and another, until we had a stable of games that could be easily modified for a host of applications—quickly and profitably! The only problem was that Macromedia kept improving Director with a host of new features, so the chapters had to be written and new screen captures completed. So it was with Director 6 and 7, but when Director 8 was released, we were experienced and ready to go.

So I have to thank more than a dozen people who have contributed their efforts to the completion of this book. Yet there is one person, whom above all others drove himself relentlessly to get the book completed on time. His name is Cliff Jones. Cliff is an individual blessed with both artistic talent as well as deep analytical skills. Just point him in the right direction and you can be assured the job will come back better than you had ever hoped for. Besides his other duties, Cliff heads up our team of student interns. Cliff, I thank you for your attention to detail, and for all the long hours you put in on the project.

My thanks also go to Susan Kurtin who managed the day-to-day production along with the technical editing for each chapter. The book has benefited enormously from the numerous and extensive revisions that her suggestions prompted.

Programmers Duke Banerjee, Lars Doucet, Rod Afshar, Nick Toboada, and Vic M. Cherubini, worked relentlessly on revising each chapter of the book until it was perfect. And thanks to our resident 2D and 3D artists Derek Hughes, Danny Duhon, and Cean Aubrey for the wonderful eye candy.

I am also grateful to Robert Bailey for his general management skills, his loyalty, friendship, and his willingness to do whatever it takes to get the job done. If it can be done in Director, Robert knows how to do it! I am also thankful to Sharon Howerton, our office manager, for the many things you do every day that keep our ship afloat.

There are many other people who have helped to create this book and it would be impossible to thank them all by name, but we are very appreciative of their creativity and hard work.

Vic Cherubini

President

epic software group, inc.

Macromedia Director Game Development
From Concept to Creation

CONTENTS AT A GLANCE

Table of Contents

Macromedia Director Game Development
From Concept to Creation

Table of Contents

Macromedia Director Game Development
From Concept to Creation

Introduction

A DIFFERENT APPROACH

Instead of simply being a rewrite of the user's manual, this book uses existing Macromedia Director games to teach you about professional techniques and strategies essential to game development. Each game will teach you a specific skill relating to game production. Working with games is a good way to become familiar with a new development tool like Director, because games are not only fun to make but also cover all the major elements of normal applications.

HISTORY OF MACROMEDIA DIRECTOR

A company called Macromind created the major precursor to Director in June of 1985. It was entitled VideoWorks and was available only for Macintosh computers. A few years later, Macromind combined an updated version of VideoWorks with a few other multimedia utilities such as GraphicWorks and MusicWorks to create Director 1.0. Director was known internally by Macromind as "VideoWorks Interactive." Its major purpose was the creation of graphical presentations, guided tours, and kiosks.

Eventually, Macromind changed its name to Macromedia and created a Windows version of Director. Originally, Director was going to be split into two separate tools. One version would handle interactive development and allow powerful programming, while the other would cover only animation. This change might have made simple animation easier for some, but overall, Director is much more convenient as a single package.

The growth of the Internet quickly prompted Macromedia to develop Web-browser plug-ins that allowed Director programs to be accessible all over the world. Director content soon became known as Shockwave, and the rush began to find new compression methods, which allowed Shockwave content to download quickly. Today, Shockwave is one of the most common forms of interactivity on the Internet.

Figure I.1 The splash screen of Director 8 Shockwave Studio.

ADVANTAGES OF USING DIRECTOR

Director allows programmers to create quality interactive multimedia quickly and easily for the Internet, Macintoshes, and PCs. Director's drag-and-drop interface and simplified programming language help to free programmers from wasting their time on common or repetitive tasks. The Shockwave player, which lets Internet users view online Director applications, is already installed on most computers with Internet access and comes pre-installed on nearly all new computers. With such a wide audience available, you can be sure that your Director games will get noticed.

OVERVIEW OF THE CHAPTERS

Chapters 1, "Designing Games," and 2, "Using Director," of this book cover the basic skills you will need to develop in order to produce quality Director games. Each chapter begins with four figures that should be viewed clockwise to show the game in action. The first chapter covers basic aspects of game design such as story-line and character development, interface design, writing the code, and debugging. Chapter 2 walks you through the creation of a simple Director movie including all the basic features with which you must become familiar. If you are unfamiliar with Lingo, Director's built-in programming language, you should refer to Appendix A, "Lingo Programmer's Guide." For specific questions about Lingo commands, look up the commands in Appendix B, "Lingo Quick Reference."

Chapter 3, "*Scramble*: Manipulating Graphical Sprites," uses the *Scramble* game to explain the process of manipulating graphical sprites. The *Scramble* game is a perfect example of the basic procedures necessary for almost any game involving graphical sprites. Such sprite manipulations include adding sprites to the Score, applying behaviors, and changing basic sprite properties. The *Scramble* game is shown in Figure I.2.

Figure I.2 Scrambling the pieces within the *Scramble* game.

Macromedia Director Game Development
From Concept to Creation

Chapter 4, "*Painter*: Painting with Sprite Trails," uses the *Painter* game to explain the process of painting with sprite trails. The *Painter* game moves a single sprite of a custom size and color based on user input. Because the sprite is set to leave trails behind as it moves, the user can, in effect, paint on a canvas with a custom brush. Director provides other methods to accomplish such a task, but they are either too slow or too complicated for the purposes of Chapter 4. The *Painter* game is shown in Figure I.3.

Figure 1.3 Using custom colors within the Painter game.

Chapter 5, "*Monk Mania*: Playing Sounds," uses the *Monk Mania* game to explain the process of playing sound effects and music in your games. Most games use sound effects to enhance their entertainment value, but the *Monk Mania* game actually focuses on its sound effects. *Monk Mania* is a memory game in which random sequences of monks sing their individual notes, and you must remember the correct order. The game uses not only sounds played through Lingo but also through the Score. The *Monk Mania* game is shown in Figure I.4.

Figure I.4 Listening to the music of the *Monk Mania* game.

Chapter 6, "*Tic-Tac-Toe Challenge*: Elaborating on a Simple Game," uses the *Tic-Tac-Toe Challenge* game to explain the process of elaborating on a simple game. By adding characters, a story line, and eye-catching graphics to a simple tic-tac-toe game, *Tic-Tac-Toe Challenge* increases its playability and entertainment value. Artificial intelligence is essential to the game's story, because the player's objective is to defeat an abnormally smart opponent. The *Tic-Tac-Toe Challenge* game is shown in Figure I.5.

Figure I.5 Seizing victory within the *Tic-Tac-Toe Challenge* game.

Chapter 7, "*Gremlins*: Generating Random Motion," uses the *Gremlins* game to explain the process of generating random motion. Every dynamic item within the *Gremlins* game makes use of random motion, including items directly controlled by the user. As the user picks up a gremlin dart to throw at a passing plane, the gremlin wriggles around randomly. The planes not only move across the screen randomly but also change their images to show different angles of the planes. The *Gremlins* game is shown in Figure I.6.

Figure I.6 Preparing a shot within the *Gremlins* game.

Macromedia Director Game Development
From Concept to Creation

Chapter 8, "*Go*: Providing Two Methods of Play," uses the *Go* game to explain the process of providing two methods of play for your games. The three-dimensional *Go* board attracts the attention of the user and adds to the overall playability of the game. Some players, however, prefer the more straightforward overhead view of the game board. The *Go* game provides both methods of play so that all users are satisfied. The *Go* game is shown in Figure I.7.

Figure I.7 Battling it out within the *Go* game.

Chapter 9, "*Smac-Man*: Utilizing Keyboard Control," uses the *Smac-Man* game to explain the process of utilizing keyboard control. Without the use of keyboard control, users would have to rely on the mouse to move the main character around the screen. Such an unusual method of play could prove ridiculously inconvenient in such a simple game with only four directions available in which to move. The *Smac-Man* game is shown in Figure I.8.

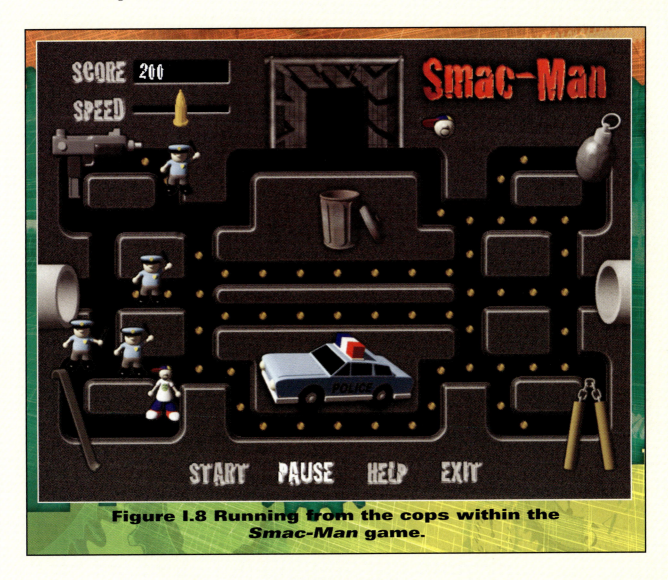

Figure I.8 Running from the cops within the *Smac-Man* game.

Chapter 10, "The *Great Erudini*: Animating with Film Loops," uses the *Great Erudini* game to explain the process of animating with film loops. The *Great Erudini* is the only game in the book to make use of film-loop animations. Although film loops are generally not a component of most Shockwave games, they do add a great deal of functionality to Director. Animations more than a few frames long are simply easier to work with in the form of film loops, and the *Great Erudini* game illustrates this well. The *Great Erudini* game is shown in Figure I.9.

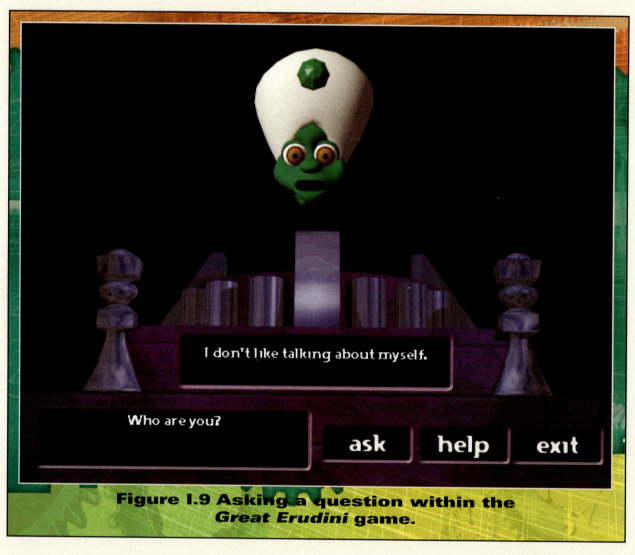

Figure I.9 Asking a question within the *Great Erudini* game.

Chapter 11, *"Old-Fashioned Pinball*: Applying Realistic Physics,"* uses the *Old-Fashioned Pinball* game to explain the process of applying realistic physics to your games. The entire *Old-Fashioned Pinball* game uses basic physics principles to create realistic movement for the pinball, but the simplest example of these principles is the game's introduction screen. The draggable pinballs of the introduction screen use inertia, friction, gravity, and magnetism to enhance their realism as well as entertain the user. The *Old-Fashioned Pinball* game is shown in Figure I.10.

Figure I.10 Keeping the ball alive within the *Old-Fashioned Pinball* game.

Macromedia Director Game Development
From Concept to Creation

Chapter 12, "*Backyard Brawl*: Creating Dynamic Characters," uses the *Backyard Brawl* game to explain the process of creating dynamic characters for your games. Based on the user's choices in the opening screen of the *Backyard Brawl* game, the two character sprites set several of their properties before each fight, including strength, weight, and aggression. As the user or computer controls a fighter, its cast member changes based on the character's name and current action. The *Backyard Brawl* game is shown in Figure I.11.

Figure I.11 Pairing up the characters of the *Backyard Brawl* game.

Chapter 13, "*Covert Mayhem*: Animating in Three Dimensions," uses the *Covert Mayhem* game to explain the process of animating in three dimensions. Although Director does not lend itself to the creation of hard-core three-dimensional engines, the *Covert Mayhem* game provides a good example of the sort of basic pseudo-3-D engine you can build within Director. Within a given level of the game, the room's walls and floor are distorted to show perspective. All mobile elements of the level move about the room and resize themselves realistically, but all stationary elements appear actual size in a set location on the Stage. The *Covert Mayhem* game is shown in Figure I.12.

Figure I.12 Bombing the art gallery within the *Covert Mayhem* game.

Chapter 14, "*Martian Dogfight*: Producing Complex Vector Graphics," uses the *Martian Dogfight* game to explain the process of producing complex vector graphics. The *Martian Dogfight* game uses only vector graphics for all dynamic foreground elements. Both of the spaceships use layering techniques to produce complex vector images of multiple colors and fill styles. Each ship takes up a few sprite channels in the Score—one to translate user input into ship movement, rotation, and scaling, and the others simply to mimic the first sprite. The *Martian Dogfight* game is shown in Figure I.13.

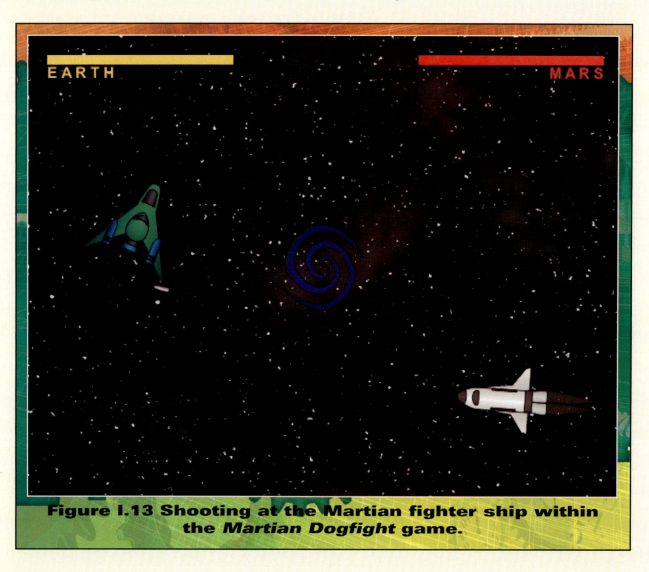

Figure I.13 Shooting at the Martian fighter ship within the *Martian Dogfight* game.

Chapter 15, "*Froggy*: Publishing Internet Content," uses the *Froggy* game to explain the process of publishing Internet content. Director offers a wide assortment of pre-set HTML templates for your Shockwave games, but it also allows you to create your own HTML files. In addition to customizing the way your game appears on an HTML page, you can customize various aspects of the Shockwave movie's compression. So many options make Director an unbelievably powerful tool for creating Internet content. The *Froggy* game is shown in Figure I.14.

Figure I.14 Crossing the street within the *Froggy* game.

Macromedia Director Game Development
From Concept to Creation

Chapter 16, "*Robo-Pong*: Exporting Digital Video," uses the *Robo-Pong* game to explain the process of exporting digital video. The *Robo-Pong* game's opening sequence is a perfect example of a portion of a Director game that you might like to export as digital video. Director offers a number of ways to customize your video file's compression method and format. Or, if you prefer, you can export a series of bitmap images. Such a series of images would be perfect if you wanted to create an animated GIF image or even a film loop within another Director movie. The *Robo-Pong* game is shown in Figure I.15.

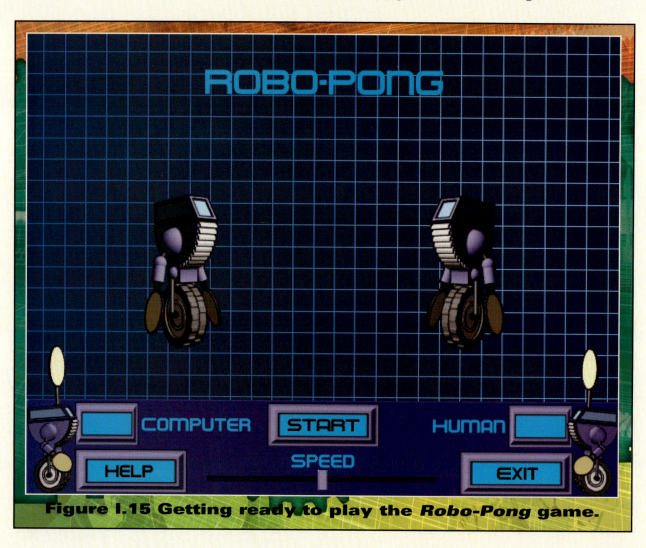

Figure I.15 Getting ready to play the *Robo-Pong* game.

Chapter 17, "*Epic-Sketch*: Incorporating Flash Movies," uses the *Epic-Sketch* game to explain the process of incorporating Flash movies into your games. *Epic-Sketch* is the only game in the book to make use of Flash movies. Generally, Director games do not incorporate Flash movies both because they tend to slow down Shockwave games and because they are often inconvenient to work with. In some cases, however, game producers like to combine the specialized graphics capabilities of Flash with the power of Director. The *Epic-Sketch* game is shown in Figure I.16.

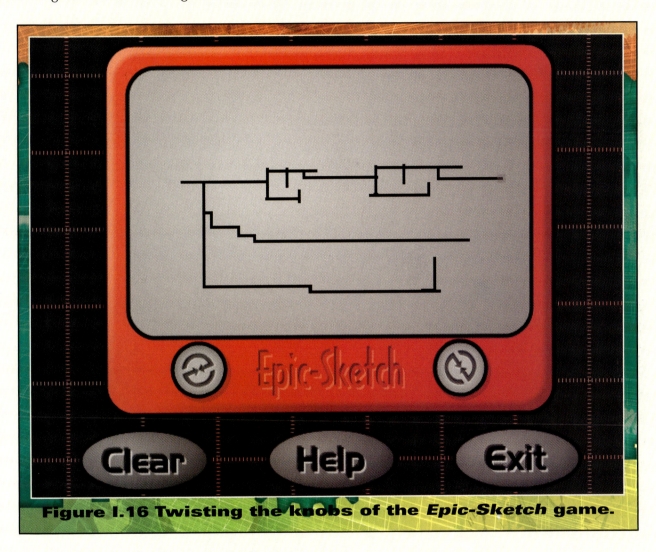

Figure I.16 Twisting the knobs of the *Epic-Sketch* game.

USING THE CD-ROM

You can access virtually all elements of the accompanying CD-ROM through its multimedia interface. For example, if you want to play one of the games featured in this book, you should choose its button from the main menu of the CD-ROM's interface. Then, when you see a screen featuring several screenshots of the game, you should click your mouse on the Run Game button. When you have finished playing the game, simply press the Esc key or use the game's Exit button.

If you choose not to run the multimedia interface, however, you can access all files on the CD-ROM from your operating system's browsing utility. Within the browsing utility, you may want to copy the contents of the CD-ROM onto your hard drive for increased speed and convenience. Or if you prefer, you can open source files through Director and then save them to your hard drive.

GETTING STARTED

If you are already familiar with Lingo and you just want to learn more about different aspects of Shockwave game development, then you can jump to any chapter you want and complete its tutorial. Each lesson is designed in such a way that it is independent from other lessons. However, if you have never used Director before, you should definitely read Chapter 2 and look through Appendix A, "Lingo Programmer's Guide," before proceeding to any game chapters. Each game chapter assumes that you have a basic understanding of Director and its programming language, Lingo.

Chapter 1
Designing Games

Chapter

1

- Approaching Game Development

- Focusing Your Game

- Developing a Story Line and Characters

- Designing the Interface

- Formulating Good Gameplay

- Developing the Logic

- Writing the Code

- Checking for Errors

- Preparing Your Game for Distribution

APPROACHING GAME DEVELOPMENT

Whether you are an experienced game developer, a master of video games, or even new to computers, a great computer game will offer you entertainment and often some type of competition. Over the years, basic games have evolved to encompass numerous genres such as role-playing, first-person shooter, side-scrolling, strategy, educational, and simulations. Role-playing games involve a main character or characters thrust into a heroic plot. A first-person shooter, however, involves adrenaline-fed killing and destruction. Although simulations are generally designed to be as realistic as possible, most side-scrolling, strategy, and educational games tend to be a bit more simplistic. With the wide variety of games available today, the average person will have no trouble finding a game that suits his or her desires. As you develop your game-design skills, avoid simply mimicking existing games. In most cases, however, any game you develop will fit clearly into a specific genre.

FOCUSING YOUR GAME

When you begin the process of designing a game, you must first decide how to approach the task. Determining the focus of your game is the best way to begin. You should decide on a topic, purpose, and theme for your game. Listing objectives that you want to accomplish through your game is often a smart way to begin. You might have objectives that direct the activities you will build into the game and a different set of objectives for the person who plays the game to accomplish. Through your thinking process, you will determine exactly what your game is about and how you should go about creating it. The manner in which you focus your game will affect all the decisions you make later in the design process.

DEVELOPING A STORY LINE
AND CHARACTERS

The focus of your game will affect the development of the story line. A first-person shooter, for example, does not require very much depth. The player wants to shoot things, not listen to a story. However, you can never completely ignore the character and plot. Even the simple arcade classic *Pac-Man* had a story. Over the course of the game and its two sequels, *Pac-Man* apparently fell in love, got married, and had a kid, all while avoiding pixelated ghosts. Even the bloodiest and most mindless adrenaline-based shooter game could always use *some* justification for the rampant killing. If the game is of a different genre, such as a role-playing or strategy, plot and characters will become much more important, as these types of games use storytelling to capture and maintain player interest.

Generally, the plot is not all that advances during play. To attract the player and make the game more interesting, the game designer must determine the events that brought the conflict that the player faces to existence, known as the background story. You can effectively present the background story in a brief introductory scene of the game. If the story is a bit complicated, you can go into more detail in a manual accompanying the game. Even if you decide not to go into detail about the story line, you should at least have some idea why the game's events occur. The story and setting provide ideas for designing the artwork such as characters and scenes and the interface through which the player interacts with the game.

DESIGNING THE INTERFACE

Perhaps the most logistically important feature of your game is the interface. The interface is the layout through which the player interacts with the game. The design is important to the theme of the game. In addition, the interface must offer clear navigation. Your player must never have to fight the interface in order to get something to work. When you design your interface, therefore, you should keep several things in mind.

First, keep the interface simple. Your interface should be straightforward enough that someone who has never used a computer before will be able to pick up your game and intuitively be able to use the controls with little or no awkwardness. The controls should allow the player to play the game effectively without even having to open the manual.

Next, make your interface appropriate for the type of game you design. Control elements are classified as either virtual or physical. Physical controls are hardware such as keyboards, mice, and joysticks that the player actually makes physical contact with in order to play the game. Physical controls are the first part of your interface with which the player will actually interact. Virtual controls are the interface features of your game, such as buttons and drop-down lists, that the player uses to control certain aspects of the game.

The types of controls you use in your game depend largely on the game's focus. A fighting game that involves quick reflexes should include a minimal amount of virtual control and consist almost entirely of physical control. Because the player must use physical controls to access virtual controls, too many virtual controls can make your game seem cluttered. A strategy game, however, with many menus and interactive charts and maps, should implement a great deal of virtual control.

The next consideration in designing the interface is delivering feedback to the player. *Feedback* is a term that encompasses all information that the player receives from the game. Feedback is an important part of the interface, but you must control and shape it depending on the necessity of using it in the game. For a simple side-scrolling game, you would probably only need to provide the player with the level number, the number of extra lives remaining, the player's score, and the time left to complete the level. In a strategy game you would have to provide the player with troop counts, reconnaissance and intelligence reports, weapons and armament statistics, as well as demographics and troop morale, for example. In short, the more thought your game requires, the more feedback you should include. On the other hand, if your game is more fast-paced, you should tone down the feedback as it will distract the player and is probably unnecessary.

FORMULATING GOOD GAMEPLAY

Good gameplay never gives the user a chance to get bored. Poor gameplay will result in an unbalanced game that is too hard, too easy, or simply awkward and dull. Balance is the most important aspect of gameplay. There are several ways to make your game balanced and therefore fun to play.

Often the best way to balance a game is to prevent the player from having too much power. Good balancing tools often come from real life. For example, when developing a shooting game, you should limit the player's ammunition supply. If the player never runs out of ammunition, he or she has no reason to ever stop firing at all. Therefore, pressing the shoot button simply becomes a chore, and the user becomes more likely to lose interest.

Next, there should always be a good conflict working against the player that he or she must overcome in order to proceed with the game. The level of difficulty should not be easy, nor should it be impossible. It is all right for certain parts of a game to be so difficult that it takes the player many tries to overcome them, but the game should not be so difficult that the average player can never make any progress. The average player probably can't beat all 256 levels of *Pac-Man* before the game runs out of memory and crashes, but at least he or she can have fun trying.

When creating any game, you should try to make it easy to learn but hard to master. The game should not be so cryptic and complicated that the average beginning player would not be able to play with relative ease. Some power must be reserved so that to truly get good at the game, you must continue playing and practicing for some time. Games that require little or no skill can be just as annoying as those that are impossible even for the most adept gamers to master. The skill level of your game must fall somewhere in the middle.

When developing single-player games, you might face a dilemma. Without good artificial-intelligence routines, the player will always beat the computer in an equal match. Although good artificial intelligence allows decent competition against the player, the computer characters still sometimes lack the spark of human smarts, leaving them predictable and exploitable. In this case, it is necessary to give the computer a few extra advantages, such as omniscience or a large supply of weapons.

DEVELOPING THE LOGIC

Although developing the logic of the game is perhaps the least fun, it is the stonework of the bridge between the design and the birth of the actual game. You should plan the methods you will use to create your game before you begin typing in the code. Break out the old-fashioned paper and pencil and turn off the computer for now. The logic should come first.

Divide your game into various sections, and simplify until you have isolated a single task. Pretend for a moment that you are programming a falling-blocks puzzle game in the spirit of *Tetris*. When the player presses the left- or right-arrow keys, you want the block to rotate to the left or right respectively. Now that you have isolated a single task, break it down and write it out in "pseudo code." Pseudo code is simply a rough draft of a program's logic, not an actual programming language, so it has no real rules. Just write your pseudo code so that it makes sense to you. Do not worry about syntax right now. The pseudo code for the block rotation algorithm could appear as follows:

```
if the left-arrow key is pressed then
   rotate the currentBlock 90 degrees to the left
end if
if the right-arrow key is pressed then
   rotate the currentBlock 90 degrees to the left
end if
```

Notice how the *if* statements are written in plain English and the conditions for the key presses are expressed as literal words, instead of ASCII code. Do not worry about syntax or programming-language specifications right now. Just think it out and put it down on paper.

If you are already familiar with Lingo, you may notice that the preceding code looks similar to the verbose syntax used in previous versions of Director that is now becoming archaic. Do not even think about the similarities between pseudo code and actual programming languages. Your pseudo code can look however you want. Not until you actually write the code will you need to worry about details.

WRITING THE CODE

For hard-core game programmers, writing the code is the most fun part of the entire project. For those concerned only with design, however, actually programming the code can seem like a chore. But the fact remains that programming is the most necessary part of game development. Even the best-designed game gets nowhere if you do not sit down and write the code for it. Consequently, programming is usually the most time-consuming part of the project.

However, writing the code is not as hard and scary as many people think it is, providing you have a good grasp of your programming language. When writing a program, you are fighting an endless battle against code entropy. As you write your game, you will notice that it will become increasingly complicated and messy. You can avoid unnecessary clutter by taking advantage of a technique called compartmentalization.

Compartmentalization is the process of breaking your code up into as many small reusable parts as possible. You should try to make your functions as generic as possible so that you can use the same basic function for several similar purposes throughout your game. For example, when developing the falling-block algorithm, you should assign falling speed and block shape as parameters of a function. *Parameters*, or *arguments*, allow you to change how a function behaves by specifying different values in different situations.

By using compartmentalization, you can organize your code to make finding and isolating bugs easier. Sloppily written code causes several problems. First, determining the cause of a bug can become extremely difficult. In addition, changing code can become awkward and difficult. If you write generic functions instead of countless sections of scattered code, you will know exactly where to look when you run into a specific problem, and the entire program will be easy to fix.

To be an effective programmer, you should also take advantage of *objects*. The use of objects differs between languages, but the idea is generally the same. Objects allow you to assign various properties and functions to a single item. For example, an object named "car" might include a "model" property, a "year" property, and a "drive" function. By creating properties and functions specific to objects, programming becomes a much more organized and less complicated task.

To keep your games clean and organized, you should always comment sections of ambiguous code. A comment is a line of programming code completely ignored by the compiler. The main purpose of a comment is to keep your thoughts organized and make your code easier for other programmers to understand. Comments can also be useful when debugging your games. You can keep the compiler from seeing specific lines of code to help you find potential bugs.

CHECKING FOR ERRORS

Now that you have written your programming code, you should check over it to make sure you have not overlooked any errors in syntax or logic. Syntax errors cause your program to crash or often prevent your program from even compiling. If you understand the programming language, syntax errors are easy enough to fix. However, logic errors, commonly called *bugs* or *glitches*, are much harder to catch, because your compiler will never even be aware that a problem exists. You must test your work after each finished aspect of your program to find bugs as they come and be able to deal with them one at a time. Never let bugs build up, or you will have to deal with them later, and they may become so overwhelming that you find yourself unable to continue. Whenever you find a bug, try to fix it immediately, or you might create even more bugs.

PREPARING YOUR GAME FOR DISTRIBUTION

Preparing and packaging your game is the final stage of game development. First, you must compile your program into an executable file and organize it, along with any other files required to run your game, into logically named folders. After your game is completely finished, you must decide on the method of distribution you will use. You might decide to give your game away as shareware or even freeware depending on your motivation for creating the game. If you plan on selling your game, you should probably find a publisher who will market and distribute your game and give you a share of the proceeds. If you choose to market the game yourself, you will be limited to selling only as many copies as you can burn onto CDs. Most likely, without any advertising or large-scale distribution, only a limited market of consumers will be aware of your game. If you plan to give your program away, it will be easiest to upload your game to a Web site where people can download or view it.

Chapter 2
Using Director

Chapter

2

- Using the Stage Window

- Using the Property Inspector Window

- Using the Score Window

- Creating Bitmap and Vector Graphics

- Importing Media into a Cast

- Writing Lingo Scripts

- Compiling and Compressing Your Game

Macromedia Director Game Development
From Concept to Creation

Director is a graphically oriented development utility with all the most common algorithms built in. Most multimedia development tools are either designed for non-interactive presentations, such as Microsoft PowerPoint, or powerful but complicated applications such as Borland C++. Director is a hybrid that allows developers to explore game ideas and display them on the Internet and requires considerably less effort than its predecessors. With enough practice, anyone can create impressive games in no time. To install the trial version of Director 8 Shockwave Studio on your computer, perform the following steps:

1. Insert the companion CD-ROM into your CD drive. If a full-screen interface is not automatically displayed, then run start.exe off your CD drive.

2. Follow the on-screen instructions to install the correct version of Director 8 Shockwave Studio for your operating system.

3. When the Director installation program finishes, run director.exe from your Director 8 folder.

With so many unusual-looking windows, Director's interface may seem overwhelming at first. However, if you learn Director one piece at a time, everything will fall into place. Each window in Director serves a specific and unique purpose. You will not need every window open all the time, but to keep confusion to a minimum, do not close any windows unless instructed to do so.

USING THE STAGE WINDOW

Within Director, the Stage is the static canvas that contains all the visible elements of a movie. Much like its theatrical counterpart, Director's Stage is where everything happens. The Stage itself is simply a solid rectangle that appears behind everything else. In fact, most major Director games cover the Stage up completely with a background image. Nevertheless, the Stage is the most important part of any Director game. To view the Stage window within Director, perform the following steps:

1. If you do not see the Stage window, click your mouse on the Toolbar Stage button, which is shown in Figure 2.1. Director will display the Stage window.

Figure 2.1 The Stage button within the Toolbar.

2. If you wish to reposition the Stage window within Director, use your mouse to drag its title bar to the position you desire.

3. If you wish to resize the Stage window within Director, use your mouse to drag its lower-right corner until the window is the size you desire.

4. If you wish to zoom the Stage in or out, click your mouse on the Zoom Menu drop-down list and select an option. Director will update the Stage window, as shown in Figure 2.2.

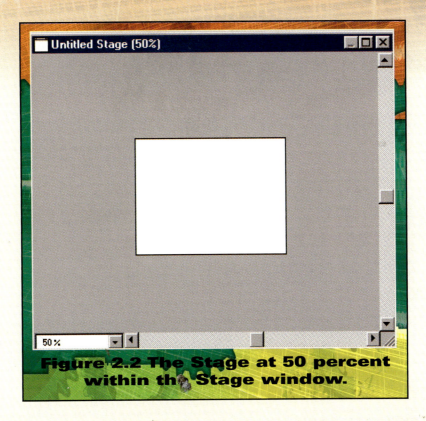

Figure 2.2 The Stage at 50 percent within the Stage window.

To build any Director game, you must create at least a few sprites. A *sprite* is any visible object, such as text or an image, that exists on the Stage. One simple method of creating sprites is to use the Tool Palette window. To add customized text to the Stage using the Tool Palette window, perform the following steps:

1. If you do not see the Tool Palette window within Director, click your mouse on the Window menu, and select the Tool Palette option. Director will display the Tool Palette window.

2. Within the Tool Palette window, click your mouse on the Text button. Director will select the Text tool, as shown in Figure 2.3.

3. Within the Stage window, click your mouse near the middle of the Stage. Director will display an editable text field within the Stage.

4. Within the Stage window, in the new text field, type whatever text you desire.

Figure 2.3 The Text button within the Tool Palette window.

5. Within the Stage window, in the new text field, select all your text. Click your mouse on the Modify menu, and select the Font option. Director will display the Font dialog box, as shown in Figure 2.4.

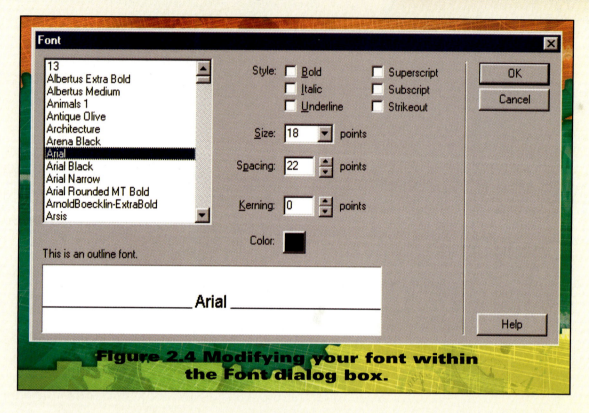

Figure 2.4 Modifying your font within the Font dialog box.

6. Within the Font dialog box, click your mouse on the Color button, and select a color swatch of your choice. Director will set the color of your text to whatever color you select.

7. Within the Font dialog box, in the Font selection box, click your mouse on the font of your choice. Director will set the font of your text to whatever you select.

8. Within the Font dialog box, click your mouse on the Size drop-down arrow, and select the size of your choice. Director will set the size of your text to whatever you select.

9. Within the Font dialog box, click your mouse on the OK button. Director will apply your font selections to your text in the text field.

10. Within the Stage window, drag one of the new text field's corners to the size you desire.

So far, you have already learned how to create customized text within a Director movie. Surprisingly, Director doesn't get all that much more complicated. You are already on your way to developing interactive, graphically oriented games. Now that you know how to use the Stage window, you are ready to scratch through the next layer of Director's interface.

USING THE PROPERTY INSPECTOR WINDOW

The Property Inspector window is the easiest way to customize the properties of anything and everything within Director. You will use the Property Inspector at least as much as any other of Director's windows. Before you begin creating your movie, you should change a few of its properties such as size and color. To modify your movie's properties, perform the following steps:

1. If you do not see the Property Inspector, then within the Toolbar, click your mouse on the Property Inspector button. Director will display the Property Inspector window, as shown in Figure 2.5.

Property Inspector (Ctrl+Alt+S)

Figure 2.5 The Property Inspector button within the Toolbar.

2. Within the Property Inspector window, click your mouse on the Movie tab. Director will display the Movie sheet.

3. Within the Property Inspector window, click your mouse on the Stage Size button, and select the 640×480 option. Director will size the Stage window to 640 pixels wide and 480 pixels tall.

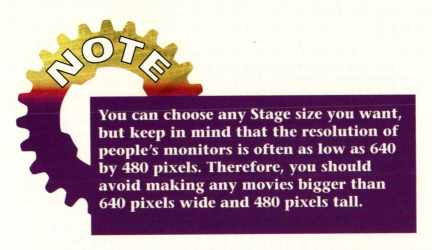

You can choose any Stage size you want, but keep in mind that the resolution of people's monitors is often as low as 640 by 480 pixels. Therefore, you should avoid making any movies bigger than 640 pixels wide and 480 pixels tall.

4. Within the Property Inspector window, click your mouse on the Stage Fill Color button and select a color swatch of your choice. Director will change the color of the Stage to whatever color you select.

The Property Inspector window can do more than just modify your movie's properties. You can use the Property Inspector window to modify the properties of anything related to a sprite. To modify the properties of the text you created earlier, perform the following steps:

1. Within the Stage, click your mouse on the text you created earlier. Director will update the Property Inspector window.

2. Within the Property Inspector window, click your mouse on the Member tab. Director will display the Member sheet.

3. Within the Property Inspector window, in the Name field, type **Tweening**, and press the Enter key. Director will name the text you created earlier "Tweening."

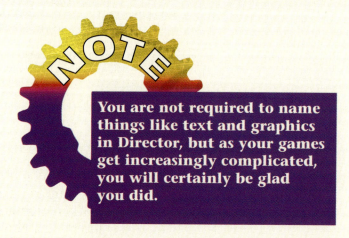

You are not required to name things like text and graphics in Director, but as your games get increasingly complicated, you will certainly be glad you did.

4. Within the Property Inspector window, click your mouse on the Sprite tab. Director will display the Sprite sheet.

5. Within the Property Inspector window, click your mouse on the Ink drop-down list. Select the Matte option, as shown in Figure 2.6. Director will remove the background rectangle from the Tweening text.

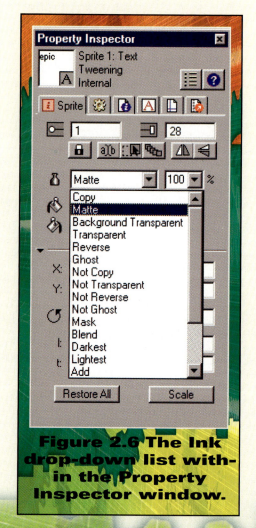

Figure 2.6 The Ink drop-down list within the Property Inspector window.

6. Within the Property Inspector window, in the Rotation Angle field, type a number between 0 and 360 and press the Enter key. Director will rotate the Tweening text to whatever angle you type.

7. Within the Property Inspector window, click your mouse on the Moveable button. Director will allow the user to drag the Tweening text around the Stage while the game is running.

8. Within the Toolbar, click your mouse on the Play button. Director will preview your game within the Stage window. Drag the Tweening text around the Stage to make sure that your game is working properly.

9. Within the Toolbar, click your mouse on the Rewind button. Director will return your game to its original state within the Stage window.

By now, you have a fully functioning, interactive Director movie. However, dragging text around an empty screen really isn't very high in entertainment value. Although your Director skills are improving, you are a long way from creating a truly impressive game. Keep your chin up. You are about to get to the fun stuff.

USING THE SCORE WINDOW

The Score is the element that sets Director apart from other development tools. You can use the Score tool to position graphical elements of your game in different frames to create an animation. Because the Score uses a graphical interface, you can use it to create an entire multimedia presentation with no programming. Interactive games usually have more complex animation requirements, however, which require a great deal of programming to make happen. Thus, game-developers often do not use the Score for animation at all. Nonetheless, it is still important for you to understand the Score because it is an important tool for layering and organizing your game's sprites. To view the Score window within Director, perform the following steps:

1. If you do not see the Score window, then within the Toolbar, click your mouse on the Score Window button, as shown in Figure 2.7. Director will display the Score window.

Score Window (Ctrl+4)

Figure 2.7 The Score button within the Toolbar.

2. If you want to reposition the Score window within Director, drag its title bar to the position you desire.

3. If you want to resize the Score window within Director, drag its lower-right corner until the window is the size you desire.

To move a sprite using the Score, it must be under Score control. By default, all sprites are under the control of the Score, but the Tweening text is draggable. If a sprite is supposed to follow the user's mouse, then of course Director will ignore any attempt to move it in the Score. To remove the draggability of the Tweening text and create movement for it using the Score, perform the following steps:

1. Within the Stage window, click your mouse on the Tweening text. Director will update the Property Inspector window.

2. Within the Property Inspector window, click your mouse on the Moveable button. Director will no longer allow the user to drag the Tweening text around the Stage while the game is running.

3. Within the Score window, drag cell 28 of channel 1 to frame 50. Director will extend the Tweening text to frame 50, as shown in Figure 2.8.

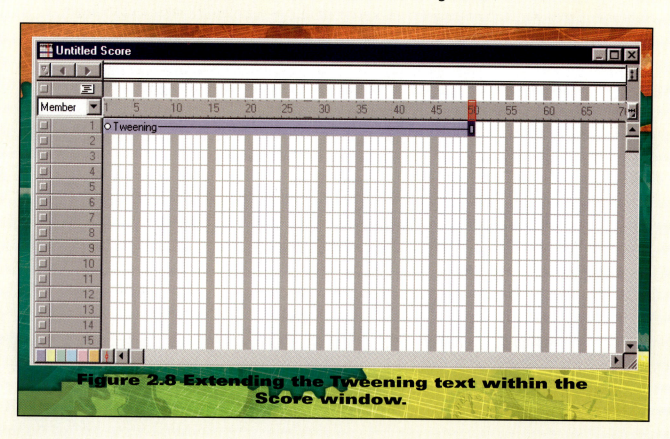

Figure 2.8 Extending the Tweening text within the Score window.

4. Within the Score window, click your mouse on cell 50 of channel 1. Director will display frame 50 of your movie within the Stage.

5. Click your mouse on the Insert menu, and select the Keyframe option. Director will mark cell 50 of channel 1 as a keyframe.

6. Within the Score window, click your mouse on cell 10 of channel 1. Director will display frame 10 of your movie within the Stage.

7. Click your mouse on the Insert menu and select the Keyframe option. Director will mark cell 10 of channel 1 as a keyframe.

8. Within the Stage window, drag the Tweening text to a new location on the Stage. Director will display a path outline between the old and new positions of the Tweening text within the Stage.

9. Within the Score window, click your mouse on cell 40 of channel 1. Director will display frame 40 of your movie within the Stage.

10. Click your mouse on the Insert menu and select the Keyframe option. Director will mark cell 40 of channel 1 as a keyframe.

11. Within the Stage window, drag the Tweening text to a new location on the Stage. Director will display a path outline between the old and new positions of the Tweening text within the Stage.

12. Click your mouse on the Modify menu, select the Sprite submenu, and select the Tweening option. Director will display the Sprite Tweening dialog box.

13. Within the Sprite Tweening dialog box, drag the Ease-In slider to around 25 percent. Director will update the path outline preview to show acceleration at the beginning of the path.

14. Within the Sprite Tweening dialog box, drag the Ease-Out slider to around 25 percent. Director will update the path outline preview to show deceleration at the end of the path.

15. Within the Sprite Tweening dialog box, click your mouse on the Continue at Endpoints checkbox. Director will update the path outline preview to show a smooth, connected path.

16. Within the Sprite Tweening dialog box, click your mouse on the OK button. Director will update the path outline of the Tweening text within the Stage as shown in Figure 2.9.

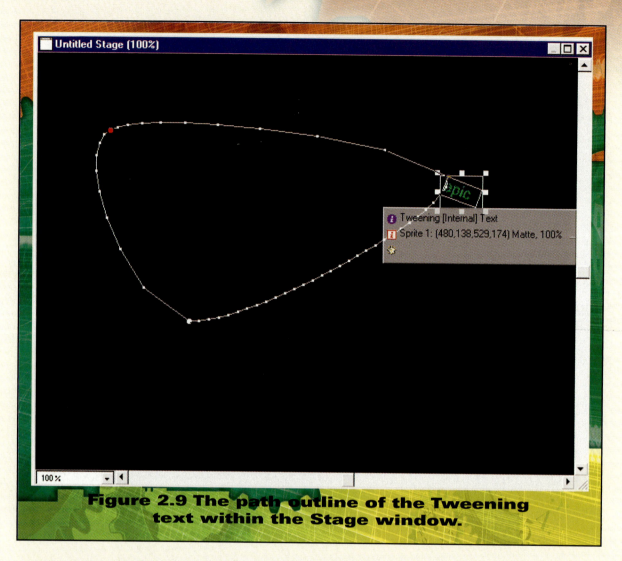

Figure 2.9 The path outline of the Tweening text within the Stage window.

17. Within the Toolbar, click your mouse on the Play button. Director will preview your game within the Stage window. Notice how the text accelerates at the beginning of the game and decelerates at the end.

18. Within the Toolbar, click your mouse on the Rewind button. Director will return your game to its original state within the Stage window.

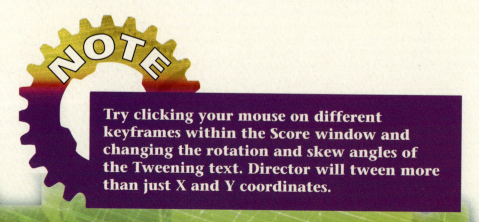

Try clicking your mouse on different keyframes within the Score window and changing the rotation and skew angles of the Tweening text. Director will tween more than just X and Y coordinates.

I know what you are thinking: Moveable text is no more entertaining than draggable text. You learned how to create and animate text first because text is the simplest of all Director media types. Now that you know how to manipulate text sprites, you can move on to graphics.

CREATING BITMAP AND VECTOR GRAPHICS

Director stores all media elements and programming code in groups called *casts*. In every new movie, Director creates a cast named "Internal." Until you get a little more practice with Director, you will store all your text, graphics, and other cast members in the Internal cast. To view the Cast window within Director, perform the following steps:

1. If you do not see the Cast window, then within the Toolbar, click your mouse on the Cast Window button, as shown in Figure 2.10. Director will display the Cast window.

Cast Window (Ctrl+3)

Figure 2.10 The Cast Window button within the Toolbar.

2. If you wish to reposition the Cast window within Director, drag its title bar to the position you desire.

3. If you wish to resize the Cast window within Director, drag its lower-right corner until the window is the size you desire.

4. Within the Cast window, click your mouse on the Cast View Style button a few times. Director will change the way it displays cast members within the Cast window.

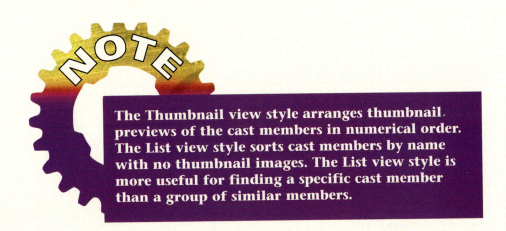

NOTE

The Thumbnail view style arranges thumbnail previews of the cast members in numerical order. The List view style sorts cast members by name with no thumbnail images. The List view style is more useful for finding a specific cast member than a group of similar members.

Macromedia Director Game Development
From Concept to Creation

One of the most important aspects of games these days is the graphics. You can develop all the realistic physics and artificial intelligence you want, but unless you have the graphics to make it interesting, no one will want to play your game. Most of the graphics that game developers use right now are *bitmap*, or *raster*, graphics. Bitmap graphics are simply a matrix of thousands of little squares of color called *pixels*. Vector graphics consist of shapes instead of pixels. Unlike bitmap graphics, vector graphics usually have a small file size and do not lose quality when they change scale. In addition, vector graphics can look very smooth on the screen through a method called *anti-aliasing*. The only problem is that vector graphics are often more difficult to create than bitmap graphics, so they are rarely very detailed.

Creating Bitmap Graphics

To create a new bitmap graphic in the Internal cast and add it to the Stage, perform the following steps:

1. Within the Toolbar, click your mouse on the Paint Window button, as shown in Figure 2.11. Director will display the Paint window and add a new bitmap member to the Internal cast.

Figure 2.11 The Paint Window button within the Toolbar.

2. Within the Paint window, click your mouse on the Foreground Color button and select a color swatch of your choice. Director will set the foreground color to whatever color you select.

3. Within the Paint window, click your mouse on the Pencil button. Director will select the Pencil tool.

4. Within the Paint window, drag your mouse around on the canvas. Director will leave a continuous trail of pixels behind your cursor as it moves.

5. Within the Paint window, click your mouse on the Brush button. Director will select the Brush tool.

6. Within the Paint window, drag your mouse around on the canvas. Director will leave a trail of brush markings behind your cursor as it moves.

7. Within the Paint window, click your mouse on the Ink drop-down list and select the Smear option. Director will set the Brush Ink effect to "Smear."

8. Within the Paint window, drag your mouse around on the canvas. Director will leave a trail of smeared pixels behind your cursor as it moves.

9. Within the Paint window, click your mouse on the Air Brush button. Director will select the Air Brush tool.

10. Within the Paint window, drag your mouse around on the canvas. Director will leave a spray of brush markings behind your cursor as it moves.

11. Within the Paint window, click your mouse on the Ink drop-down list and select the Blend option. Director will set the Air Brush Ink effect to "Blend."

12. Within the Paint window, drag your mouse around on the canvas. Director will leave a translucent spray of brush markings behind your cursor as it moves. Figure 2.12 shows the results of steps 2–12.

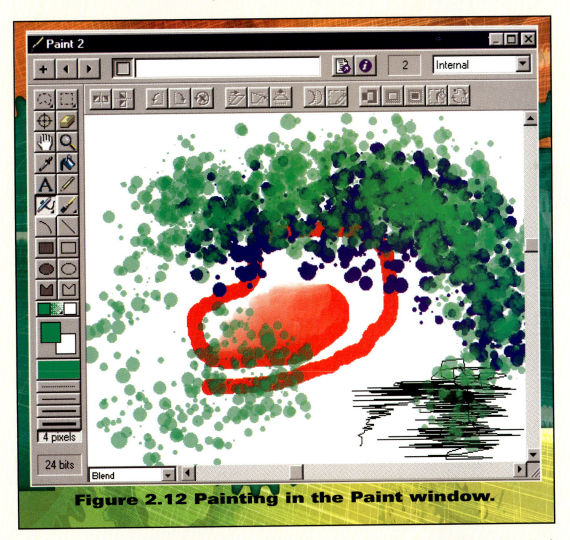

Figure 2.12 Painting in the Paint window.

13. Within the Paint window, click and hold your mouse on the Air Brush button and select the Settings option. Director will display the Air Brush Settings dialog box.

14. Within the Air Brush Settings dialog box, drag the various sliders around as you see fit. Director will update the Air Brush Settings dialog box.

15. Within the Air Brush Settings dialog box, click your mouse on the OK button. Director will update the Air Brush tool.

16. Within the Paint window, drag your mouse around on the canvas. Director will leave a customized spray of brush markings behind your cursor as it moves.

17. Within the Paint window, in the Cast Member Name field, type **Bitmap Graphic** and press the Enter key. Director will name the bitmap you created "Bitmap Graphic."

18. Within the Toolbar, click your mouse on the Paint Window button. Director will close the Paint window.

19. Drag the Bitmap Graphic member from the Cast window into cell 1 of channel 2 of the Score window. Director will display the Bitmap Graphic bitmap within the Stage.

20. Within the Score window, drag cell 28 of channel 2 to frame 50. Director will extend the Bitmap Graphic bitmap to frame 50.

Now that you have created a graphic, you can use it as many times as you want within your game in the form of a sprite. A sprite is simply an instance of a cast member that shows up on the Stage and in the Score. If you delete a cast member, all sprites associated with it in the Score and on the Stage will appear blank. While the differences between sprites and cast members may seem confusing at first, you'll get the hang of it in no time.

Creating Vector Graphics

By now, you have the skills required to create and implement a bitmap graphic in your game. Vector graphics may seem more complicated than bitmaps at first, but they behave in nearly the same way. To create a new vector graphic in the Internal cast and add it to the Stage, perform the following steps:

1. Within the Toolbar, click your mouse on the Vector Shape Window button, as shown in Figure 2.13. Director will display the Vector Shape window and add a new shape member to the Internal cast.

Figure 2.13 The Vector Shape Window button within the Toolbar.

2. Within the Vector Shape window, click your mouse on the Fill Color button and select a color swatch of your choice. Director will set the fill color to whatever color you select.

3. Within the Vector Shape window, click your mouse on the Filled Rectangle button. Director will select the Filled Rectangle tool.

4. Within the Vector Shape window, drag your mouse around on the canvas. Director will draw a filled rectangle based on the starting and ending points of your mouse movement.

5. Within the Vector Shape window, drag any of the rectangle's four handles around on the canvas. Director will distort the rectangle based on the position of its handles.

6. Within the Vector Shape window, click your mouse on the Filled Ellipse button. Director will select the Filled Ellipse tool.

7. Within the Vector Shape window, drag your mouse around on the canvas. Director will draw a filled ellipse based on the starting and ending points of your mouse movement.

8. Within the Vector Shape window, drag any of the ellipse's four handles around on the canvas. Director will distort the ellipse based on the position of its handles.

9. Within the Vector Shape window, click your mouse on the Filled Round Rectangle button. Director will select the Filled Round Rectangle tool.

10. Within the Vector Shape window, drag your mouse around on the canvas. Director will draw a filled round rectangle based on the starting and ending points of your mouse movement.

11. Within the Vector Shape window, drag any of the round rectangle's eight handles around on the canvas. Director will distort the round rectangle based on the position of its handles.

12. Within the Vector Shape window, click your mouse on the Stroke Width drop-down list and select the 4 pt option. Director will change the outline of your vector shapes to be four points thick.

13. Within the Vector Shape window, click your mouse on the Gradient button. Director will change the fill of your vector shapes to fade between two colors.

14. Within the Vector Shape window, click your mouse on the second Gradient Color button and select a color swatch of your choice. Director will change the second gradient fill color to whatever color you select. Figure 2.14 shows the results of steps 2–12.

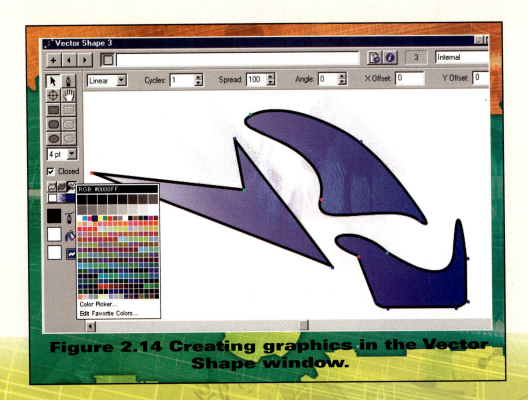

Figure 2.14 Creating graphics in the Vector Shape window.

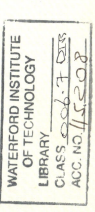

WATERFORD INSTITUTE
OF TECHNOLOGY
LIBRARY
CLASS 006.7 BAR
ACC. NO. 115208

15. Within the Vector Shape window, in the Gradient Spread field, type **75** and press the Enter key. Director will change the gradient fill to take up 75 percent of the width of your vector shapes.

16. Within the Vector Shape window, in the Gradient Angle field, type **45** and press the Enter key. Director will change the gradient angle to start in the upper-left corner of your vector shapes.

17. Within the Vector Shape window, click your mouse on the Gradient Type drop-down list and select the Radial option. Director will change the gradient fill to start in the center of your vector shapes.

18. Within the Vector Shape window, in the Gradient Cycles field, type **7** and press the Enter key. Director will change the gradient fill to cycle seven times within your vector shapes.

19. Within the Vector Shape window, in the Cast Member Name field, type **Vector Graphic** and press the Enter key. Director will name the shape you created "Vector Graphic."

20. Within the Toolbar, click your mouse on the Vector Shape Window button. Director will close the Vector Shape window.

21. Drag the Vector Graphic member from the Cast window into cell 1 of channel 3 of the Score window. Director will display the Vector Graphic shape within the Stage.

22. Within the Score window, drag cell 28 of channel 3 to frame 50. Director will extend the Vector Graphic shape to frame 50.

You can create very detailed, complex bitmap graphics within Director's Paint window and smooth, impressive vector graphics within Director's Vector Shape window. However, quite often you will need to import graphics, sounds, or other media that you are not able to create within Director.

IMPORTING MEDIA INTO A CAST

Director recognizes several media types that you can import, including JPEG photos, GIF animations, WAV sounds, AVI movies, and Flash movies. Importing media files is not only convenient, but also often completely necessary. To import external media files into your game, perform the following steps:

1. Within the Toolbar, click your mouse on the Import button. Director will display the Import Files dialog box.

2. Within the Import Files dialog box, click your mouse on the Look In drop-down list and select your CD drive. Director will display the contents of your CD drive.

3. Within the Import Files dialog box, double-click your mouse on the *Graphics* folder. Director will display the contents of the *Graphics* folder.

4. Within the Import Files dialog box, click your mouse on the *redball.bmp* file. Director will update the Import Files dialog box.

5. Within the Import Files dialog box, click your mouse on the Import button. Director will display the Image Options dialog box.

6. Within the Image Options dialog box, click your mouse on the OK button. Director will import *redball.bmp* into your game.

7. Within the Property Inspector window, click your mouse on the Member tab. Director will display the Member sheet.

8. Within the Property Inspector window, in the Name field, type **Red Ball** and press the Enter key. Director will rename the graphic you imported "Red Ball," as shown in Figure 2.15.

Figure 2.15 The properties of the Red Ball member within the Property Inspector window.

9. Drag the Red Ball member from the Cast window into cell 1 of channel 4 of the Score window. Director will display the Red Ball bitmap within the Stage.

10. Within the Score window, drag cell 28 of channel 4 to frame 50. Director will extend the Red Ball bitmap to frame 50.

11. Within the Stage window, click your mouse on the Red Ball bitmap. Director will update the Property Inspector window.

12. Within the Property Inspector window, click your mouse on the Ink drop-down list and select the Matte option. Director will remove the background rectangle from the Red Ball bitmap.

So far, your Director game should contain four cast members and four sprites. While your game is running, the Tweening text should move around the screen as the other three sprites just sit there. With your current skill level, you could use Director to create a multimedia presentation. However, if you want a truly interactive game, you must add a bit of programming code.

WRITING LINGO SCRIPTS

The programming language associated with Director is Lingo. Lingo is an attempt to make graphical programming easy. Earlier in the chapter, you created draggable text by simply clicking your mouse on a button. To write a Lingo script that makes a sprite draggable, perform the following steps:

1. Within the Toolbar, click your mouse on the Script Window button, as shown in Figure 2.16. Director will display the Script window.

Figure 2.16 The Script Window button within the Toolbar.

2. Within the Script window, in the Cast Member Name text field, type **Drag** and press the Enter key. Director will name the new script "Drag."

3. Within the Properties window, click your mouse on the Script tab. Director will display the Script sheet.

4. Within the Properties window, click your mouse on the Script Type drop-down list and select the Behavior option. Director will mark the Drag script as a behavior script.

5. Within the Script window, type the following code:

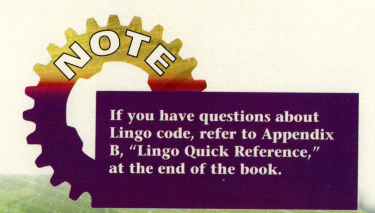

If you have questions about Lingo code, refer to Appendix B, "Lingo Quick Reference," at the end of the book.

```
property isDragging
on beginSprite
   isDragging = false
end
on enterFrame me
   if the mouseUp then isDragging = false
```

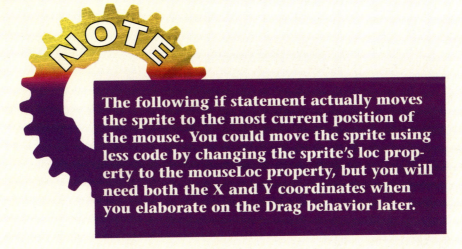

NOTE

The following if statement actually moves the sprite to the most current position of the mouse. You could move the sprite using less code by changing the sprite's loc property to the mouseLoc property, but you will need both the X and Y coordinates when you elaborate on the Drag behavior later.

```
   if isDragging then
      sprite(me.spriteNum).locH = the mouseH
      sprite(me.spriteNum).locV = the mouseV
   end if
end
on mouseDown
   isDragging = true
end
```

6. Within the Toolbar, click your mouse on the Script Window button. Director will close the Script window.

7. Within the Stage, click your mouse on the Red Ball bitmap. Director will update the Property Inspector window.

8. Within the Property Inspector window, click your mouse on the Behavior pop-up button and select the Drag option, as shown in Figure 2.17. Director will apply the Drag behavior to the Red Ball bitmap.

**Figure 2.17
Associating the
Drag behavior with
the Red Ball bitmap.**

9. Within the Toolbar, click your mouse on the Play button. Director will preview your game within the Stage window. Notice how the Red Ball bitmap behaves much as the draggable text did earlier.

10. Within the Toolbar, click your mouse on the Rewind button. Director will return your game to its original state within the Stage window.

Of course, if dragging the sprite was all you wanted to do, you could have used the method you used to make text draggable earlier in the chapter. Fortunately, Lingo enables you to program behavior that's a little more complicated. For example, to elaborate on the Drag behavior and make the user be able to throw the ball, perform the following steps:

1. Within the Cast window, click your mouse on the Drag member. Director will update the Cast window.

2. Within the Cast window, click your mouse on the Cast Member Script button. Director will display the Script window.

3.   Within the Script window, update the code to appear as follows:

```
property x, y, addX, addY, isDragging
```

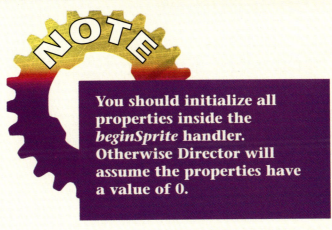

You should initialize all properties inside the *beginSprite* handler. Otherwise Director will assume the properties have a value of 0.

```
on beginSprite me
    x = sprite(me.spriteNum).locH
    y = sprite(me.spriteNum).locV
    addX = 0
    addY = 0
    isDragging = false
  end
on enterFrame me
    if the mouseUp then isDragging = false
```

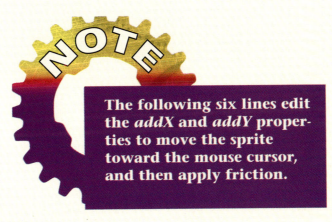

The following six lines edit the *addX* and *addY* properties to move the sprite toward the mouse cursor, and then apply friction.

```
    if isDragging then
        addX = addX + (the mouseH - x)
        addY = addY + (the mouseV - y)
      end if
    addX = addX*0.95
    addY = addY*0.95
```

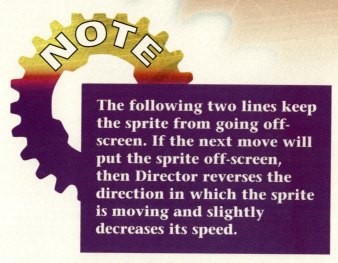

The following two lines keep the sprite from going off-screen. If the next move will put the sprite off-screen, then Director reverses the direction in which the sprite is moving and slightly decreases its speed.

```
if x + addX < 0 or x + addX > 640 then addX = -addX*0.9
if y + addY < 0 or y + addY > 480 then addY = -addY*0.9
```

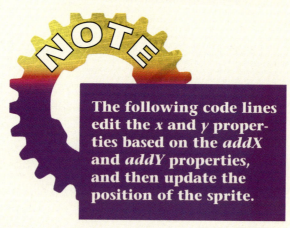

The following code lines edit the x and y properties based on the addX and addY properties, and then update the position of the sprite.

```
x = x + addX
  y = y + addY
  sprite(me.spriteNum).locH = x
  sprite(me.spriteNum).locV = y
end
on mouseDown
  isDragging = true
end
```

4. Within the Toolbar, click your mouse on the Script Window button. Director will close the Script window.

5. Within the Toolbar, click your mouse on the Play button. Director will preview your game within the Stage window. Notice how the Red Ball bitmap now trails behind your cursor when you move your mouse quickly and bounces around the screen when you throw it.

6. Within the Toolbar, click your mouse on the Rewind button. Director will return your game to its original state within the Stage window.

By now, you have the basic skills required to create a game in Director. The main difference between the Director movie you just created and the games in the following chapters is the complex Lingo programming code. As you read through the book, you will gain the skill and experience needed to create as complex a game as you wish.

COMPILING AND COMPRESSING YOUR GAME

If you create a game that you want to show your friends, or perhaps sell for profit, you should create an executable Projector file. Director allows quite a bit of customization when it comes to compression. The more you compress a file, the more quality you will lose. You must decide how much quality you are willing to sacrifice to make your game easier to download. To create an executable Project file, perform the following steps:

1. Click your mouse on the File menu and select the Save As option. Director will display the Save Movie dialog box.

2. Within the Save Movie dialog box, click your mouse on the Save In drop-down list and select your primary hard drive. Director will display the contents of your primary hard drive.

3. Within the Save Movie dialog box, click your mouse on the Create New Folder button. Director will create a new folder on your primary hard drive.

4. Within the Save Movie dialog box, type **Director Games** as the name of your new folder and press the Enter key. Director will name your new folder "Director Games."

5. Within the Save Movie dialog box, double-click your mouse on the *Director Games* folder. Director will display the contents of the *Director Games* folder.

6. Within the Save Movie dialog box, in the File Name text field, type **myfirstgame.dir** and press the Enter key. Director will save your work into a file named *myfirstgame.dir*.

7. Click your mouse on the File menu, and select the Create Projector option. Director will display the Create Projector dialog box.

8. Within the Create Projector dialog box, click your mouse on the Look In drop-down list and select your primary hard drive. Director will display the contents of your primary hard drive.

9. Within the Create Projector dialog box, double-click your mouse on the *Director Games* folder. Director will display the contents of the *Director Games* folder.

10. Within the Create Projector dialog box, click your mouse on the *myfirstgame.dir* file. Director will update the Create Projector dialog box.

11. Within the Create Projector dialog box, click your mouse on the Options button. Director will display the Projector Options dialog box, as shown in Figure 2.18.

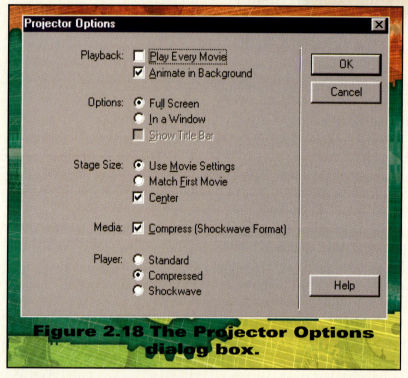

Figure 2.18 The Projector Options dialog box.

12. Within the Projector Options dialog box, customize the various playback and compression options. You will most likely want Director to compress your media in Shockwave format so that your images will not lose any quality.

13. Within the Projector Options dialog box, click your mouse on the OK button. Director will close the Projector Options dialog box.

14. Within the Create Projector dialog box, click your mouse on the Create button. Director will display the Save Projector As dialog box.

15. Within the Save Projector As dialog box, click your mouse on the Save In drop-down list and select your primary hard drive. Director will display the contents of your primary hard drive.

16. Within the Save Projector As dialog box, double-click your mouse on the *Director Games* folder. Director will display the contents of the *Director Games* folder.

17. Within the Save Projector As dialog box, in the File Name text field, type **myfirstgame.exe** and press the Enter key. Director will create an executable Projector file named *myfirstgame.exe* from the *myfirstgame.dir* file.

If you want to distribute your game, you must send people the *myfirstgame.exe* file that Director created. Most people do not have Director, so they would not even be able to view your *myfirstgame.dir* file. In addition, DIR files are uncompressed, so they are generally too large to conveniently send over the Internet. As you create more and more games, you will build a library of executable Projector files to showcase your skills.

Chapter 3
Scramble: Manipulating Graphical Sprites

"It's a job that's never started that takes the longest to finish."—J.R.R. Tolkien

Chapter

3

- Approaching the *Scramble* Game

- Opening the *Scramble* Game's Template

- Understanding the *Scramble* Game

- Adding the Scramble Button

- Applying the Generic Button Behavior

- Comparing and Changing Sprite Locations

- Changing a Sprite's Cast Member

- Creating a Soft Blink Behavior

- Applying Your Skills

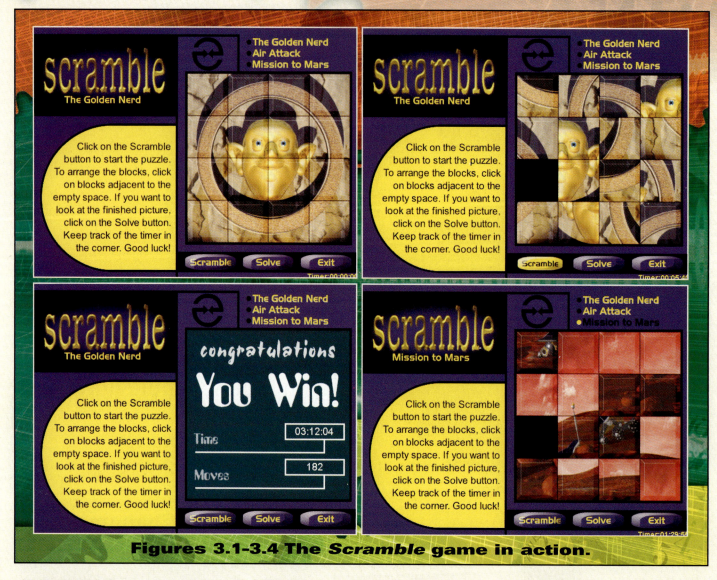

Figures 3.1–3.4 The *Scramble* game in action.

APPROACHING THE *SCRAMBLE* GAME

Graphics are usually the most noticeable part of any game. Director's strongest feature is the ability to manipulate graphics easily in a variety of ways. Although the *Scramble* game contains very little sprite movement and few effects, it is a perfect example of the basic graphical features required for almost any game. The *Scramble* game will teach you how to apply multiple behaviors to a graphical sprite, compare and change the locations of sprites, and even change the cast member associated with a sprite.

OPENING THE *SCRAMBLE* GAME'S TEMPLATE

On the companion CD-ROM is a partially completed version of the *Scramble* game that you will use to learn about manipulating graphical sprites. The partially completed game, called a *template*, will allow you to use Director as a learning tool. To open the *Scramble* game's template in Director and save a copy to your hard drive, perform the following steps:

1. If the companion CD-ROM is not currently in your CD drive, then insert it in your CD-ROM drive now.

2. Within Director, in the Toolbar, click your mouse on the Open button. Director will display the Open dialog box.

3. Within the Open dialog box, click your mouse on the Look In drop-down list and select your CD drive. Director will display the contents of your CD drive.

4. Within the Open dialog box, double-click your mouse on the *Scramble* folder. Director will display the contents of the *Scramble* folder.

5. Within the Open dialog box, click your mouse on the *scrambletemplate.dir* file. Director will update the Open dialog box.

6. Within the Open dialog box, click your mouse on the OK button. Director will open the *scrambletemplate.dir* file.

7. Click your mouse on the File menu and select the Save As option. Director will display the Save Movie dialog box.

8. Within the Save Movie dialog box, click your mouse on the Save In drop-down list and select your primary hard drive. Director will display the contents of your primary hard drive.

9. Within the Save Movie dialog box, double-click your mouse on the *Director Games* folder you created in Chapter 2, "Using Director." Director will display the contents of the *Director Games* folder.

10. Within the Save Movie dialog box, in the File Name text field, type **myscramble.dir** and press the Enter key. Director will save the *Scramble* game's template as a file named *myscramble.dir*.

As you create more and more games in Director, you will develop your own system of organization. For the purpose of clarity, however, you will keep all your edited template files in a single folder.

UNDERSTANDING THE *SCRAMBLE* GAME

The logic behind the *Scramble* game is no more complex than the game itself. To create the illusion of sliding puzzle pieces easily and efficiently, the *Scramble* game simply swaps the appropriate puzzle piece with an invisible puzzle piece. Each time the user tells the *Scramble* game to swap a puzzle piece, the *Scramble* game checks whether the puzzle is in the correct order. As most puzzle games do, the *Scramble* game uses a list to keep track of all the puzzle pieces. As the user plays the *Scramble* game, he or she is actually sorting the list manually. When the user switches between the different puzzles, literally all that changes is the graphics. The *Scramble* game requires a relatively small amount of programming. To view the various Lingo scripts in the Code cast, perform the following steps:

1. Within the Cast window, click your mouse on the Choose Cast button and select the Code option. Director will display the Code cast within the Cast window. The Code cast contains 15 Lingo scripts, as shown in Table 3.1.

Table 3.1 The 15 Lingo scripts of the Code cast and their descriptions.

Script Name	Description
Global	Stores all the global variables, such as *grid* and *gridMoves*, and global functions, such as *scrambleGrid*, *checkWin*, and *resetWin*.
Generic Button	Makes its associated sprite behave as a button complete with specified image, cursor, and sound options.
Generic Stopwatch	Makes its associated sprite behave as a stopwatch to a specified precision.
Wait	Keeps the *Scramble* game looping on one frame until otherwise specified.
Default Visible	Sets its associated sprite's *visible* property to true when the sprite begins.
Default Invisible	Sets its associated sprite's *visible* property to false when the sprite begins.
Block	If possible, swaps the location of its associated sprite with that of the invisible first puzzle piece when the user clicks on its associated sprite.
Scramble Button	Scrambles and shows the puzzle pieces when the user clicks on its associated sprite.
Solve Button	Hides the puzzle pieces with an image of the finished puzzle when the user clicks on its associated sprite.
Exit Button	Plays the game's Exit frame when the user clicks on its associated sprite.
Face Button	Changes the puzzle graphics to the "The Golden Nerd" theme when the user clicks on its associated sprite.
Planes Button	Changes the puzzle graphics to the "Air Attack" theme when the user clicks on its associated sprite.
Mars Button	Changes the puzzle graphics to the "Mission to Mars" theme when the user clicks on its associated sprite.
Yes Button	Ends the game when the user clicks on its associated sprite.
No Button	Resets the game when the user clicks on its associated sprite.

2. Within the Cast window, click your mouse on the Global member. Director will update the Cast window, as shown in Figure 3.5.

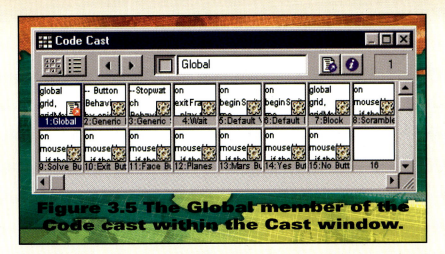

Figure 3.5 The Global member of the Code cast within the Cast window.

3. Within the Cast window, click your mouse on the Cast Member Script button. Director will display the Script window.

4. Within the Script window, use the Previous Cast Member and Next Cast Member buttons to view each of the Lingo scripts in the Code cast.

By now, you should have a good understanding of the logic behind the *Scramble* game. You will find that using Director to edit an existing game is nearly impossible unless you first understand how the game works.

ADDING THE SCRAMBLE BUTTON

The cleanest way add a cast member to the Stage is through the Score window. By default, new sprites take up 28 frames. However, if you have frame markers that are fewer than 28 frames apart, the sprite will only exist until the next frame marker. If you do not want a sprite to exist at the beginning of a game, you actually need to use the Score window to position the sprite in its correct channel. To add the Scramble button to the *Scramble* game, perform the following steps:

1. Within the Cast window, click your mouse on the Choose Cast button and select the Graphics option, as shown in Figure 3.6. Director will display the Graphics cast within the Cast window.

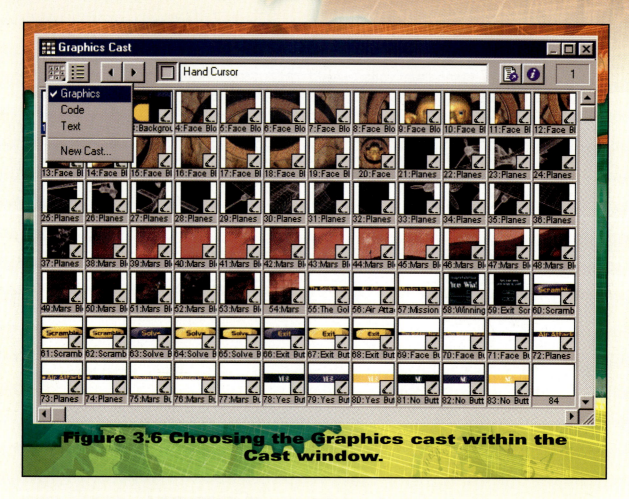

Figure 3.6 Choosing the Graphics cast within the Cast window.

2. Using your mouse, drag the Scramble Button member from the Cast window into cell 1 of channel 23 of the Score window. Director will display the Scramble Button bitmap within the Stage.

3. Within the Score window, drag cell 14 of channel 23 to frame 29. Director will extend the Scramble bitmap to frame 29, as shown in Figure 3.7.

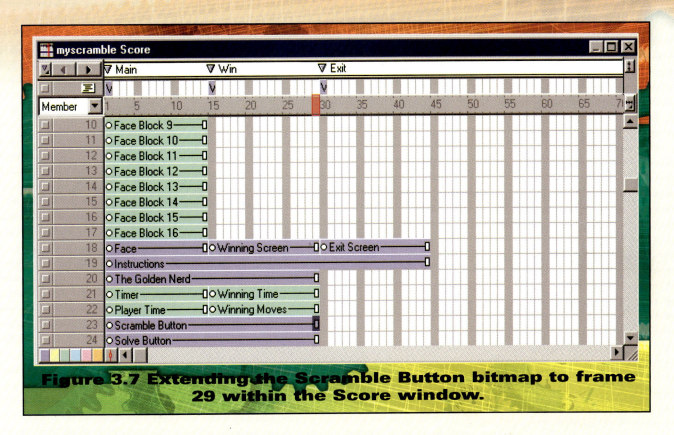

Figure 3.7 Extending the Scramble Button bitmap to frame 29 within the Score window.

4.   Within the Stage window, drag the Scramble Button bitmap to its appropriate position. Director will update the Property Inspector window.

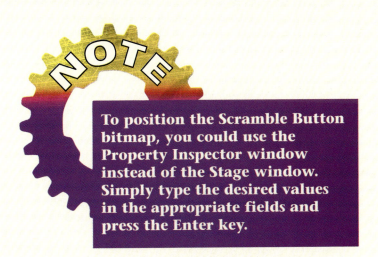

To position the Scramble Button bitmap, you could use the Property Inspector window instead of the Stage window. Simply type the desired values in the appropriate fields and press the Enter key.

5. Within the Property Inspector window, click your mouse on the Behavior tab. Director will display the Behavior sheet.

6. Within the Property Inspector window, click your mouse on the Behavior pop-up button and select the Scramble Button option. Director will apply the Scramble Button behavior to the Scramble Button bitmap.

If you were to preview your game now, the Scramble button should function properly. It would not, however, appear to be functioning as a button. As you are aware, most buttons change the way they look when you click your mouse on them or sometimes even hold your mouse over them. Usually, buttons appear to be pressed because their actual image changes slightly. The changing images are often accompanied by a cursor change, a sound, or both.

APPLYING THE GENERIC BUTTON BEHAVIOR

The Generic Button behavior packages all the aspects of a button besides it actual functionality into a single, customizable behavior. Unlike most behaviors, the Generic Button behavior accepts arguments, or parameters, that set the values of its different properties. To apply the Generic Button behavior to the Scramble Button bitmap, perform the following steps:

1. Within the Property Inspector window, click your mouse on the Behavior pop-up button and select the Generic Button option. Director will display the Parameters dialog box, as shown in Figure 3.8.

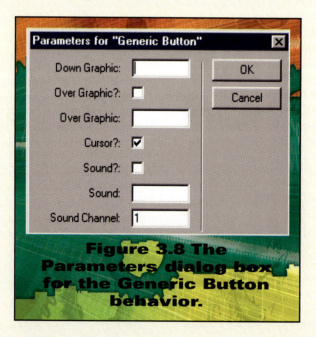

Figure 3.8 The Parameters dialog box for the Generic Button behavior.

2. Within the Parameters dialog box, in the Down Graphic field, type **Scramble Button Down**. Director will set the graphic used to represent the down state of the Scramble button to the Scramble Button Down member.

3. Within the Parameters dialog box, click your mouse on the Over Graphic check-box. Director will set the Scramble button to use a graphic that represents the over state.

4. Within the Parameters dialog box, in the Over Graphic field, type **Scramble Button Over**. Director will set the over graphic of the Scramble button to the Scramble Button Over member.

5. Within the Parameters dialog box, click your mouse on the OK button. Director will apply the Generic Button behavior to the Scramble Button bitmap.

6. Within the Toolbar, click your mouse on the Play button. Director will preview your game within the Stage window. The Scramble button should be fully functional.

7. Within the Toolbar, click your mouse on the Rewind button. Director will return your game to its original state within the Stage window.

Because almost every game uses some sort of button in its interface, the Generic Button behavior is extraordinarily convenient. Some programmers, however, feel that using programming code that someone else originally created is morally wrong. You will have to decide for yourself whether you want to type all the code for a standard button each time you create a new game.

COMPARING AND CHANGING SPRITE LOCATIONS

Lingo allows you to distort and move sprites in a wide variety of ways. The most commonly used method is to set a sprite's *locH* property to an X coordinate and its *locV* property to a Y coordinate. You can accomplish the same task in a single line by setting the sprite's *loc* property to a point value that consists of the X and Y coordinates. If you wanted your code to be a bit more specific, you could even edit the sprite's *width*, *height*, *left*, *right*, *top*, *bottom*, and *quad* properties. To add the code to the Block behavior that swaps the location of the invisible first puzzle piece with that of another puzzle piece, perform the ollowing steps:

1. Within the Cast window, click your mouse on the Choose Cast button and select the Code option. Director will display the Code cast within the Cast window.

2. Within the Cast window, click your mouse on the Block member. Director will update the Cast window.

3. Within the Cast window, click your mouse on the Cast Member Script button. Director will display the Script window, as shown in Figure 3.9.

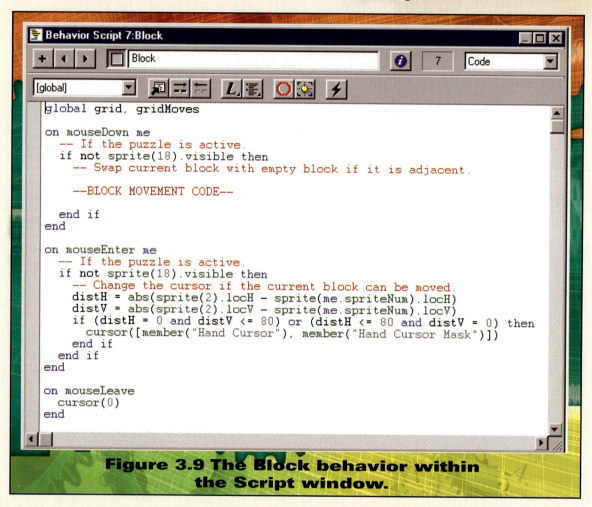

Figure 3.9 The Block behavior within the Script window.

4. Within the Script window, replace —*BLOCK MOVEMENT CODE*— with the following code:

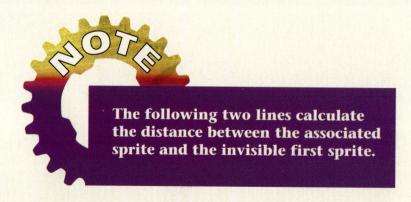

The following two lines calculate the distance between the associated sprite and the invisible first sprite.

```
distH = abs(sprite(2).locH - sprite(me.spriteNum).locH)
distV = abs(sprite(2).locV - sprite(me.spriteNum).locV)
```

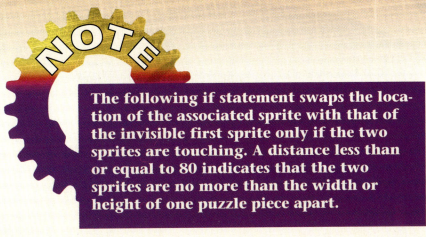

NOTE

The following if statement swaps the location of the associated sprite with that of the invisible first sprite only if the two sprites are touching. A distance less than or equal to 80 indicates that the two sprites are no more than the width or height of one puzzle piece apart.

```
if (distH = 0 and distV <= 80) or (distH <= 80 and distV = 0) then
    temp = sprite(2).loc
    sprite(2).loc = sprite(me.spriteNum).loc
    sprite(me.spriteNum).loc = temp
    temp = getPos(grid, 1)
    grid[getPos(grid, me.spriteNum - 1)] = 1
    grid[temp] = me.spriteNum - 1
    gridMoves = gridMoves + 1
    checkWin
end if
```

5.   Within the Toolbar, click your mouse on the Script Window button. Director will close the Script window.

6.   Within the Toolbar, click your mouse on the Play button. Director will preview your game within the Stage window. The puzzle should be fully functional.

7.   Within the Toolbar, click your mouse on the Rewind button. Director will return your game to its original state within the Stage window.

If you strip away all the different sections and effects, the block movement code is essentially the entire game. If the block clicked is adjacent to the invisible first puzzle piece, the *Scramble* game swaps its location with that of the invisible piece. Then, the game checks whether the puzzle is in the correct order.

CHANGING A SPRITE'S CAST MEMBER

In the course of a game, you can change a sprite in any way you like. Not only can you change a sprite's location, size, and effects, but you can also change the cast member with which it is associated. To add the code to the Mars Button behavior that changes the puzzle images to the "Mission to Mars" theme, perform the following steps:

1.   Within the Cast window, click your mouse on the Mars Button member. Director will update the Cast window.

2. Within the Cast window, click your mouse on the Cast Member Script button. Director will display the Script window, as shown in Figure 3.10.

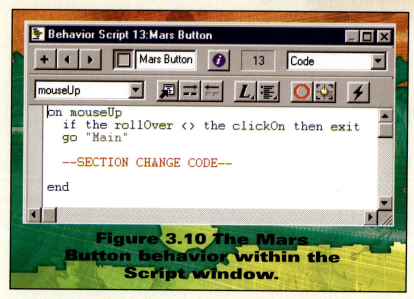

Figure 3.10 The Mars Button behavior within the Script window.

3. Within the Script window, replace —*SECTION CHANGE CODE*— with the following code:

```
sprite(18).member = "Mars"
sprite(20).member = "Mission to Mars"
repeat with count = 1 to 16
    sprite(count+1).member = "Mars Block" & count
end repeat
```

4. Within the Toolbar, click your mouse on the Script Window button. Director will close the Script window.

5. Within the Toolbar, click your mouse on the Play button. Director will preview your game within the Stage window. The "Mission to Mars" button should be fully functional.

6. Within the Toolbar, click your mouse on the Rewind button. Director will return your game to its original state within the Stage window.

If you change a sprite's cast member to a new cast member of a different size, the sprite behaves a bit unpredictably. By default, the sprite will not distort the new cast member to fit its current size unless you have explicitly changed its *width* and *height* properties. You can keep the new cast member from distorting by setting the sprite's *stretch* property to false. Keep in mind, however, that the sprite's *width* and *height* properties will change automatically.

CREATING A SOFT BLINK BEHAVIOR

The variety of effects you can create using the various properties of sprites is virtually endless. Refer to Appendix B, "Lingo Quick Reference," for a complete listing of sprite properties. One of the most useful sprite properties is the *blend* property. The *blend* property can be any value from 0 to 100 representing a percentage of visibility. A value of 50 indicates that the associated sprite is 50 percent transparent. To create and apply a behavior using the *blend* property, perform the following steps:

1. Within the Toolbar, click your mouse on the Script Window button. Director will display the Script window.

2. Within the Script window, click your mouse on the New Cast Member button. Director will add a new script to the Code cast.

3. Within the Script window, in the Cast Member Name text field, type **Soft Blink** and press the Enter key. Director will name the new script "Soft Blink."

4. Within the Properties window, click your mouse on the Script tab. Director will display the Script sheet.

5. Within the Properties window, click your mouse on the Script Type drop-down list and select the Behavior option. Director will mark the Soft Blink script as a behavior script, as shown in Figure 3.11.

Figure 3.11 Marking the Soft Blink script as a behavior script.

6. **Within the Script window, type the following code:**

```
property addBlend
on beginSprite me
   addBlend = 5
   sprite(me.spriteNum).blend = 100
end
```

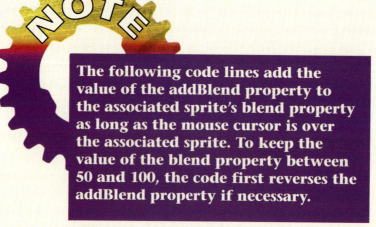

NOTE

The following code lines add the value of the addBlend property to the associated sprite's blend property as long as the mouse cursor is over the associated sprite. To keep the value of the blend property between 50 and 100, the code first reverses the addBlend property if necessary.

```
on mouseWithin me
   if sprite(me.spriteNum).blend + addBlend < 50 or sprite(me.spriteNum).\
   blend + addBlend > 100 then
      addBlend = -addBlend
   end if
   sprite(me.spriteNum).blend = sprite(me.spriteNum).blend + addBlend
end
on mouseLeave me
   sprite(me.spriteNum).blend = 100
end
```

7. Within the Toolbar, click your mouse on the Script Window button. Director will close the Script window.

8. Within the Stage, click your mouse on the Scramble Button bitmap. Director will update the Property Inspector window.

9. Within the Property Inspector window, click your mouse on the Behavior pop-up button and select the Soft Blink option, as shown in Figure 3.12. Director will apply the Soft Blink behavior to the Scramble Button bitmap.

Figure 3.12 Applying the Soft Blink behavior to the Scramble Button bitmap.

10. Within the Toolbar, click your mouse on the Play button. Director will preview your game within the Stage window. The Scramble button should slowly fade in and out.

11. Within the Toolbar, click your mouse on the Rewind button. Director will return your game to its original state within the Stage window.

Try applying the Soft Blink behavior to other sprites in the *Scramble* game. Notice the translucent appearance of the associated sprites when they overlap. Similar algorithms dealing with rotation, distortion, size, and location are useful to spice up any boring interface.

APPLYING YOUR SKILLS

Now that you have the skills required to manipulate graphical sprites in a variety of ways, you can create a simple game like the *Scramble* game. You could create a *Whack-a-Mole* style game by placing a mole image at random locations on the Stage and using its *mouseDown* handler to change the image and add a point to the player's score. Even the simplest of games can seem impressive with the right graphics.

Chapter 4
Painter: Painting with Sprite Trails

"It took me four years to paint like Raphael, but a lifetime to paint like a child."—Pablo Picasso

Chapter

4

- Approaching the *Painter* Game

- Opening the *Painter* Game's Template

- Understanding the *Painter* Game

- Painting Smooth Lines

- Adding the Paper Mask

- Keeping the Paint Inside of the Mask

- Adding Randomness to the Paint

- Applying Your Skills

Figures 4.1–4.4 The *Painter* game in action.

APPROACHING THE *PAINTER* GAME

To create a movement effect with most software development tools, you must draw an image, make any necessary calculations, erase the image, and then quickly redraw it in a new location. By default, Director erases images automatically before changing their properties. However, Director still provides the option to leave trails behind instead of automatically erasing them. The *Painter* game allows the user to draw simply by moving an image around and leaving trails behind. The *Painter* game will teach you how to move the paint graphic smoothly while limiting it to a specific area of the screen.

OPENING THE *PAINTER* GAME'S TEMPLATE

On this book's companion CD-ROM is a template of the *Painter* game that you will use to learn about painting with sprite trails. The template will allow you to use Director as a learning tool. To open the

Painter game's template in Director and save a copy to your hard drive, perform the following steps:

1. If the companion CD-ROM is not currently in your CD drive, then insert it in your CD-ROM drive now.

2. Within Director, in the Toolbar, click your mouse on the Open button. Director will display the Open dialog box.

3. Within the Open dialog box, click your mouse on the Look In drop-down list and select your CD drive. Director will display the contents of your CD drive.

4. Within the Open dialog box, double-click your mouse on the *Painter* folder. Director will display the contents of the *Painter* folder.

5. Within the Open dialog box, click your mouse on the *paintertemplate.dir* file. Director will update the Open dialog box.

6. Within the Open dialog box, click your mouse on the OK button. Director will open the *paintertemplate.dir* file.

7. Click your mouse on the File menu and select the Save As option. Director will display the Save Movie dialog box.

8. Within the Save Movie dialog box, click your mouse on the Save In drop-down list and select your primary hard drive. Director will display the contents of your primary hard drive.

9. Within the Save Movie dialog box, double-click your mouse on the *Director Games* folder you created in Chapter 2, "Using Director." Director will display the contents of the *Director Games* folder.

10. Within the Save Movie dialog box, in the File Name text field, type **mypainter.dir** and press the Enter key. Director will save the *Painter* game's template as a file named "mypainter.dir."

As you create more and more games in Director, you will develop your own system of organization. For the purpose of clarity, however, you will keep all your edited template files in a single folder.

UNDERSTANDING THE *PAINTER* GAME

The *Painter* game utilizes Director's built-in *trails* sprite property. If a sprite's *trails* property is true, Director will not erase the sprite each time just before it moves. However, if a different sprite with its *trails* property set to false crosses the original sprite's path, the trail will disappear. To keep the trail of paint from being overwritten, the *Painter* game avoids updating any sprites that overlap the paper in the *Painter* game. To keep the paint only on the paper, the Painter game uses a separate mask image. The mask image is an invisible outline of the paintable area. If the user tries to paint outside the mask's outline, the *Painter* game hides the paint with a Lingo script. To view the various Lingo scripts in the Code cast, perform the following steps:

1. Within the Cast window, click your mouse on the Choose Cast button and select the Code option. Director will display the Code cast within the Cast window. The Code cast contains 20 Lingo scripts, as shown in Table 4.1.

Table 4.1 The 20 Lingo scripts of the Code cast and their descriptions.

Script Name	Description
Global	Updates the color of the paper and paint based on the six text fields.
Generic Button	Makes its associated sprite behave as a button complete with specified image, cursor, and sound options.
Wait	Keeps the *Painter* game looping on one frame until otherwise specified.
Default Invisible	Sets its associated sprite's *visible* property to false when the sprite begins.
Paper	Continuously moves the Paint bitmap toward the mouse cursor while the user is painting.
Brush 1	Changes the width and height of the Paint bitmap to 20 pixels when the user clicks on its associated sprite.
Brush 2	Changes the width and height of the Paint bitmap to 16 pixels when the user clicks on its associated sprite.
Brush 3	Changes the width and height of the Paint bitmap to 12 pixels when the user clicks on its associated sprite.
Brush 4	Changes the width and height of the Paint bitmap to 8 pixels when the user clicks on its associated sprite.
Brush 5	Changes the width and height of the Paint bitmap to 4 pixels when the user clicks on its associated sprite.
Eraser	Changes the color of the Paint bitmap to the color of the Paper shape when the user clicks on its associated sprite.
Blue	Changes the color of the Paint bitmap to blue when the user clicks on its associated sprite.
Red	Changes the color of the Paint bitmap to red when the user clicks on its associated sprite.
Green	Changes the color of the Paint bitmap to green when the user clicks on its associated sprite.
Yellow	Changes the color of the Paint bitmap to yellow when the user clicks on its associated sprite.
Purple	Changes the color of the Paint bitmap to purple when the user clicks on its associated sprite.

Table 4.1 The 20 Lingo scripts of the Code cast and their descriptions. (cont.)

Script Name	Description
Black	Changes the color of the Paint bitmap to black when the user clicks on its associated sprite.
Reset Button	Clears the paper when the user clicks on its associated sprite.
Help Button	Plays game's Help frame when the user clicks on its associated sprite.
Exit Button	Ends the game when the user clicks on its associated sprite.

2. Within the Cast window, click your mouse on the Global member, as shown in Figure 4.5. Director will update the Cast window.

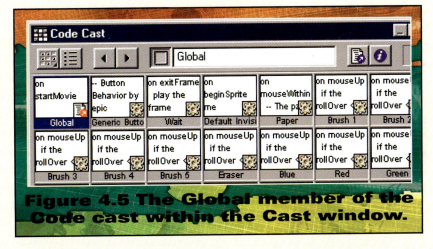

Figure 4.5 The Global member of the Code cast within the Cast window.

3. Within the Cast window, click your mouse on the Cast Member Script button. Director will display the Script window.

4. Within the Script window, use the Previous Cast Member and Next Cast Member buttons to view each of the Lingo scripts in the Code cast.

By now, you should have a good understanding of the logic behind the *Painter* game. You will find that using Director to edit an existing game is nearly impossible unless you first understand how the game works.

PAINTING SMOOTH LINES

If you were to preview your game now, you would see a technically functional painting game. However, the paint only draws itself in a new position when it receives a new set of mouse coordinates. Moving the paint immediately to the current mouse coordinates often leaves large gaps between spots of paint. A relatively simple way to leave a solid trail of paint behind the mouse cursor no matter how fast it moves is to draw straight lines between mouse coordinates as quickly as possible. Because the computer receives mouse coordinates much quicker than the *Painter* game can draw paint on the screen, drawing straight

Macromedia Director Game Development
From Concept to Creation

lines between points often results in mechanical-looking trails with sharp corners. To make the trails appear as smooth as possible, the *Painter* game only draws a small piece of a line at a time. By the time the paint is ready to move again, the mouse coordinates have most likely changed. To add the code to the Paper behavior that makes the Paint bitmap smoothly follow the mouse cursor, perform the following steps:

1. Within the Cast window, click your mouse on the Paper member. Director will update the Cast window.

2. Within the Cast window, click your mouse on the Cast Member Script button. Director will display the Script window, as shown in Figure 4.6.

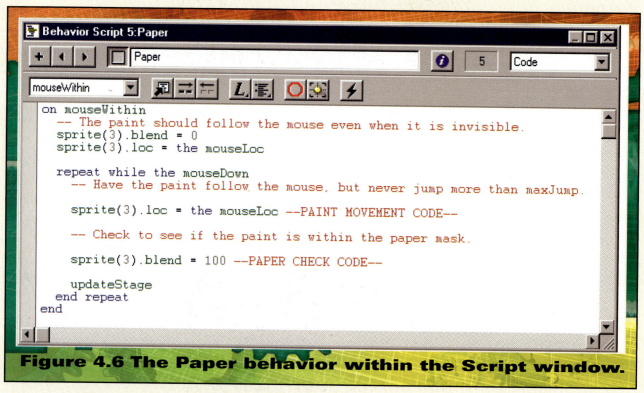

```
on mouseWithin
  -- The paint should follow the mouse even when it is invisible.
  sprite(3).blend = 0
  sprite(3).loc = the mouseLoc

  repeat while the mouseDown
    -- Have the paint follow the mouse, but never jump more than maxJump.

    sprite(3).loc = the mouseLoc --PAINT MOVEMENT CODE--

    -- Check to see if the paint is within the paper mask.

    sprite(3).blend = 100 --PAPER CHECK CODE--

    updateStage
  end repeat
end
```

Figure 4.6 The Paper behavior within the Script window.

3. Within the Script window, replace *sprite(3).loc = the mouseLoc —PAINT MOVEMENT CODE—* with the following code:

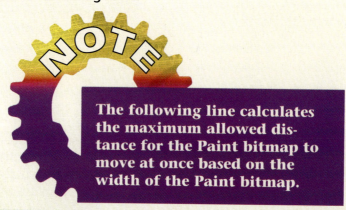

The following line calculates the maximum allowed distance for the Paint bitmap to move at once based on the width of the Paint bitmap.

```
maxJump = integer(sprite(3).width/3) + 1
```

52

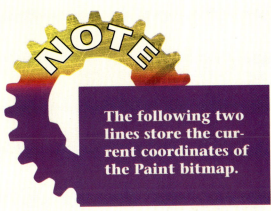

NOTE

The following seven lines calculate a value for the jumps variable based on either the horizontal or the vertical distance between the Paint bitmap and the mouse cursor. The jumps variable indicates how many movements of maxJump pixels are required for the Paint bitmap to catch up to the mouse cursor.

```
distH = abs(sprite(3).locH - the mouseH)
distV = abs(sprite(3).locV - the mouseV)
if distH > distV then
  jumps = distH/maxJump + 1
else
  jumps = distV/maxJump + 1
end if
```

NOTE

The following two lines store the current coordinates of the Paint bitmap.

```
tempH = sprite(3).locH
tempV = sprite(3).locV
```

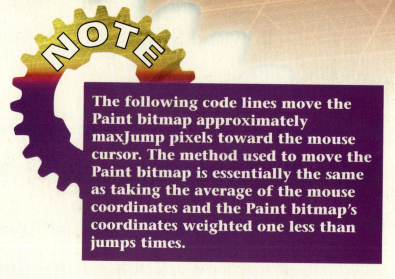

NOTE

The following code lines move the Paint bitmap approximately maxJump pixels toward the mouse cursor. The method used to move the Paint bitmap is essentially the same as taking the average of the mouse coordinates and the Paint bitmap's coordinates weighted one less than jumps times.

```
sprite(3).locH = integer(sprite(3).locH*(jumps-1) + the mouseH)/jumps
sprite(3).locV = integer(sprite(3).locV*(jumps-1) + the mouseV)/jumps
```

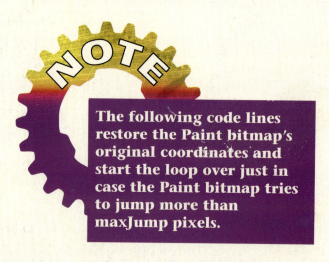

NOTE

The following code lines restore the Paint bitmap's original coordinates and start the loop over just in case the Paint bitmap tries to jump more than maxJump pixels.

```
if abs(tempH - sprite(3).locH) > maxJump or abs(tempV - sprite(3).locV) \
> maxJump then
   sprite(3).locH = tempH
   sprite(3).locV = tempV
   next repeat
end if
```

4. Within the Toolbar, click your mouse on the Script Window button. Director will close the Script window.

5. Within the Toolbar, click your mouse on the Play button. Director will preview your game within the Stage window. You should be able to paint smoothly anywhere on the screen, as shown in Figure 4.7.

Figure 4.7 Painting smoothly within the Stage.

6. Within the Toolbar, click your mouse on the Rewind button. Director will return your game to its original state within the Stage window.

If you wanted to use the entire screen for painting, the *Painter* game would be complete. However, the *Painter* game allows the user to paint only on the paper. The simplest way to avoid having the user draw outside of the paper is to use a separate bitmap as a sort of a mask.

ADDING THE PAPER MASK

The Paper Mask bitmap consists of a black outline of the entire useable area of the paper. The *Painter* application uses the Paper Mask bitmap to determine whether it should draw the Paint bitmap. Both bitmaps are of irregular shape. In order to determine if two non-rectangular bitmaps are touching each other, both bitmaps must be of the Matte ink style. The Matte ink style ignores all white pixels around the edge of an image. Therefore, the background of the Paper Mask bitmap must be white for the mask to work. To add the Paper Mask bitmap to the *Painter* game, perform the following steps:

1. Within the Cast window, click your mouse on the Choose Cast button and select the Graphics option, as shown in Figure 4.8. Director will display the Graphics cast within the Cast window.

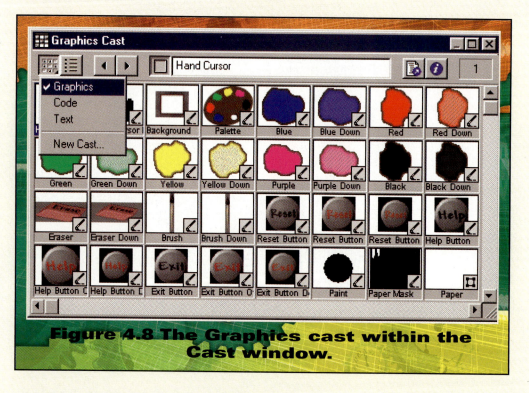

Figure 4.8 The Graphics cast within the Cast window.

2. Drag the Paper Mask member from the Cast window into cell 1 of channel 4 of the Score window. Director will display the Paper Mask bitmap within the Stage.

3. Within the Stage window, drag the Paper Mask bitmap to its appropriate position. Director will update the Property Inspector window.

4. Within the Property Inspector window, click your mouse on the Sprite tab. Director will display the Sprite sheet.

5. Within the Property Inspector window, click your mouse on the Ink drop-down list and select the Matte option, as shown in Figure 4.9. Director will remove the background rectangle from the Paper Mask bitmap.

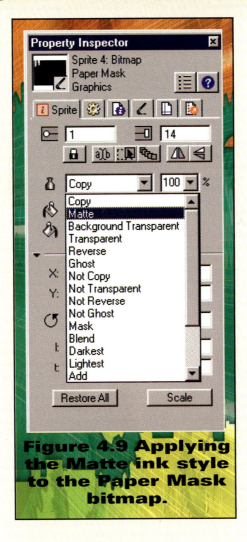

Figure 4.9 Applying the Matte ink style to the Paper Mask bitmap.

6. Within the Property Inspector window, click your mouse on the Behavior tab. Director will display the Behavior sheet.

7. Within the Property Inspector window, click your mouse on the Behavior pop-up button and select the Default Invisible option. Director will apply the Default Invisible behavior to the Paper Mask bitmap.

Although the Paper Mask bitmap is now positioned correctly on the Stage, you'll notice that it is functionless. This is because the *Painter* game's template does not contain any of the programming code needed to use the Paper Mask bitmap properly.

KEEPING THE PAINT INSIDE OF THE MASK

A simple way to keep the Paint bitmap within the border of the Paper Mask bitmap is to hide the Paint bitmap when it is out of bounds. The *trails* sprite property can sometimes be tricky, though. If you simply set the Paint bitmap's *visible* property to false when it goes out of bounds, the sprite will leave a white square behind and erase a part of its trails. One way to avoid this is by instead setting the Paint bitmap's *blend* property to zero. A *blend* value of zero means that the sprite is 0 percent visible. (As you can see, sometimes you must work around specific problems, and your code will look different than originally expected.) To add the code to the Paper behavior that makes the Paint bitmap stay inside the border of the Paper Mask bitmap, perform the following steps:

1. Within the Cast window, click your mouse on the Paper member. Director will update the Cast window.

2. Within the Cast window, click your mouse on the Cast Member Script button. Director will display the Script window.

3. Within the Script window, replace *sprite(3).blend = 100 —PAPER CHECK CODE—* with the following code:

The following two lines store the current size of the Paint bitmap.

```
tempWidth = sprite(3).width
tempHeight = sprite(3).height
```

The following nine lines determine whether the Paint bitmap should be visible based on its intersection with the Paper Mask bitmap.

```
sprite(3).width = 2
sprite(3).height = 2
sprite(3).blend = 0
updateStage
if sprite(3).intersects(4) then
  sprite(3).blend = 100
else
  sprite(3).blend = 0
end if
```

NOTE

The following two lines restore the Paint bitmap's original size.

```
sprite(3).width = tempWidth
sprite(3).height = tempHeight
```

4.   Within the Toolbar, click your mouse on the Script Window button. Director will close the Script window.

5.   Within the Toolbar, click your mouse on the Play button. Director will preview your game within the Stage window. The *Painter* game should be fully functional.

6.   Within the Toolbar, click your mouse on the Rewind button. Director will return your game to its original state within the Stage window.

By now, the *Painter* game's template is fully functional. Your template file contains all the features of the original *Painter* game. However, that shouldn't stop you from adding new features. No game is complete until the programmer decides it is.

ADDING RANDOMNESS TO THE PAINT

If you change a sprite's properties as it leaves trails behind, you can produce amazing fade effects. Because the user sees all the steps of a gradual change at once, the change is more apparent. When changing properties randomly, you should generally add a small random number to the existing value. If you set the property to a completely random value, you will lose the fade effect. To add code to the Paper behavior that makes the Paint bitmap randomly resize and shift colors, perform the following steps:

1. Within the Cast window, click your mouse on the Paper member. Director will update the Cast window.

2. Within the Cast window, click your mouse on the Cast Member Script button. Director will display the Script window.

3. Within the Script window, immediately following the paper check code and preceding the *updateStage* command, type the following code:

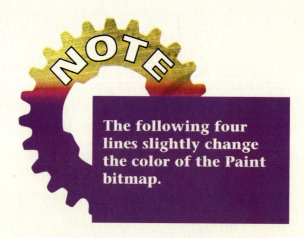

The following four lines slightly change the color of the Paint bitmap.

```
newRed = sprite(3).color.red + random(7)-4
newGreen = sprite(3).color.green + random(7)-4
newBlue = sprite(3).color.blue + random(7)-4
sprite(3).color = rgb(newRed, newGreen, newBlue)
```

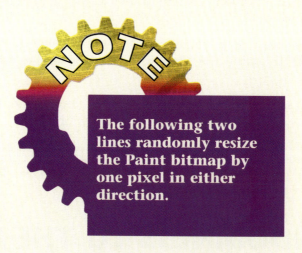

The following two lines randomly resize the Paint bitmap by one pixel in either direction.

```
sprite(3).width = sprite(3).width + random(3) - 2
sprite(3).height = sprite(3).height + random(3) - 2
```

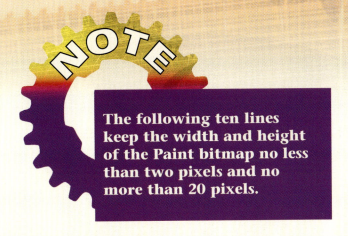

The following ten lines keep the width and height of the Paint bitmap no less than two pixels and no more than 20 pixels.

```
if sprite(3).width < 2 then
   sprite(3).width = sprite(3).width + 1
else if sprite(3).width > 20 then
   sprite(3).width = sprite(3).width - 1
end if
if sprite(3).height < 2 then
   sprite(3).height = sprite(3).width + 1
else if sprite(3).height > 20 then
   sprite(3).height = sprite(3).height - 1
end if
```

4. Within the Toolbar, click your mouse on the Script Window button. Director will close the Script window.

5. Within the Toolbar, click your mouse on the Play button. Director will preview your game within the Stage window. As you drag your mouse across the paper, the paint should randomly resize and shift colors, as shown in Figure 4.10.

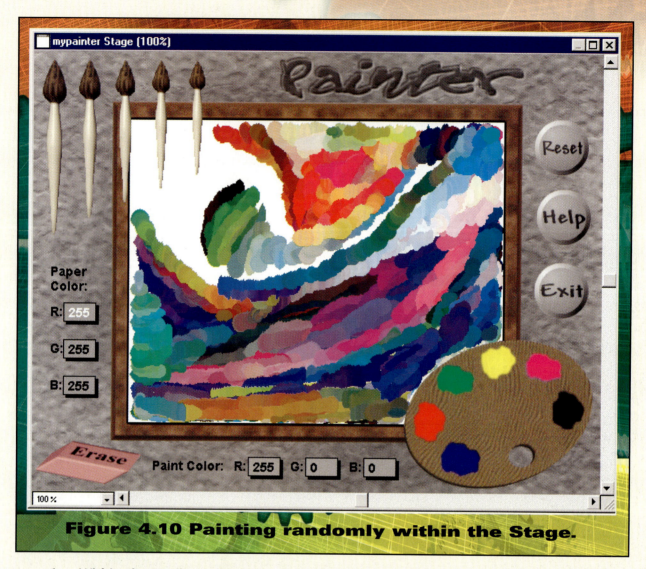

Figure 4.10 Painting randomly within the Stage.

6. Within the Toolbar, click your mouse on the Rewind button. Director will return your game to its original state within the Stage window.

You can expand on the *Painter* game as long as you wish. You can change the Paint bitmap to some kind of stamp image. Alternatively, if you want to create an airbrush effect, you can change the Paint bitmap to a light spray of single pixels and set its *rotation* property to a random value each frame. The *Painter* game is quite versatile.

APPLYING YOUR SKILLS

Now that you have the skills required to paint with sprite trails, you can create all kinds of impressive effects. To produce an eye-catching intro for a game, try gradually enlarging or fading a sprite as it moves. For a simple side-scrolling game in which the character shoots projectiles, set one of the projectile sprites to leave trails behind it for a laser effect. Though the *trails* sprite property seems simple, you must always remember to clear the sprite trails manually so as not to leave unwanted trails on the screen.

Chapter 5
Monk Mania: Playing Sounds

"Music is the best." —Frank Zappa

Chapter

5

- Approaching the *Monk Mania* Game

- Opening the *Monk Mania* Game's Template

- Understanding the *Monk Mania* Game

- Adding Sound to the Score

- Puppetting Sounds in Lingo

- Using Other Methods to Play Sounds

- Interrupting Sounds to Speed Up the Game

- Applying Your Skills

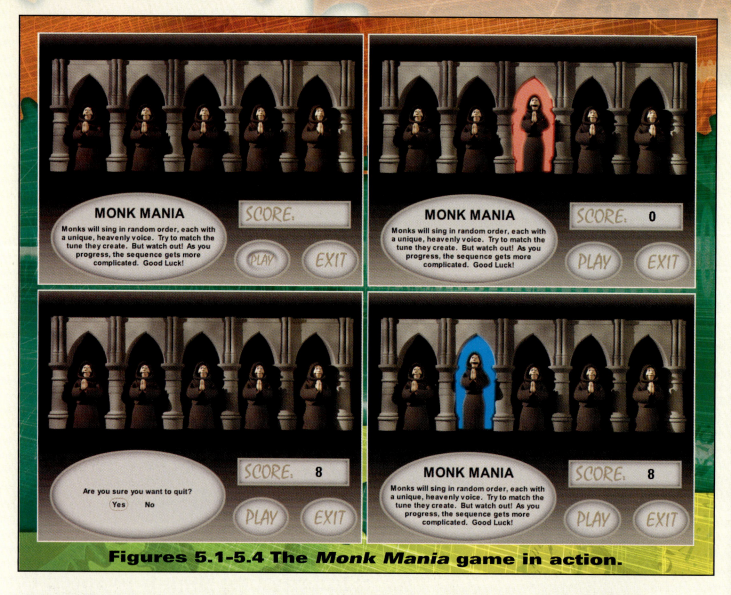

Figures 5.1-5.4 The *Monk Mania* game in action.

APPROACHING THE *MONK MANIA* GAME

Sound effects and music add atmosphere to any game. Although Director is mostly a graphically oriented development tool, playing sounds in Director is just as easy as drawing graphics. Without sounds, the *Monk Mania* game would be quite boring. The *Monk Mania* game will teach you how to play sounds through the Score and manipulate sounds through Lingo in a variety of ways.

OPENING THE *MONK MANIA* GAME'S TEMPLATE

On this book's companion CD-ROM is a template of the *Monk Mania* game that you will use to learn about playing sounds. The template will allow you to use Director as a learning tool. To open the *Monk Mania* game's template in Director and save a copy to your hard drive, perform the following steps:

1. If the companion CD-ROM is not currently in your CD drive, then insert it in your CD-ROM drive now.

2. Within Director, in the Toolbar, click your mouse on the Open button. Director will display the Open dialog box.

3. Within the Open dialog box, click your mouse on the Look In drop-down list, and select your CD drive. Director will display the contents of your CD drive.

4. Within the Open dialog box, double-click your mouse on the *Monk Mania* folder. Director will display the contents of the *Monk Mania* folder.

5. Within the Open dialog box, click your mouse on the *monkmaniatemplate.dir* file. Director will update the Open dialog box.

6. Within the Open dialog box, click your mouse on the OK button. Director will open the *monkmaniatemplate.dir* file.

7. Click your mouse on the File menu, and select the Save As option. Director will display the Save Movie dialog box.

8. Within the Save Movie dialog box, click your mouse on the Save In drop-down list, and select your primary hard drive. Director will display the contents of your primary hard drive.

9. Within the Save Movie dialog box, double-click your mouse on the *Director Games* folder you created in Chapter 2, "Using Director." Director will display the contents of the *Director Games* folder.

10. Within the Save Movie dialog box, in the File Name text field, type **mymonkmania.dir**, and press the Enter key. Director will save the *Monk Mania* game's template as a file named "mymonkmania.dir."

As you create more and more games in Director, you will develop your own system of organization. For the purpose of clarity, however, you will keep all your edited template files in a single folder.

UNDERSTANDING THE *MONK MANIA* GAME

The *Monk Mania* game's background image contains all five monks in their normal states. The singing versions of the monks are in front of the normal versions, but they all start off invisible. The *playMonk* function displays the singing version of a specified monk, plays its sound, and returns the monk to normal. Each time the user chooses the correct sequence of monks, the *Monk Mania* game adds another monk to the list, and calls the *playMonk* function for each monk in the sequence. To view the various Lingo scripts in the Code cast, perform the following steps:

1. Within the Cast window, click your mouse on the Choose Cast button, and select the Code option. Director will display the Code cast within the Cast window. The Code cast contains 12 Lingo scripts, as shown in Table 5.1.

Table 5.1 The 12 Lingo scripts of the Code cast and their descriptions.

Script Name	Description
Global	Contains the *playMonk* function, which makes a specified monk sing.
Generic Button	Makes its associated sprite behave as a button complete with specified image, cursor, and sound options.
Wait	Keeps the *Monk Mania* game looping on one frame until otherwise specified.
Start Game	Initializes global variables and chooses a random monk to play first.
Default Invisible	Sets its associated sprite's *visible* property to false when the sprite begins.
Change Cursor	Set the mouse cursor to the Hand Cursor bitmap while the mouse is over its associated sprite.
Monk Hot Spot	Checks whether or not the user chose the correct monk in the sequence when the user clicks on its associated sprite.
Play Button	Plays game's Game frame when the user clicks on its associated sprite.
Exit Button	Plays game's Exit frame when the user clicks on its associated sprite.
Highlight Hot Spot	Changes the color of its associated sprite to indicate mouse events.
Quit Yes	Ends the game when the user releases a click on its associated sprite.
Quit No	Plays game's Game frame when the user releases a click on its associated sprite.

2. Within the Cast window, click your mouse on the Global member. Director will update the Cast window, as shown in Figure 5.5.

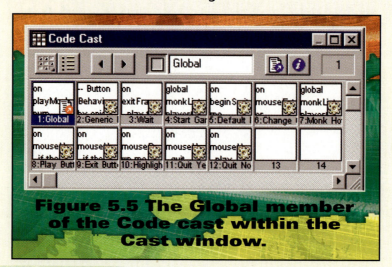

Figure 5.5 The Global member of the Code cast within the Cast window.

3. Within the Cast window, click your mouse on the Cast Member Script button. Director will display the Script window.

4. Within the Script window, use the Previous Cast Member and Next Cast Member buttons to view each of the Lingo scripts in the Code cast.

By now, you should have a good understanding of the logic behind the *Monk Mania* game. You will find that using Director to edit an existing game is nearly impossible unless you first understand how the game works.

ADDING SOUND TO THE SCORE

In addition to the visual channels of the Score, Director also provides six effects channels. The six effects channels consist of a tempo channel, a palette channel, a transition channel, two sound channels, and a script channel. The effects channels allow you to affect Director movies in various ways by using the Score. None of the effects channels are completely necessary, but they sometimes make things easier for the programmer. To add the Bells sound to the first sound channel, perform the following steps:

1. Within the Score window, click your mouse on the Hide/Show Effects Channels button. Director will display the effects channels, as shown in Figure 5.6.

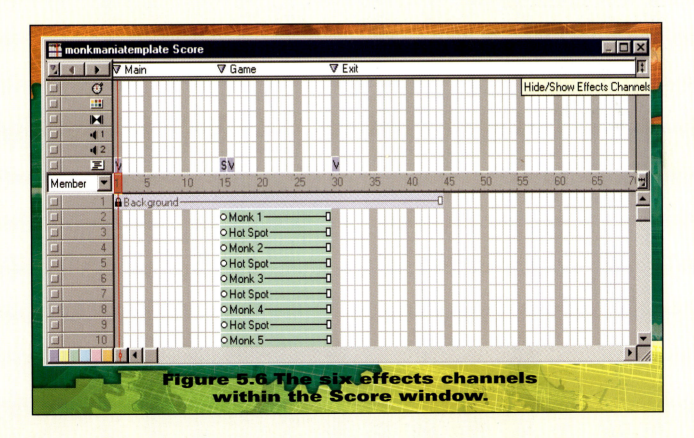

Figure 5.6 The six effects channels within the Score window.

2. Within the Cast window, click your mouse on the Choose Cast button, and select the Sound option. Director will display the Sound cast within the Cast window.

3. Drag the Bells member from the Cast window into cell 1 of the first sound channel of the Score window. Director will play the Bells sound when the game begins, as shown in Figure 5.7.

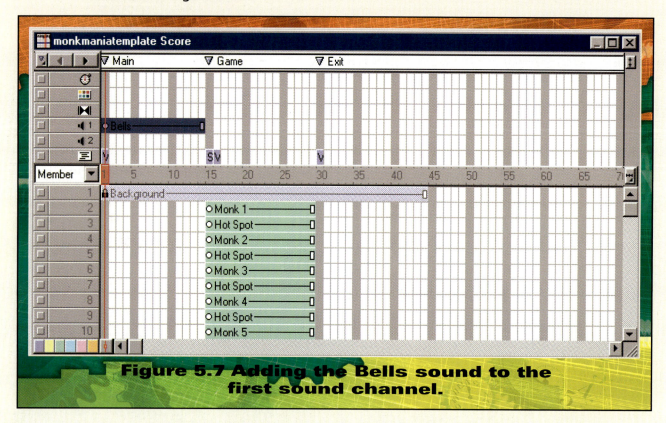

Figure 5.7 Adding the Bells sound to the first sound channel.

4. Within the Toolbar, click your mouse on the Play button. Director will preview your game within the Stage window. The Bells sound should loop as long as you remain in frame 1.

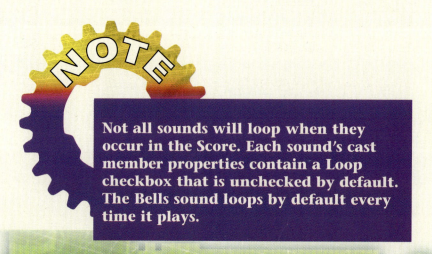

NOTE

Not all sounds will loop when they occur in the Score. Each sound's cast member properties contain a Loop checkbox that is unchecked by default. The Bells sound loops by default every time it plays.

5. Within the Toolbar, click your mouse on the Rewind button. Director will return your game to its original state within the Stage window.

Trying to use the two sound channels for all sound effects and music can sometimes prove nearly impossible. Quite often, the most convenient way to play sounds is through Lingo, and sometimes Lingo is completely necessary. For instance, if you would like to allow the user to pause and resume a sound, you must use a Lingo script.

PUPPETING SOUNDS IN LINGO

A sprite under the control of Lingo as opposed to the Score is called a "puppet." When you edit the values of graphical sprites in Lingo, Director considers them puppets unless you specify otherwise. If you puppet a sound manually, Director will play the sound until it ends or another sound overwrites it. Puppetting a sound is probably not the most elegant way to play a sound, but it is the most convenient. To add the code to the Global script that plays a chord sound and waits for it to finish, perform the following steps:

1. Within the Cast window, click your mouse on the Choose Cast button, and select the Code option. Director will display the Code cast within the Cast window.

2. Within the Cast window, click your mouse on the Global member. Director will update the Cast window.

3. Within the Cast window, click your mouse on the Cast Member Script button. Director will display the Script window, as shown in Figure 5.8.

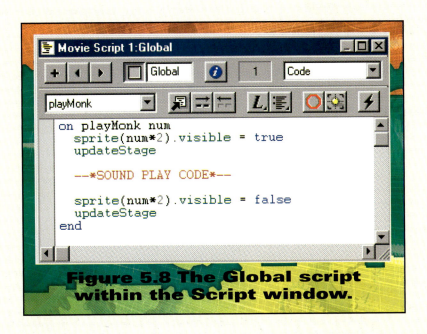

Figure 5.8 The Global script within the Script window.

4. Within the Script window, replace —*SOUND PLAY CODE*— with the following code:

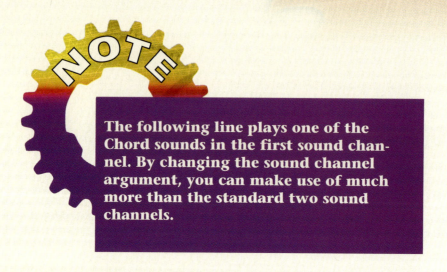

NOTE

The following line plays one of the Chord sounds in the first sound channel. By changing the sound channel argument, you can make use of much more than the standard two sound channels.

```
puppetSound(1, "Chord" && num)
```

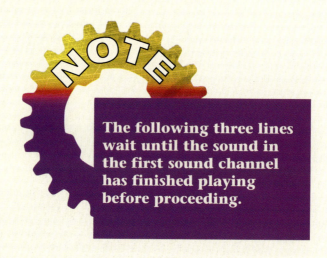

NOTE

The following three lines wait until the sound in the first sound channel has finished playing before proceeding.

```
repeat while soundBusy(1)
   nothing
end repeat
```

5. Within the Toolbar, click your mouse on the Script Window button. Director will close the Script window.

6. Within the Toolbar, click your mouse on the Play button. Director will preview your game within the Stage window. The *playMonk* function should be fully functional.

7. Within the Toolbar, click your mouse on the Rewind button. Director will return your game to its original state within the Stage window.

By now, the Monk Mania game should be fully functional. However, you have explored only one method of playing sounds through Lingo. Although the puppetSound function is a very simple and common way to play sounds, its functionality stops there. Other functions in Lingo have more specific purposes relating to sound playback.

USING OTHER METHODS TO PLAY SOUNDS

The various sound playback functions of Lingo include *play*, *pause*, *stop*, and *rewind* along with several others. The *play* function does not require an argument if a sound is already queued in the specified sound channel. However, even when one of the playback functions does not require an argument, you must still type the parentheses. To add code to the Global script that plays a chord sound, pauses it for a moment, then resumes play, perform the following steps:

1. Within the Cast window, click your mouse on the Choose Cast button, and select the Code option. Director will display the Code cast within the Cast window.

2. Within the Cast window, click your mouse on the Global member. Director will update the Cast window.

3. Within the Cast window, click your mouse on the Cast Member Script button. Director will display the Script window.

4. Within the Script window, replace the code you typed earlier with the following code:

NOTE

The following line plays one of the Chord sounds in the first sound channel.

```
sound(1).play(member("Chord" && num))
```

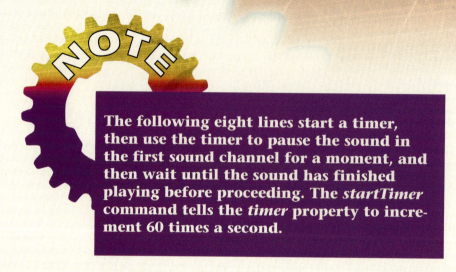

NOTE

The following eight lines start a timer, then use the timer to pause the sound in the first sound channel for a moment, and then wait until the sound has finished playing before proceeding. The *startTimer* command tells the *timer* property to increment 60 times a second.

```
startTimer
repeat while soundBusy(1)
  if the timer = 10 then
    sound(1).pause()
  else if the timer = 100 then
    sound(1).play()
  end if
end repeat
```

5. Within the Toolbar, click your mouse on the Script Window button. Director will close the Script window.

6. Within the Toolbar, click your mouse on the Play button. Director will preview your game within the Stage window. When a monk sings, it should pause in the middle for just a moment.

7. Within the Toolbar, click your mouse on the Rewind button. Director will return your game to its original state within the Stage window.

Although the sound playback functions offer more control over sounds, they are rarely necessary. Usually, you will only need to play sounds and allow them to finish on their own. For short, simple sound effects, the simplest method continues to be the most popular.

INTERRUPTING SOUNDS TO SPEED UP THE GAME

If you still prefer the *puppetSound* function over the *play* function, you should be aware of a method commonly used to interrupt manually puppetted sounds. The method may not be as elegant as the *stop* function, but it gets the job done. To stop a sound in the middle, simply replace the sound's name with the number zero. To add code to the Global script that plays a sound, waits a moment, then interrupts the sound, perform the following steps:

1. Within the Cast window, click your mouse on the Choose Cast button, and select the Code option. Director will display the Code cast within the Cast window.

2. Within the Cast window, click your mouse on the Global member. Director will update the Cast window.

3. Within the Cast window, click your mouse on the Cast Member Script button. Director will display the Script window.

4. Within the Script window, replace the code you typed earlier with the following code:

```
puppetSound(1, "Chord" && num)
```

The following four lines wait almost two seconds before proceeding.

```
startTimer
repeat while the timer < 100
   nothing
end repeat
```

The following line interrupts the sound playing in the first sound channel.

```
puppetSound(1, 0)
```

5. Within the Toolbar, click your mouse on the Script Window button. Director will close the Script window.

6. Within the Toolbar, click your mouse on the Play button. Director will preview your game within the Stage window. When a monk sings, it should pause in the middle for just a moment.

7. Within the Toolbar, click your mouse on the Rewind button. Director will return your game to its original state within the Stage window.

Very rarely will you need to stop a short sound before it completes. Interrupting sounds is most useful for those that loop. For instance, if you want music to play only while a certain character is on-screen, the music should be a looping sound. If the sound is set to loop, you can use the *puppetSound* function to both begin and end the loop.

APPLYING YOUR SKILLS

Now that you have the skills required to play sounds in a variety of ways, your games can be much more immersive. Any good shooting game can use a few explosion sound effects. Try looping background music during certain sections of your game. When creating Internet games, however, you must be careful not to include too many long sounds. Sounds generally take up more room than graphics. If you want to include music in a game, you should consider using several short sounds to build the music in Director. For instance, you might have a bass loop, a drum loop, and a few short drum sounds for variety. You will find that sound effects are almost a necessity in most games.

Chapter 6
Tic-Tac-Toe Challenge: Elaborating on a Simple Game

"You've got to learn to survive a defeat. That's when you develop character." —Richard Nixon

Chapter 6

- Approaching the *Tic-Tac-Toe Challenge* Game

- Opening the *Tic-Tac-Toe Challenge* Game's Template

- Understanding the *Tic-Tac-Toe Challenge* Game

- Creating the *Tic-Tac-Toe Challenge* Game's Introduction Screen

- Applying the Take Turns Behavior

- Building Artificial Intelligence

- Tweening the Winner and Loser Bitmaps

- Applying Your Skills

Figures 6.1–6.4 *The Tic-Tac-Toe Challenge game in action.*

APPROACHING THE *TIC-TAC-TOE* CHALLENGE GAME

Simple puzzle games can be the most addictive of all computer games. In order to attract the user's attention, however, a puzzle game must offer more than just strategy. What makes the *Tic-Tac-Toe Challenge* game more entertaining than the average puzzle game is the added graphics, sound, and story line. The computer opponent is just annoying enough to really keep the user trying to beat him. The *Tic-Tac-Toe Challenge* game will teach you how to display an introduction screen, create a computer player with artificial intelligence, and add extra effects to make a simple game such as tic-tac-toe more interesting.

OPENING THE *TIC-TAC-TOE CHALLENGE* GAME'S TEMPLATE

On this book's companion CD-ROM is a partially completed version of the *Tic-Tac-Toe Challenge* game that you will use to learn about elaborating on a simple game. This template will allow you to use Director as a learning tool. To open the *Tic-Tac-Toe Challenge* game's template in Director and save a copy to your hard drive, perform the following steps:

1. If the companion CD-ROM is not currently in your CD drive, then insert it in your CD-ROM drive now.

2. Within Director, in the Toolbar, click your mouse on the Open button. Director will display the Open dialog box.

3. Within the Open dialog box, click your mouse on the Look In drop-down list, and select your CD drive. Director will display the contents of your CD drive.

4. Within the Open dialog box, double-click your mouse on the *Tic-Tac-Toe Challenge* folder. Director will display the contents of the *Tic-Tac-Toe Challenge* folder.

5. Within the Open dialog box, click your mouse on the *tic-tac-toechallengetemplate.dir* file. Director will update the Open dialog box.

6. Within the Open dialog box, click your mouse on the OK button. Director will open the *tic-tac-toechallengetemplate.dir* file.

7. Click your mouse on the File menu, and select the Save As option. Director will display the Save Movie dialog box.

8. Within the Save Movie dialog box, click your mouse on the Save In drop-down list, and select your primary hard drive. Director will display the contents of your primary hard drive.

9. Within the Save Movie dialog box, double-click your mouse on the *Director Games* folder you created in Chapter 2, "Using Director." Director will display the contents of the *Director Games* folder.

10. Within the Save Movie dialog box, in the File Name text field, type **mytic-tactoechallenge.dir**, and press the Enter key. Director will save the *Tic-Tac-Toe Challenge* game's template as a file named "mytic-tac-toechallenge.dir".

As you create more and more games in Director, you will develop your own system of organization. For the purpose of clarity, however, you will keep all your edited template files in a single folder.

UNDERSTANDING THE *TIC-TAC-TOE CHALLENGE* GAME

To create a simple puzzle game such as tic-tac-toe, you must set up some sort of list to keep track of all the pieces on the board. In the case of the *Tic-Tac-Toe Challenge* game, an element of the list may equal a space, an X, or an O. Because the standard tic-tac-toe board is a three by three grid, the list consists of nine elements. As with a normal tic-tac-toe game, the *Tic-Tac-Toe Challenge* game ends either when one of the players lines up three pieces in a row or when all nine spots on the grid are full. To view the various Lingo scripts in the Code cast, perform the following steps:

1. Within the Cast window, click your mouse on the Choose Cast button, and select the Code option. Director will display the Code cast within the Cast window. The Code cast contains nine Lingo scripts, as shown in Table 6.1.

Table 6.1 The nine Lingo scripts of the Code cast and their descriptions.

Script Name	Description
Global	Stores all the global variables, such as *winner*, *board*, and *playersTurn*, and global functions, such as *resetGame*, *playerMoves*, and *computerMoves*.
Generic Button	Makes its associated sprite behave as a button complete with specified image, cursor, and sound options.
Wait	Keeps the *Tic-Tac-Toe Challenge* game looping on one frame until otherwise specified.
Take Turns	Allows the user or the computer to take a turn and then checks the board to see if there is a winner.
End Game	Assigns the graphics for the Results frame and resets the game.
Play Button	Resets the game and plays the game's Game frame when the user clicks on its associated sprite.
Help Button	Plays game's Help frame when the user clicks on its associated sprite.
Exit Button	Plays game's Exit frame when the user clicks on its associated sprite.
Yup Button	Ends the game when the user releases a click on its associated sprite.

2. Within the Cast window, click your mouse on the Global member. Director will update the Cast window, as shown in Figure 6.5.

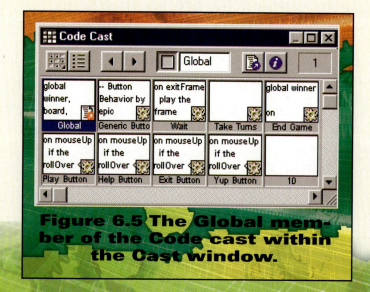

Figure 6.5 The Global member of the Code cast within the Cast window.

3. Within the Cast window, click your mouse on the Cast Member Script button. Director will display the Script window.

4. Within the Script window, use the Previous Cast Member and Next Cast Member buttons to view each of the Lingo scripts in the Code cast.

By now, you should have a good understanding of the logic behind the *Tic-Tac-Toe Challenge* game. You will find that using Director to edit an existing game is nearly impossible unless you first understand how the game works.

CREATING THE INTRODUCTION SCREEN

The *Tic-Tac-Toe Challenge* game's introduction screen immediately catches the user's attention with the cartoon characters and displays a story to give a reason for playing. Without at least some amount of a story, a game may seem incomplete or confusing. Therefore, the introduction screen is often an essential part of the game. To add the story and graphics to the introduction screen in the Main frame, perform the following steps:

1. Within the Cast window, click your mouse on the Choose Cast button, and select the Text option, as shown in Figure 6.6. Director will display the Text cast within the Cast window.

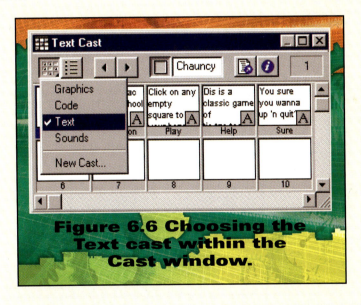

Figure 6.6 Choosing the Text cast within the Cast window.

2. Drag the Introduction member from the Cast window into cell 1 of channel 2 of the Score window. Director will display the Introduction text within the Stage.

3. Within the Stage window, drag the Introduction text to its appropriate position near the top of the Stage. Director will update the Property Inspector window.

4. Within the Cast window, click your mouse on the Choose Cast button, and select the Graphics option. Director will display the Graphics cast within the Cast window.

5. Drag the Names member from the Cast window into cell 1 of channel 3 of the Score window. Director will display the Names bitmap within the Stage.

6. Within the Stage window, drag the Names bitmap to its appropriate position near the bottom of the Stage. Director will update the Property Inspector window, as shown in Figure 6.7.

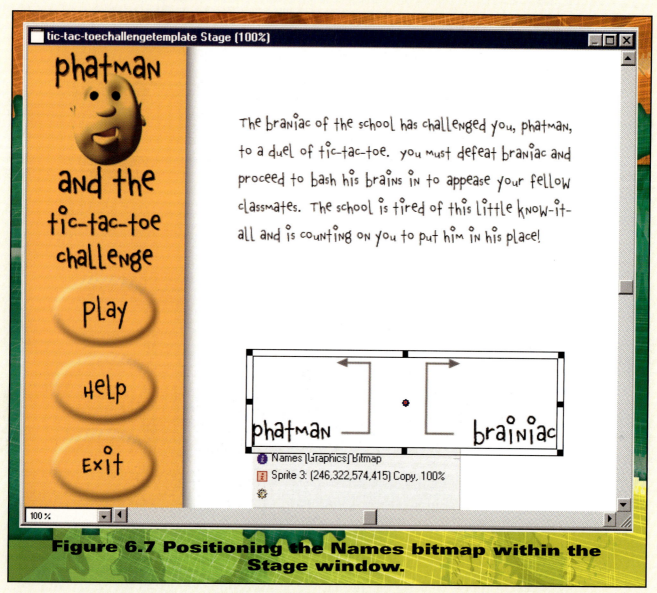

Figure 6.7 Positioning the Names bitmap within the Stage window.

7. Drag the Phatman member from the Cast window into cell 1 of channel 4 of the Score window. Director will display the Phatman bitmap within the Stage.

8. Within the Stage window, drag the Phatman bitmap to its appropriate position directly above and to the left of the Names bitmap. Director will update the Property Inspector window.

9. Within the Property Inspector window, click your mouse on the Sprite tab. Director will display the Sprite sheet.

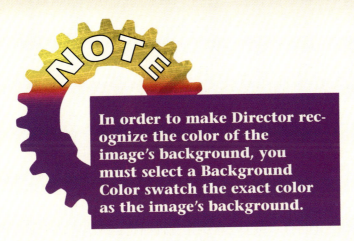

In order to make Director recognize the color of the image's background, you must select a Background Color swatch the exact color as the image's background.

10. Within the Property Inspector window, click your mouse on the Background Color button, and select the cyan (RGB: #00FFFF) swatch. Director will set the background color of the Phatman bitmap to cyan.

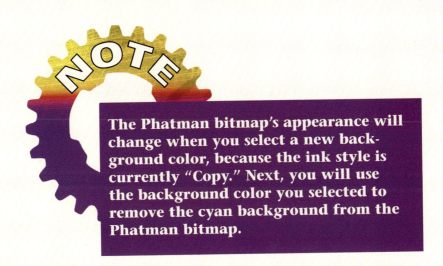

The Phatman bitmap's appearance will change when you select a new background color, because the ink style is currently "Copy." Next, you will use the background color you selected to remove the cyan background from the Phatman bitmap.

11. Within the Property Inspector window, click your mouse on the Ink drop-down list, and select the Background Transparent option, as shown in Figure 6.8. Director will remove the cyan background from the Phatman bitmap.

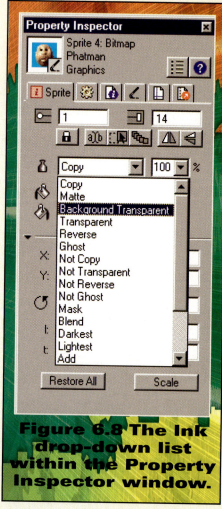

Figure 6.8 The Ink drop-down list within the Property Inspector window.

12. Drag the Brainiac member from the Cast window into cell 1 of channel 5 of the Score window. Director will display the Brainiac bitmap within the Stage.

13. Within the Stage window, drag the Brainiac bitmap to its appropriate position directly above and to the right of the Names bitmap. Director will update the Property Inspector window.

14. Within the Property Inspector window, click your mouse on the Sprite tab. Director will display the Sprite sheet.

15. Within the Property Inspector window, click your mouse on the Background Color button, and select the cyan (RGB: #00FFFF) swatch. Director will set the background color of the Brainiac bitmap to cyan.

16. Within the Property Inspector window, click your mouse on the Ink drop-down list, and select the Background Transparent option. Director will remove the cyan background from the Brainiac bitmap.

While the introduction screen is an integral part of most games, no game can survive without a good amount of content. In order to keep the user busy in a single-player puzzle game such as *Tic-Tac-Toe Challenge*, you must add a script that alternates between the player and his or her computer opponent.

APPLYING THE TAKE TURNS BEHAVIOR

The Take Turns behavior is a very simple script that chooses either the player or the computer to take a turn based on mouse events and the *playersTurn* variable. Without the Take Turns behavior, the *Tic-Tac-Toe Challenge* game is unplayable. To apply the Take Turns behavior to the Game frame, perform the following steps:

1. Within the Cast window, click your mouse on the Choose Cast button, and select the Code option. Director will display the Code cast within the Cast window.

2. Within the Cast window, click your mouse on the Take Turns member. Director will update the Cast window.

3. Within the Cast window, click your mouse on the Cast Member Script button. Director will display the Script window, as shown in Figure 6.9.

Figure 6.9 The blank Take Turns behavior within the Script window.

4. Within the Script window, type the following code:

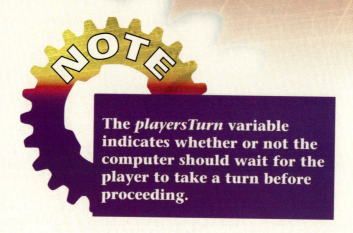

The *playersTurn* variable indicates whether or not the computer should wait for the player to take a turn before proceeding.

```
global playersTurn
```

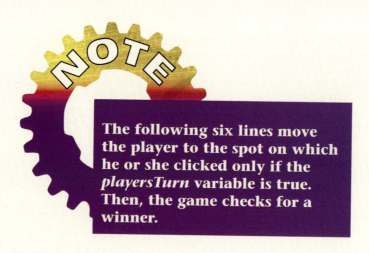

The following six lines move the player to the spot on which he or she clicked only if the *playersTurn* variable is true. Then, the game checks for a winner.

```
on mouseDown
  if playersTurn then
    playerMoves the rollOver - 5
    checkBoard
  end if
end
```

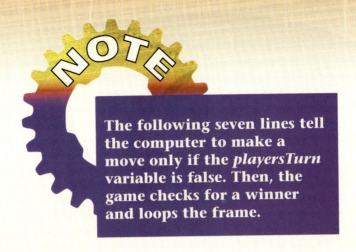

NOTE

The following seven lines tell the computer to make a move only if the *playersTurn* variable is false. Then, the game checks for a winner and loops the frame.

```
on exitFrame
    if not playersTurn then
        computerMoves
        checkBoard
    end if
    play the frame
end
```

5. Within the Toolbar, click your mouse on the Script Window button. Director will close the Script window.

6. Drag the Take Turns member from the Cast window into cell 45 of the script channel of the Score window. Director will apply the Take Turns behavior to frame 45.

Although the game should now alternate properly between the player and the computer, the *Tic-Tac-Toe Challenge* game is not complete. First, you must complete the artificial intelligence routine within the Global script. The computer must know how to take a turn much as a human player would.

BUILDING ARTIFICIAL INTELLIGENCE

When the computer decides to make a move, it must methodically consider every option so it does not overlook anything. First, the computer checks to see if it or its human opponent is about to complete a line of three pieces. If so, the computer fills in the empty space either to complete a line and win the game or to block its opponent from doing so. If no line needs to be completed, then based on the current placement of the pieces on the board, the computer chooses the center square, a random corner square, or a random side square. Because the computer randomly decides between equal moves, it is unpredictable and therefore difficult to exploit. To complete the artificial intelligence for the *computerMoves* function in the Global script, perform the following steps:

1. Within the Cast window, click your mouse on the Global member. Director will update the Cast window.

2. Within the Cast window, click your mouse on the Cast Member Script button. Director will display the Script window.

3. Within the Script window, replace —*HORIZONTAL CHECK CODE*— with the following code:

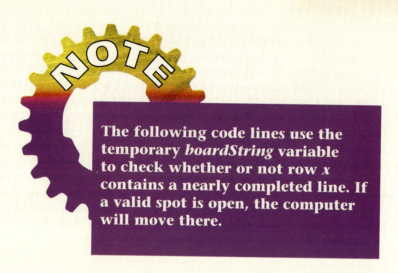

NOTE

The following code lines use the temporary *boardString* variable to check whether or not row *x* contains a nearly completed line. If a valid spot is open, the computer will move there.

```
boardString = board[3*(x-1) + 1] & board[3*(x-1) + 2] board[3*(x-1) + 3]
if boardString = " 00" or boardString = " XX" then
   square = 3*(x-1) + 1
else if boardString = "0 0" or boardString = "X X" then
   square = 3*(x-1) + 2
else if boardString = "00 " or boardString = "XX " then
   square = 3*(x-1) + 3
end if
```

4. Within the Script window, replace —*COMPUTER MOVE CODE*— with the following code.

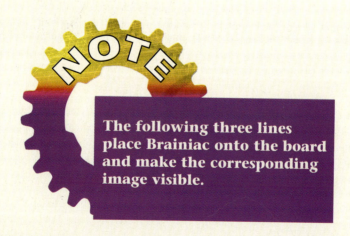

NOTE

The following three lines place Brainiac onto the board and make the corresponding image visible.

```
board[square] = "0"
sprite(square + 5).member = "Brainiac"
sprite(square + 5).blend = 100
```

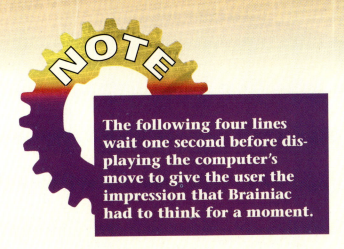

The following four lines wait one second before displaying the computer's move to give the user the impression that Brainiac had to think for a moment.

```
startTimer
repeat while the timer < 60
   nothing
end repeat
```

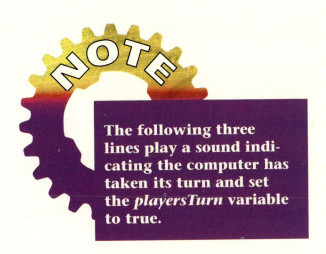

The following three lines play a sound indicating the computer has taken its turn and set the *playersTurn* variable to true.

```
updateStage
puppetSound(1, "Place")
playersTurn = true
```

5. Within the Toolbar, click your mouse on the Script Window button. Director will close the Script window.

6. Within the Toolbar, click your mouse on the Play button. Director will preview your game within the Stage window. The *Tic-Tac-Toe Challenge* game should be fully functional.

7. Within the Toolbar, click your mouse on the Rewind button. Director will return your game to its original state within the Stage window.

After the bulk of the game is complete, your only remaining task is adding effects to spice up the interface. You may want images to move around the screen, zoom, fade, or rotate. You can create virtually any motion effect with a simple tween in the Score.

TWEENING THE WINNER AND LOSER BITMAPS

At the end of each round of tic-tac-toe, the Results frame displays images to let the user know who won the game. You will notice that the Phatman and Brainiac bitmaps fade in simply to make the game look nicer. While the tweening fade effect has no practical purpose, it does add a great deal to the atmosphere of the game. To add tweening effects to the Winner and Loser bitmaps, perform the following steps:

1. Within the Score window, click your mouse on cell 74 of channel 15. Director will select the Winner bitmap within the Stage window.

2. Click your mouse on the Insert menu and select the Keyframe option. Director will mark cell 74 of channel 15 as a keyframe, as shown in Figure 6.10.

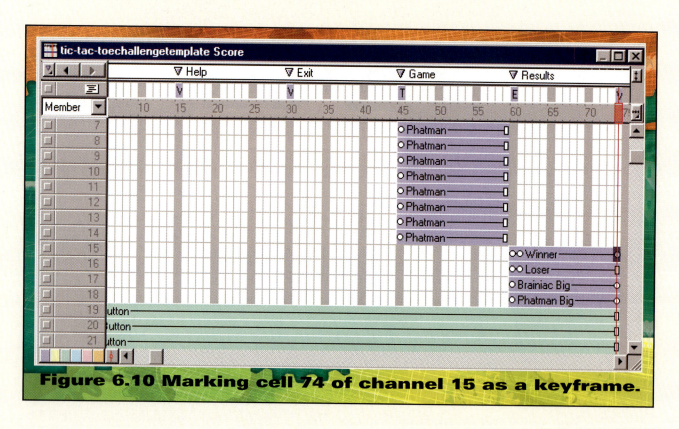

Figure 6.10 Marking cell 74 of channel 15 as a keyframe.

3. Within the Score window, click your mouse on cell 61 of channel 15. Director will select the Winner bitmap within the Stage window.

4. Within the Property Inspector window, click your mouse on the Sprite tab. Director will display the Sprite sheet.

5. Within the Property Inspector window, in the Rotation Angle text field, type **500**, and press the Enter key. Director will rotate the Winner bitmap to 500 degrees.

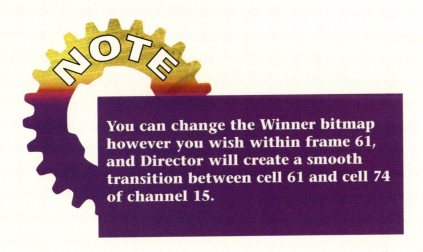

You can change the Winner bitmap however you wish within frame 61, and Director will create a smooth transition between cell 61 and cell 74 of channel 15.

6. Within the Score window, click your mouse on cell 74 of channel 16. Director will select the Loser bitmap within the Stage window.

7. Click your mouse on the Insert menu and select the Keyframe option. Director will mark cell 74 of channel 16 as a keyframe.

8. Within the Score window, click your mouse on cell 61 of channel 16. Director will select the Loser bitmap within the Stage window.

9. Within the Property Inspector window, click your mouse on the Sprite tab. Director will display the Sprite sheet.

10. Within the Property Inspector window, in the Height text field, type **0**, and press the Enter key. Director will resize the Loser bitmap to 0 pixels tall, as shown in Figure 6.11.

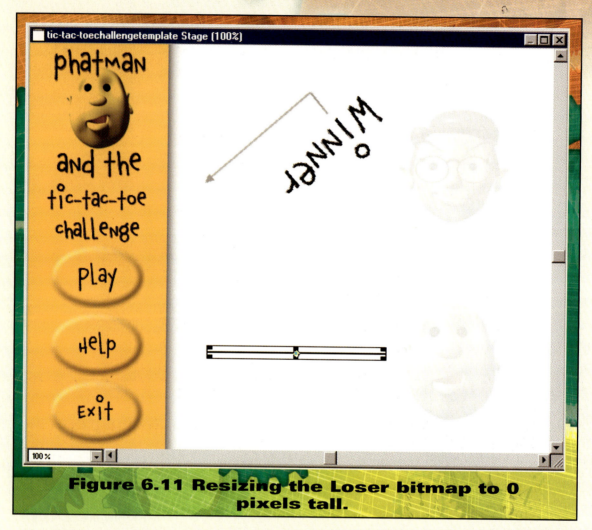

Figure 6.11 Resizing the Loser bitmap to 0 pixels tall.

11. Within the Toolbar, click your mouse on the Play button. Director will preview your game within the Stage window. The Winner and Loser bitmaps should spin and expand as the Phatman and Brainiac bitmaps fade in.

12. Within the Toolbar, click your mouse on the Rewind button. Director will return your game to its original state within the Stage window.

Many Director games incorporate Score animation into their interfaces, because it is usually easier than animating through Lingo code. For a simple introduction or ending screen, tweening can be a simple and effective way to improve upon an existing game.

APPLYING YOUR SKILLS

Now that you have the skills required to make a simple game addictive and enjoyable, you can make all your games more entertaining. Virtually every game could use a bit of improvement. With a few flashy graphics and a story to get the user involved, even the simplest game can seem like a major production. In addition to simply making your games appear more sophisticated, you should work on developing artificial intelligence to make single-player games as challenging as you want them to be.

Chapter 7
Gremlins: Generating Random Motion

"The crisis of today is the joke of tomorrow." —H.G. Wells

Chapter

7

- Approaching the *Gremlins* Game

- Opening the *Gremlins* Game's Template

- Understanding the *Gremlins* Game

- Randomly Rotating Sprites

- Randomly Moving Sprites

- Randomly Changing Cast Members

- Adding a Crazy Gremlin Behavior

- Applying Your Skills

Figures 7.1-7.4 The *Gremlins* game in action.

APPROACHING THE *GREMLINS* GAME

The logic behind a simple game of darts, such as *Gremlins*, is no more complex than any other game. What makes the *Gremlins* game unique, besides its story, is the random movement of the planes and gremlins. Adding a bit of randomness to the motion of a sprite makes its path less predictable and the game as a whole more entertaining. The *Gremlins* game will teach you how to randomly affect the rotation, position, and cast member of a sprite throughout the course of a game.

OPENING THE *GREMLINS* GAME'S TEMPLATE

On this book's companion CD-ROM is a partially completed version of the *Gremlins* game that you will use to learn about generating random movement. This template will allow you to use Director as a learning tool. To open the *Gremlins* game's template in Director and save a copy to your hard drive, perform the following steps:

1. If the companion CD-ROM is not currently in your CD drive, then insert it in your CD-ROM drive now.

2. Within Director, in the Toolbar, click your mouse on the Open button. Director will display the Open dialog box.

3. Within the Open dialog box, click your mouse on the Look In drop-down list, and select your CD drive. Director will display the contents of your CD drive.

4. Within the Open dialog box, double-click your mouse on the *Gremlins* folder. Director will display the contents of the *Gremlins* folder.

5. Within the Open dialog box, click your mouse on the *gremlinstemplate.dir* file. Director will update the Open dialog box.

6. Within the Open dialog box, click your mouse on the OK button. Director will open the *gremlinstemplate.dir* file.

7. Click your mouse on the File menu, and select the Save As option. Director will display the Save Movie dialog box.

8. Within the Save Movie dialog box, click your mouse on the Save In drop-down list, and select your primary hard drive. Director will display the contents of your primary hard drive.

9. Within the Save Movie dialog box, double-click your mouse on the *Director Games* folder you created in Chapter, 2, "Using Director." Director will display the contents of the *Director Games* folder.

10. Within the Save Movie dialog box, in the File Name text field, type **mygremlins.dir**, and press the Enter key. Director will save the *Gremlins* game's template as a file named "mygremlins.dir."

As you create more and more games in Director, you will develop your own system of organization. For the purpose of clarity, however, you will keep all your edited template files in a single folder.

UNDERSTANDING THE *GREMLINS* GAME

The *Gremlins* game is quite a bit simpler than it appears. With a little help from the *random* function, a plane flies back and forth across the screen and changes its face periodically. When the user picks up a gremlin, it changes into a randomly rotating, horizontal version of itself. When the user throws the gremlin, it shrinks and appears to fly away from the screen. The gremlin checks for a collision with a plane only if it is very small and therefore appearing far away. If the gremlin's sprite intersects the plane, the plane explodes, the score increases, and the gremlins reset. None of the *Gremlins* game's animation takes place in the Score. To view the various Lingo scripts in the Code cast, perform the following steps:

1. Within the Cast window, click your mouse on the Choose Cast button, and select the Code option. Director will display the Code cast within the Cast window. The Code cast contains 16 Lingo scripts, as shown in Table 7.1.

Table 7.1 The 16 Lingo scripts of the Code cast and their descriptions.

Script Name	Description
Global	Stores the global function *resetGame*, which resets the players score, starts a new plane, and makes all three gremlins visible.
Generic Button	Makes its associated sprite behave as a button complete with specified image, cursor, and sound options.
Wait	Keeps the *Gremlins* game looping on one frame until otherwise specified.
Wait for Click	Keeps the *Gremlins* game looping on one frame until the user clicks his or her mouse. Then resets the game and plays the Game frame.
Default Visible	Sets its associated sprite's *visible* property to true when the sprite begins.
Change Cursor	Set the mouse cursor to the Hand Cursor bitmap while the mouse is over its associated sprite.
Move Text	Moves its associated sprite up two pixels each frame until the sprite has moved completely off-screen.
Gremlin	Handles the functions of the gremlins such as dragging, rotation, and collision.
Plane	Moves the plane randomly across the screen over and over.
Speed Slider	Allows the user to change the tempo of the game by dragging the Speed Slider bitmap.
Reset Button	Resets the game and plays game's Game frame when the user clicks on its associated sprite.
Help Button	Plays game's Help frame when the user clicks on its associated sprite.
Exit Button	Plays game's Exit frame when the user clicks on its associated sprite.
Yes Button	Ends the game when the user releases a click on its associated sprite.
Gremlin Fireworks	Makes its associated sprite behave like a firework for the winning screen.
You Win	Flashes its associated sprite different shades of blue for the winning screen.

2. Within the Cast window, click your mouse on the Global member. Director will update the Cast window, as shown in Figure 7.5.

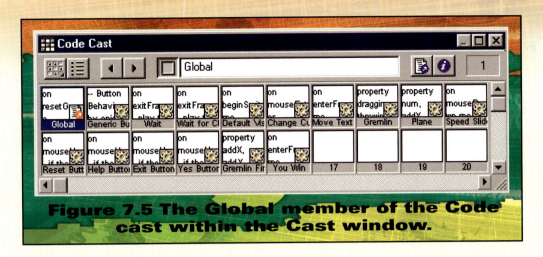

Figure 7.5 The Global member of the Code cast within the Cast window.

3. Within the Cast window, click your mouse on the Cast Member Script button. Director will display the Script window.

4. Within the Script window, use the Previous Cast Member and Next Cast Member buttons to view each of the Lingo scripts in the Code cast.

By now, you should have a good understanding of the logic behind the *Gremlins* game. You will find that using Director to edit an existing game is nearly impossible unless you first understand how the game works.

RANDOMLY ROTATING SPRITES

In older programming languages, rotating an image was a very complicated task. In Director, however, you need only to specify an angle, and Director does the rest. Rotating sprites can often eliminate the need for several similar cast members. To randomly rotate a sprite, you should not simply set the sprite's *rotation* property to a random value. You should add or subtract a random amount from the current rotation value to give the rotation a more natural appearance. To add the code to the Gremlin behavior that rotates the gremlin randomly as the user drags it, perform the following steps:

1. Within the Cast window, click your mouse on the Gremlin member. Director will update the Cast window.

2. Within the Cast window, click your mouse on the Cast Member Script button. Director will display the Script window, as shown in Figure 7.6.

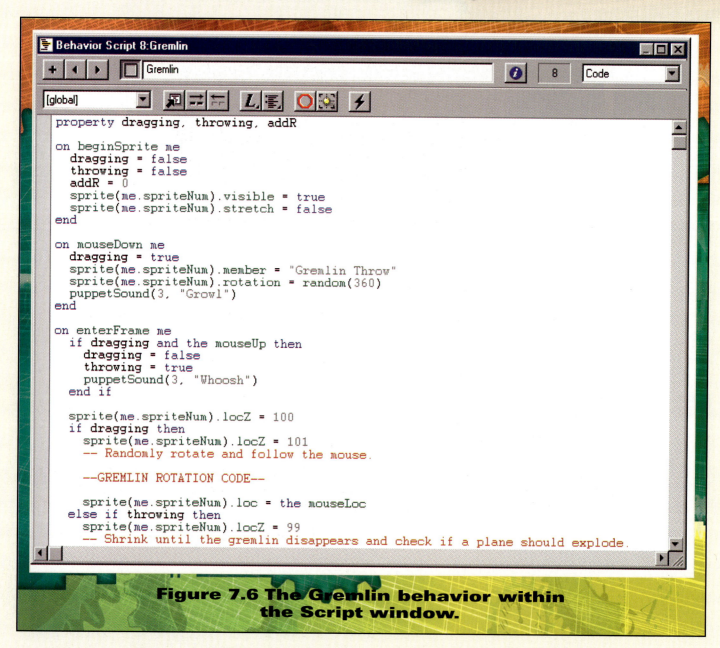

```
Behavior Script 8:Gremlin

[+] [◄] [►] [□] Gremlin                            [i]  [8]  [Code ▼]

[global ▼]  [buttons]

property dragging, throwing, addR

on beginSprite me
  dragging = false
  throwing = false
  addR = 0
  sprite(me.spriteNum).visible = true
  sprite(me.spriteNum).stretch = false
end

on mouseDown me
  dragging = true
  sprite(me.spriteNum).member = "Gremlin Throw"
  sprite(me.spriteNum).rotation = random(360)
  puppetSound(3, "Growl")
end

on enterFrame me
  if dragging and the mouseUp then
    dragging = false
    throwing = true
    puppetSound(3, "Whoosh")
  end if

  sprite(me.spriteNum).locZ = 100
  if dragging then
    sprite(me.spriteNum).locZ = 101
    -- Randomly rotate and follow the mouse.

    --GREMLIN ROTATION CODE--

    sprite(me.spriteNum).loc = the mouseLoc
  else if throwing then
    sprite(me.spriteNum).locZ = 99
    -- Shrink until the gremlin disappears and check if a plane should explode.
```

Figure 7.6 The Gremlin behavior within the Script window.

3. Within the Script window, replace —*GREMLIN ROTATION CODE*— with the following code:

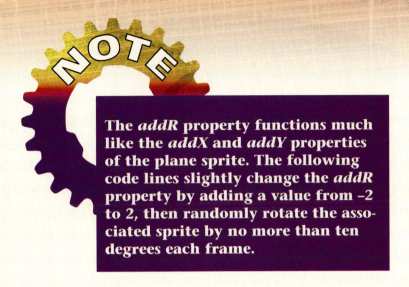

The *addR* property functions much like the *addX* and *addY* properties of the plane sprite. The following code lines slightly change the *addR* property by adding a value from –2 to 2, then randomly rotate the associated sprite by no more than ten degrees each frame.

```
addR = addR + random(5) - 3
if addR < -10 or addR > 10 then addR = -addR/5
sprite(me.spriteNum).rotation = sprite(me.spriteNum).rotation + addR
```

4. Within the Toolbar, click your mouse on the Script Window button. Director will close the Script window.

5. Within the Toolbar, click your mouse on the Play button. Director will preview your game within the Stage window. The gremlins should rotate randomly as you hold them.

6. Within the Toolbar, click your mouse on the Rewind button. Director will return your game to its original state within the Stage window.

As a gremlin rotates, it follows the movement of your mouse. You can accomplish such simple movement with only a single statement. On each new frame, you simply set the gremlin's *loc* property to the *mouseLoc* system property. To create more complex, unpredictable movement, you must add a bit more code.

RANDOMLY MOVING SPRITES

Throughout the *Gremlins* game, only one plane sprite exists. It continuously changes its location and cast member to give the impression that different planes are flying across the screen. As long as no two planes appear on the screen at once, one sprite can represent as many planes as you wish. The simplest method of resetting the plane sprite when it flies off-screen is to call its *beginSprite* handler. The *beginSprite* handler chooses a random flight direction and plane image each time it executes. To add the code to the Plane behavior that moves the plane randomly across the screen, perform the following steps:

1. Within the Cast window, click your mouse on the Plane member. Director will update the Cast window.

2. Within the Cast window, click your mouse on the Cast Member Script button. Director will display the Script window, as shown in Figure 7.7.

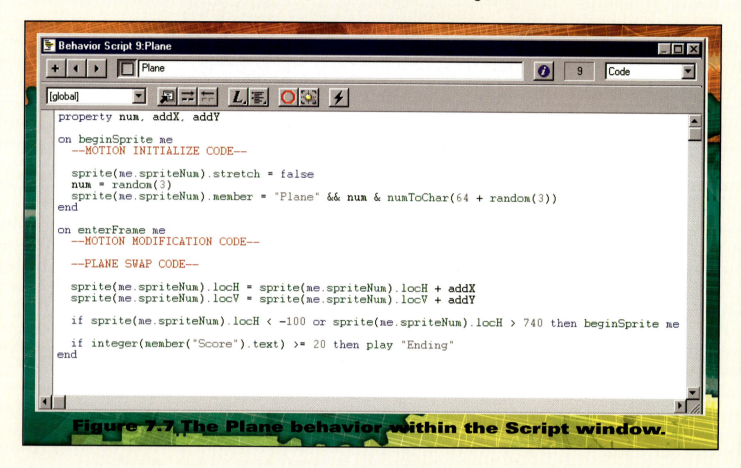

```
Behavior Script 9:Plane

[+] [◄] [►] [ ] Plane                                    [i] [9] [Code ▼]
[global ▼]   [icons...]

property num, addX, addY

on beginSprite me
  --MOTION INITIALIZE CODE--

  sprite(me.spriteNum).stretch = false
  num = random(3)
  sprite(me.spriteNum).member = "Plane" && num & numToChar(64 + random(3))
end

on enterFrame me
  --MOTION MODIFICATION CODE--

  --PLANE SWAP CODE--

  sprite(me.spriteNum).locH = sprite(me.spriteNum).locH + addX
  sprite(me.spriteNum).locV = sprite(me.spriteNum).locV + addY

  if sprite(me.spriteNum).locH < -100 or sprite(me.spriteNum).locH > 740 then beginSprite me

  if integer(member("Score").text) >= 20 then play "Ending"
end
```

Figure 7.7 The Plane behavior within the Script window.

3. Within the Script window, replace —*MOTION INITIALIZATION CODE*— with the following code:

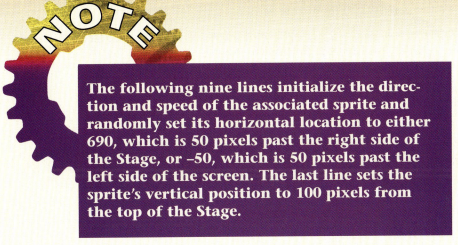

The following nine lines initialize the direction and speed of the associated sprite and randomly set its horizontal location to either 690, which is 50 pixels past the right side of the Stage, or –50, which is 50 pixels past the left side of the screen. The last line sets the sprite's vertical position to 100 pixels from the top of the Stage.

```
addX = 5 + random(10)
addY = 0
if random(2) = 1 then
  addX = -addX
  sprite(me.spriteNum).locH = 690
else
  sprite(me.spriteNum).locH = -50
end if
sprite(me.spriteNum).locV = 100
```

4. Within the Script window, replace —*MOTION MODIFICATION CODE*— with the following code.

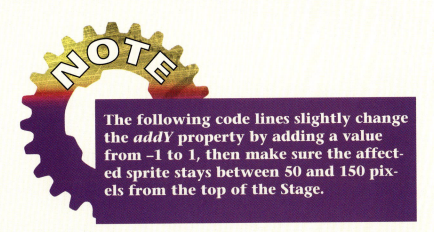

The following code lines slightly change the *addY* property by adding a value from –1 to 1, then make sure the affected sprite stays between 50 and 150 pixels from the top of the Stage.

```
addY = addY + random(3) - 2
if sprite(me.spriteNum).locV + addY < 50 or sprite(me.spriteNum).locV \
+ addY > 150 then
  addY = -addY/5
end if
```

5. Within the Toolbar, click your mouse on the Script Window button. Director will close the Script window.

6. Within the Toolbar, click your mouse on the Play button. Director will preview your game within the Stage window. The plane should fly back and forth randomly, but not mirror or change cast members while on-screen.

7. Within the Toolbar, click your mouse on the Rewind button. Director will return your game to its original state within the Stage window.

By now, the plane should fly back and forth and allow you to throw gremlins at it. The *Gremlins* game is almost fully functional. All that remains is actually changing the plane's image. To change the plane's image, all you must do is edit its *member* property.

RANDOMLY CHANGING CAST MEMBERS

The plane images consist of three different planes, referenced by number, and three images of each plane, referenced by letter. In the plane sprite's *beginSprite* handler, the sprite chooses a random plane. Every once in a while, the image of that plane should change. To add the code to the Plane behavior that changes the image of the plane randomly every once in a while, perform the following steps:

1. Within the Cast window, click your mouse on the Plane member. Director will update the Cast window.

2. Within the Cast window, click your mouse on the Cast Member Script button. Director will display the Script window.

3. Within the Script window, replace —*PLANE CHANGE CODE*— with the following code:

NOTE

About every 20 frames, the associated sprite changes its image. Then, the sprite mirrors itself if it should be moving left.

```
if random(20) = 1 then
    sprite(me.spriteNum).member = "Plane" && num & numToChar(64 + \
    random(3))
end if
if addX < 0 then
    sprite(me.spriteNum).flipH = true
```

```
else
me.spriteNum).flipH = false
end if
```

4. Within the Toolbar, click your mouse on the Script Window button. Director will close the Script window.

5. Within the Toolbar, click your mouse on the Play button. Director will preview your game within the Stage window. The gremlins should rotate randomly as you hold them.

6. Within the Toolbar, click your mouse on the Rewind button. Director will return your game to its original state within the Stage window.

By now, you should have a good understanding of how to rotate, move, and change sprites randomly. Although you can accomplish a great deal of effects with these basic techniques, you have only scratched the surface of random animation.

ADDING A CRAZY GREMLIN BEHAVIOR

Now that you have learned a few basic animation techniques, you should experiment with ink effects. So far, you have only used the Copy, Matte, and Background Transparent ink effects, but Director provides a wide variety of ink effects accessible both through the Property Inspector window and through Lingo. Along with familiar sprite properties such as *locH*, *width*, and *rotation*, you will also edit the *ink* property when you create the Crazy Gremlin behavior. To create and apply a Crazy Gremlin behavior, perform the following steps:

1. Within the Toolbar, click your mouse on the Script Window button. Director will display the Script window.

2. Within the Script window, click your mouse on the New Cast Member button. Director will add a new script to the Code cast.

3. Within the Script window, in the Cast Member Name text field, type **Crazy Gremlin**, and press the Enter key. Director will name the new script "Crazy Gremlin," as shown in Figure 7.8.

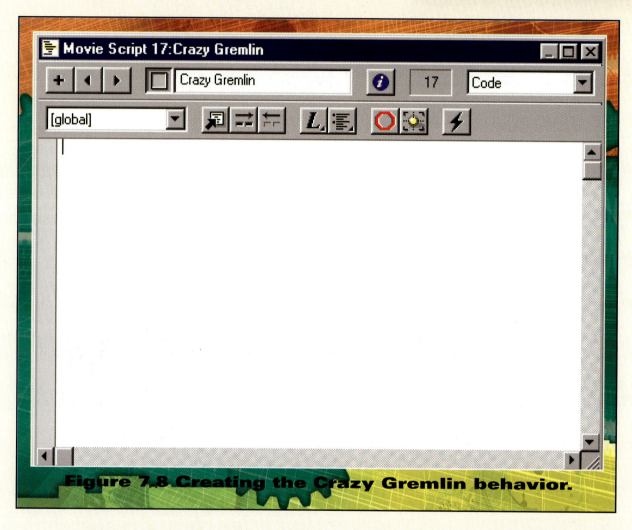

Figure 7.8 Creating the Crazy Gremlin behavior.

4. Within the Properties window, click your mouse on the Script tab. Director will display the Script sheet.

5. Within the Properties window, click your mouse on the Script Type drop-down list, and select the Behavior option. Director will mark the Crazy Gremlin script as a behavior script.

6. Within the Script window, type the following code:

NOTE

The *oldX* and *oldY* properties store the previous position of the associated sprite.

```
property oldX, oldY
on beginSprite me
   oldX = sprite(me.spriteNum).locH
   oldY = sprite(me.spriteNum).locV
end
```

NOTE

The Crazy Gremlin behavior uses the *oldX* and *oldY* properties to determine the speed of mouse movement and resize the associated sprite by adding up to three times the movement of the mouse to the sprite's original width and to the sprite's original height. The behavior then adds a random value from 1 to 20 to the rotation of the associated sprite, and sets its ink effect to either 2 (Reverse) or 3 (Ghost).

```
on enterFrame me
   if sprite(me.spriteNum).dragging then
     dist = abs(oldX - sprite(me.spriteNum).locH) + abs(oldY - \
     sprite(me.spriteNum).locV)
     sprite(me.spriteNum).width = 121 + dist*random(3)
     sprite(me.spriteNum).height = 111 + dist*random(3)
     sprite(me.spriteNum).rotation = sprite(me.spriteNum).rotation \
     + random(20)
     sprite(me.spriteNum).ink = random(2) + 1
   end if
   oldX = sprite(me.spriteNum).locH
   oldY = sprite(me.spriteNum).locV
end
```

7. Within the Toolbar, click your mouse on the Script Window button. Director will close the Script window.

8. Within the Score window, click your mouse on cell 45 of channel 11. Director will select the first gremlin sprite within the Stage window.

9. Within the Property Inspector window, click your mouse on the Behavior pop-up button, and select the Crazy Gremlin option. Director will apply the Crazy Gremlin behavior to the first gremlin sprite, as shown in Figure 7.9.

Figure 7.9 Applying the Crazy Gremlin behavior to the first gremlin sprite.

10. Within the Toolbar, click your mouse on the Play button. Director will preview your game within the Stage window. When you drag the first gremlin around, it should randomly rotate, resize based on the speed of your mouse movement, and alternate between the Reverse and Ghost ink styles.

11. Within the Toolbar, click your mouse on the Rewind button. Director will return your game to its original state within the Stage window.

Because the Crazy Gremlin behavior accesses the *dragging* property of its associated sprite, you cannot apply it to any sprite without a *dragging* property, or an error will occur. Therefore, you must only apply the Crazy Gremlin behavior to the gremlins. To learn more about ink effects, you should consult Director's Help Index and try creating your own behaviors.

APPLYING YOUR SKILLS

Now that you have the skills required to generate random sprite movement, artificial intelligence in your games can be much more interesting. Instead of enemies always walking towards you in straight lines, perhaps they could stumble around or fly like bats. The enemies' movement should not be completely random, or they will never end up getting anywhere. However, the right amount of random movement can help to make things appear quite a bit more natural.

Chapter 8
Go: Providing Two Methods of Play

"Hold out baits to entice the enemy.
Feign disorder, and crush him." —Sun Tzu

Chapter

8

- Approaching the *Go* Game

- Opening the *Go* Game's Template

- Understanding the *Go* Game

- Updating the Game Boards

- Allowing the User to Move

- Activating the Large Game Pieces

- Placing Random Pieces on the Board

- Applying Your Skills

Figures 8.1–8.4 The *Go* game in action.

APPROACHING THE GO GAME

Most games contain only a single interface. Although one interface can do the job, different people often prefer different methods of play. For instance, many people prefer to type keyboard shortcuts into applications, and many prefer to use the mouse. If you give the user more than one option, he or she is more likely to be comfortable and have fun playing your game. The *Go* game will teach you how to display two game boards based on a list of pieces, and allow user and computer interaction with that list.

OPENING THE *GO* GAME'S TEMPLATE

On the companion CD-ROM is a partially completed version of the *Go* game that you will use to learn about providing two methods of play. This template will allow you to use Director as a learning tool. To open the *Go* game's template in Director and save a copy to your hard drive, perform the following steps:

1. If the companion CD-ROM is not currently in your CD drive, then insert it in your CD-ROM drive now.

2. Within Director, in the Toolbar, click your mouse on the Open button. Director will display the Open dialog box.

3. Within the Open dialog box, click your mouse on the Look In drop-down list, and select your CD drive. Director will display the contents of your CD drive.

4. Within the Open dialog box, double-click your mouse on the *Go* folder. Director will display the contents of the *Go* folder.

5. Within the Open dialog box, click your mouse on the *gotemplate.dir* file. Director will update the Open dialog box.

6. Within the Open dialog box, click your mouse on the OK button. Director will open the *gotemplate.dir* file.

7. Click your mouse on the File menu, and select the Save As option. Director will display the Save Movie dialog box.

8. Within the Save Movie dialog box, click your mouse on the Save In drop-down list, and select your primary hard drive. Director will display the contents of your primary hard drive.

9. Within the Save Movie dialog box, double-click your mouse on the *Director Games* folder you created in Chapter 2, "Using Director." Director will display the contents of the *Director Games* folder.

10. Within the Save Movie dialog box, in the File Name text field, type **mygo.dir**, and press the Enter key. Director will save the *Go* game's template as a file named "mygo.dir."

As you create more and more games in Director, you will develop your own system of organization. For the purpose of clarity, however, you will keep all your edited template files in a single folder.

UNDERSTANDING THE *GO* GAME

The *Go* game uses a global list variable to keep track of all the pieces on the game boards. Therefore, both sets of game pieces do not directly affect their boards, but instead change the appropriate values in the list variable. Then, upon entering each frame, the *Go* game updates both boards at once based on the list variable. This method leaves very little room for error. To view the various Lingo scripts in the Code cast, perform the following steps:

1. Within the Cast window, click your mouse on the Choose Cast button, and select the Code option. Director will display the Code cast within the Cast window. The Code cast contains 10 Lingo scripts, as Table 8.1 briefly describes.

Table 8.1 The 10 Lingo scripts of the Code cast and their descriptions.

Script Name	Description
Global	Stores all the global variables, such as board and moveDelay, and global functions, such as computerMove, makeCaptures, and countNeighbors.
Generic Button	Makes its associated sprite behave as a button complete with specified image, cursor, and sound options.
Wait	Keeps the Go game looping on one frame until otherwise specified.
Game Piece	Sets its cast member to a green game piece and updates the board variable when the user clicks on its associated sprite.
Fade In	Increases its associated sprite's visibility by a specified increment if the sprite is translucent.
Play Button	Hides all text boxes and resets the game when the user clicks on its associated sprite.
Help Button	Displays the help text box when the user clicks on its associated sprite.
Exit Button	Displays the exit confirmation text box when the user clicks on its associated sprite.
Quit Yes	Ends the game when the user releases a click on its associated sprite.
Quit No	Plays game's Game frame when the user releases a click on its associated sprite.

2. Within the Cast window, click your mouse on the Global member. Director will update the Cast window, as shown in Figure 8.5.

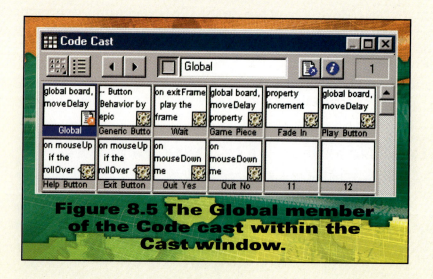

Figure 8.5 The Global member of the Code cast within the Cast window.

3. Within the Cast window, click your mouse on the Cast Member Script button. Director will display the Script window.

4. Within the Script window, use the Previous Cast Member and Next Cast Member buttons to view each of the Lingo scripts in the Code cast.

By now, you should have a good understanding of the logic behind the *Go* game. You will find that using Director to edit an existing game is nearly impossible unless you first understand how the game works.

UPDATING THE GAME BOARDS

Without the programming code to turn a list variable with 81 items into two 9×9 game boards, the *Go* game is functionless. The computer and the user both affect the *board* list variable with each turn. The *Go* game then uses the *board* variable to display the appropriate pieces on the game boards. To add the code to the Global script that updates the two game boards based on the *board* variable, perform the following steps:

1. Within the Cast window, click your mouse on the Global member. Director will update the Cast window.

2. Within the Cast window, click your mouse on the Cast Member Script button. Director will display the Script window, as shown in Figure 8.6.

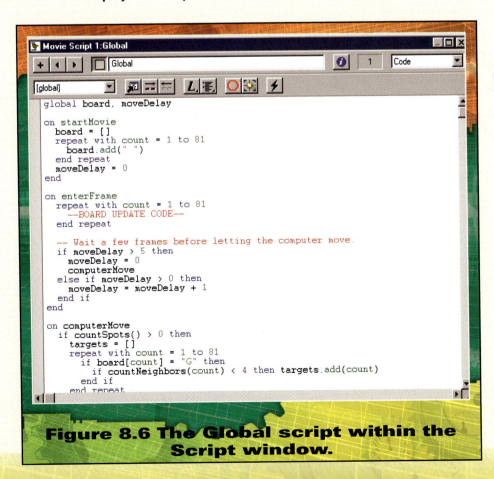

Figure 8.6 The Global script within the Script window.

3. Within the Script window, replace —*BOARD UPDATE CODE*— with the following code:

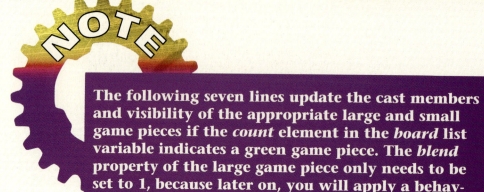

NOTE

The following seven lines update the cast members and visibility of the appropriate large and small game pieces if the *count* element in the *board* list variable indicates a green game piece. The *blend* property of the large game piece only needs to be set to 1, because later on, you will apply a behavior to the large game pieces that will increase their visibility gradually up to 100 when the *blend* property is greater than 0.

```
if board[count] = "G" then
  sprite(count + 10).member = member(count, "Green")
  sprite(count + 91).member = "Green Dot"
  if sprite(count + 91).blend = 0 then
    sprite(count + 10).blend = 1
    sprite(count + 91).blend = 100
  end if
```

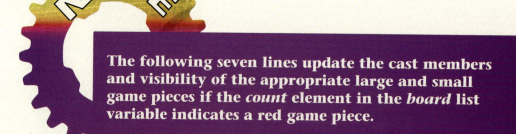

NOTE

The following seven lines update the cast members and visibility of the appropriate large and small game pieces if the *count* element in the *board* list variable indicates a red game piece.

```
else if board[count] = "R" then
  sprite(count + 10).member = member(count, "Red")
  sprite(count + 91).member = "Red Dot"
  if sprite(count + 91).blend = 0 then
    sprite(count + 10).blend = 1
    sprite(count + 91).blend = 100
  end if
```

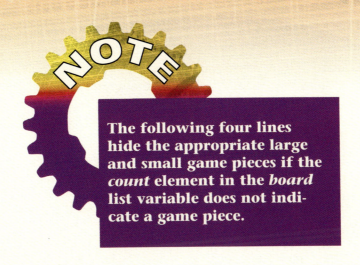

NOTE

The following four lines hide the appropriate large and small game pieces if the *count* element in the *board* list variable does not indicate a game piece.

```
else
   sprite(count + 10).blend = 0
   sprite(count + 91).blend = 0
end if
```

4. Within the Toolbar, click your mouse on the Script Window button. Director will close the Script window.

5. Within the Toolbar, click your mouse on the Play button. Director will preview your game within the Stage window. The computer's first move should show up on the small game board.

6. Within the Toolbar, click your mouse on the Rewind button. Director will return your game to its original state within the Stage window.

So far, you have set the game boards up to continuously reflect the *board* list variable. The large game pieces, however, will not show up yet, because you have not yet applied the Fade In behavior to them. Although you cannot see the large pieces, they will actually become one percent visible as the small pieces become 100 percent visible.

ALLOWING THE USER TO MOVE

The *Go* game in its current state cannot even be classified as a game. To make the game boards interactive, you must interpret user mouse clicks as piece movement and update the *board* variable accordingly. Because the Game Piece behavior uses an *offset* property, you can use the same behavior for both sets of game pieces. The game pieces are all positioned in the correct order within the Score, but they do not start in the first sprite channel. The *offset* property specifies how far past the first sprite channel the set of game pieces actually starts. Using the *offset* property, the *Go* game knows exactly which element of the *board* list variable to change when the user clicks on a game piece. To add the code to the Game Piece behavior that allows the user to affect the *board* variable, perform the following steps:

Macromedia Director Game Development
From Concept to Creation

1. Within the Cast window, click your mouse on the Game Piece member. Director will update the Cast window.

2. Within the Cast window, click your mouse on the Cast Member Script button. Director will display the Script window, as shown in Figure 8.7.

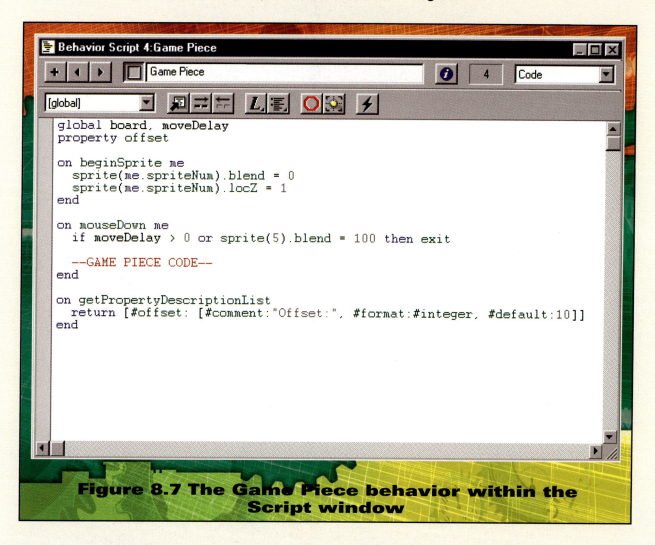

Figure 8.7 The Game Piece behavior within the Script window

3. Within the Script window, replace —*GAME PIECE CODE*— with the following code:

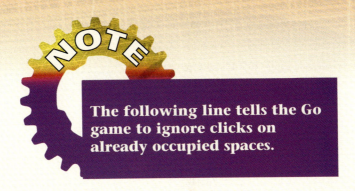

The following line tells the Go game to ignore clicks on already occupied spaces.

```
if board[me.spriteNum - offset] = " " then
```

The following three lines set the appropriate element in the board list variable to indicate a green game piece, and then check for any captures than can be made by either side.

```
board[me.spriteNum - offset] = "G"
makeCaptures("G")
makeCaptures("R")
```

The following six lines either tell the computer to make a move if a move can be made, or finish the game if only suicide moves remain. The moveDelay variable tells the computer to wait a few frames before taking its turn so the game feels more realistic.

```
if countSpots() > 0 then
    moveDelay = 1
  else
    finishGame
  end if
end if
```

4. Within the Toolbar, click your mouse on the Script Window button. Director will close the Script window.

5. Within the Toolbar, click your mouse on the Play button. Director will preview your game within the Stage window. You should be able to play the game normally through the small game board.

6. Within the Toolbar, click your mouse on the Rewind button. Director will return your game to its original state within the Stage window.

By now, you should be able to play a complete game of *Go* by using the small game board. At this point, the large game pieces will not currently make themselves visible or allow you to click on them. However, all the programming code is set up to activate the large game pieces as soon as you apply the correct behaviors to them.

ACTIVATING THE LARGE GAME PIECES

The functionality of the large game pieces is divided into two parts. The large game pieces interpret mouse clicks just like the small game pieces, but they also display a fade effect whenever they are clicked. Even when the game pieces are invisible, they still act as buttons positioned on the Stage. You have not seen the large game pieces so far, because you have not yet applied the Fade In behavior to them. The large game pieces have been remaining at one percent visibility when you click them instead of gradually becoming completely visible. To apply the Fade In behavior and the Game Piece behavior to the large game pieces, perform the following steps:

1. Within the Score window, click your mouse on cell 1 of channel 11, hold down the Shift key, and click your mouse on cell 14 of channel 91. Director will select cells 1 through 14 of channels 11 through 91, as shown in Figure 8.8.

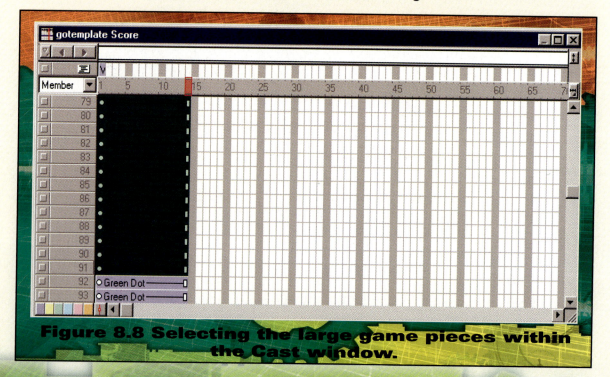

Figure 8.8 Selecting the large game pieces within the Cast window.

2. Within the Property Inspector window, click your mouse on the Behavior tab. Director will display the Behavior sheet.

3. Within the Property Inspector window, click your mouse on the Behavior pop-up button, and select the Fade In option. Director will display the Parameters dialog box.

4. Within the Parameters dialog box, in the Increment field, type **20**. Director will set the degree of visibility to add to the associated sprite each frame to 20, as shown in Figure 8.9.

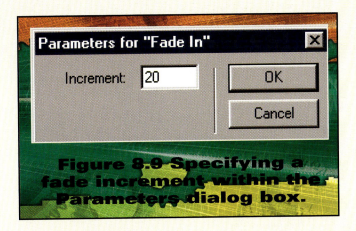

Figure 8.9 Specifying a fade increment within the Parameters dialog box.

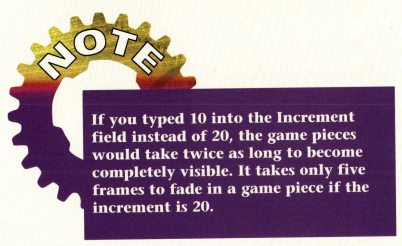

If you typed 10 into the Increment field instead of 20, the game pieces would take twice as long to become completely visible. It takes only five frames to fade in a game piece if the increment is 20.

5. Within the Parameters dialog box, click your mouse on the OK button. Director will apply the Fade In behavior to each of the large game pieces.

6. Within the Property Inspector window, click your mouse on the Behavior pop-up button, and select the Game Piece option. Director will display the Parameters dialog box.

7. Within the Parameters dialog box, in the Offset field, type **10**. Director will look for the first large game piece in sprite channel 11, the second in channel 12, and so on.

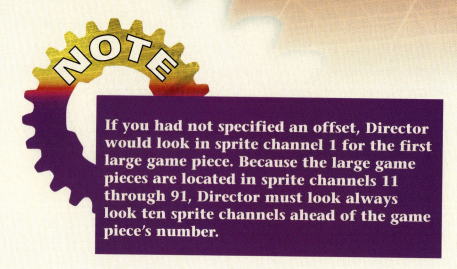

NOTE

If you had not specified an offset, Director would look in sprite channel 1 for the first large game piece. Because the large game pieces are located in sprite channels 11 through 91, Director must look always look ten sprite channels ahead of the game piece's number.

8. Within the Parameters dialog box, click your mouse on the OK button. Director will apply the Game Piece behavior to each of the large game pieces.

9. Within the Toolbar, click your mouse on the Play button. Director will preview your game within the Stage window. The *Go* game should be fully functional.

10. Within the Toolbar, click your mouse on the Rewind button. Director will return your game to its original state within the Stage window.

All aspects of the *Go* game should now work properly. You can use either of the two game boards to play the game. If you organize your games correctly, you will never need to retype similar sections of code over and over. No matter which method of play you choose, the same lines of code will execute.

PLACING RANDOM PIECES ON THE BOARD

In the game of *Go*, handicaps are often used to make the game more difficult for one of the players. A handicap involves certain pieces being positioned on the board prior to play. Because the *Go* game is controlled centrally by a single list variable, setting up handicaps is a very simple task. To add the code to the Play Button behavior that adds approximately 16 red pieces randomly to the board at the start of each game, perform the following steps:

1. Within the Cast window, click your mouse on the Play Button member. Director will update the Cast window.

2. Within the Cast window, click your mouse on the Cast Member Script button. Director will display the Script window, as shown in Figure 8.10.

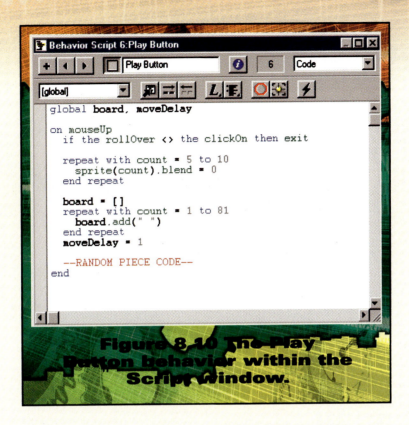

Figure 8.10 The Play Button behavior within the Script Window.

3. Within the Script window, replace —*RANDOM PIECE CODE*— with the following code.

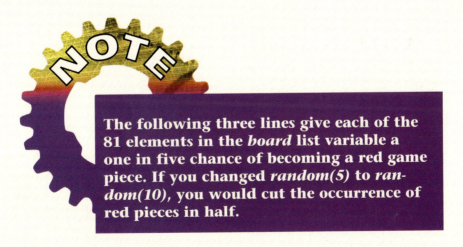

The following three lines give each of the 81 elements in the *board* list variable a one in five chance of becoming a red game piece. If you changed *random(5)* to *random(10)*, you would cut the occurrence of red pieces in half.

```
repeat with count = 1 to 81
   if random(5) = 1 then board[count] = "R"
end repeat
```

4. Within the Toolbar, click your mouse on the Script Window button. Director will close the Script window.

5. Within the Toolbar, click your mouse on the Play button. Director will preview your game within the Stage window. The game board should start with approximately 16 red pieces placed randomly on the board each time you click your mouse on the Play button, as shown in Figure 8.11.

Figure 8.11 Randomly generating red pieces within the Stage window.

6. Within the Toolbar, click your mouse on the Rewind button. Director will return your game to its original state within the Stage window.

By now, your *Go* game should not only function, but should add a random handicap at the start of each game. If you want, you can allow the user to control the number of pieces placed on the board, and even the color and location. Any time you change a value in the *board* list variable, the corresponding game pieces will immediately show up.

APPLYING YOUR SKILLS

Now that you have the skills required to provide multiple methods of play, you should have less difficulty as your games become increasingly complicated. Most commercial games are extraordinarily complex. To help keep track of every aspect of a game, the programmer should make all its parts function independently of one another. That way, the programmer can control every element of the game, either directly or indirectly, from a single section of code.

Chapter 9
Smac-Man: Utilizing Keyboard Control

"Only in a police state is the job of a policeman easy."
—Orson Wells

Chapter

9

- Approaching the *Smac-Man* Game

- Opening the *Smac-Man* Game's Template

- Understanding the *Smac-Man* Game

- Detecting Keyboard Events

- Confining Smac-Man's Movement

- Creating a Walking Animation

- Adding a Secret Cheat Command

- Applying Your Skills

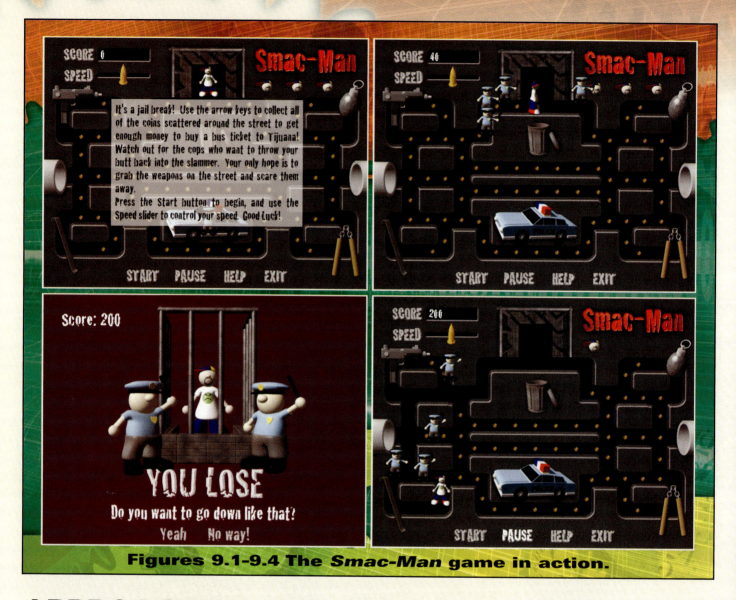

Figures 9.1–9.4 The *Smac-Man* game in action.

APPROACHING THE *SMAC-MAN* GAME

Because the number of buttons available on a mouse is so limited, most games take full advantage of keyboard control. The mouse is generally more useful for selecting specific items on the screen than controlling a game's character. While the *Smac-Man* game does require a mouse for pushing the on-screen buttons, the keyboard handles the rest of the game's commands. The *Smac-Man* game will teach you how to use keyboard events to make a character walk around specified areas of the screen.

OPENING THE *SMAC-MAN* GAME'S TEMPLATE

On this book's companion CD-ROM is a partially completed version of the *Smac-Man* game that you will use to learn about utilizing keyboard control. This template will allow you to use Director as a learning tool. To open the *Smac-Man* game's template in Director and save a copy to your hard drive, perform the following steps:

1. If the companion CD-ROM is not currently in your CD drive, then insert it in your CD-ROM drive now.

2. Within Director, in the Toolbar, click your mouse on the Open button. Director will display the Open dialog box.

3. Within the Open dialog box, click your mouse on the Look In drop-down list, and select your CD drive. Director will display the contents of your CD drive.

4. Within the Open dialog box, double-click your mouse on the *Smac-Man* folder. Director will display the contents of the *Smac-Man* folder.

5. Within the Open dialog box, click your mouse on the *smac-mantemplate.dir* file. Director will update the Open dialog box.

6. Within the Open dialog box, click your mouse on the OK button. Director will open the *smac-mantemplate.dir* file.

7. Click your mouse on the File menu, and select the Save As option. Director will display the Save Movie dialog box.

8. Within the Save Movie dialog box, click your mouse on the Save In drop-down list, and select your primary hard drive. Director will display the contents of your primary hard drive.

9. Within the Save Movie dialog box, double-click your mouse on the *Director Games* folder you created in Chapter 2, "Using Director." Director will display the contents of the *Director Games* folder.

10. Within the Save Movie dialog box, in the File Name text field, type **mysmac-man.dir**, and press the Enter key. Director will save the *Smac-Man* game's template as a file named "mysmac-man.dir."

As you create more and more games in Director, you will develop your own system of organization. For the purpose of clarity, however, you will keep all your edited template files in a single folder.

UNDERSTANDING THE *SMAC-MAN* GAME

The functionality of the *Smac-Man* game is directly linked with its background image. The background image actually functions as a color-coded map that indicates exactly where the characters may walk. All the pathways of the *Smac-Man* game's background image are colored green. However, because the background image has a transparent background color of green, all the green pathways are transparent and therefore show up as the color of the Stage. Using the *getPixel* function, the *Smac-Man* game checks before each movement to make sure that Smac-Man will still be standing on a green pathway. To view the various Lingo scripts in the Code cast, perform the following steps:

1. Within the Cast window, click your mouse on the Choose Cast button, and select the Code option. Director will display the Code cast within the Cast window. The Code cast contains 20 Lingo scripts, as shown in Table 9.1.

Table 9.1 The 20 Lingo scripts of the Code cast and their descriptions.

Script Name	Description
Global	Initializes most of the game's global variables at the start of the movie.
Generic Button	Makes its associated sprite behave as a button complete with specified image, cursor, and sound options.
Wait	Keeps the *Smac-Man* game looping on one frame until otherwise specified.
Game	Handles major aspects of the game and keeps the *Smac-Man* game looping on one frame until otherwise specified.
Default Visible	Sets its associated sprite's *visible* property to true when the sprite begins.
Smac-Man	Allows its associated sprite to be controlled by the arrow keys.
Cop	Makes its associated sprite chase Smac-Man through the background image's pathways.
Weapon	Plays an appropriate sound, disappears, and makes the cops run from Smac-Man for a short period of time when Smac-Man intersects its associated sprite.
Gold	Disappears and adds 10 to the player's score when Smac-Man walks over its associated sprite.
Score	Sets its associated sprite's text to the player's current score upon entering each frame.
Final Score	Sets its associated sprite's text to *Score:* and the player's final score at the start of the sprite.
Help Box	Fades out from 50% opacity when the game is not in Help mode.
Help Text	Fades out from 100% opacity when the game is not in Help mode.
Slider	Controls the speed of the game's characters by following the mouse when it drags over the associated sprite.
Start Button	Resets all aspects of the game when the user clicks on its associated sprite.
Pause Button	Pauses the game when the user clicks on its associated sprite.
Help Button	Pauses the game and displays help text when the user clicks on its associated sprite.
Exit Button	Plays the game's Exit frame when the user clicks on its associated sprite.
Restart Game	Resets all aspects of the game and plays the game's Main frame when the user clicks on its associated sprite.
Quit Game	Ends the game when the user clicks on its associated sprite.

2. **Within the Cast window, click your mouse on the Global member. Director will update the Cast window, as shown in Figure 9.5.**

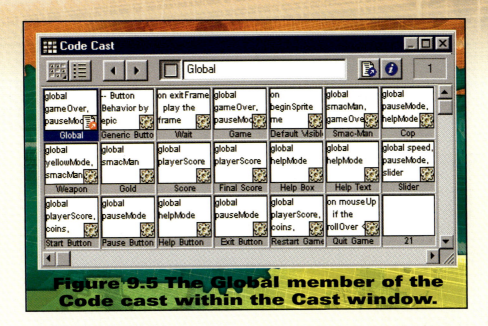

Figure 9.5 The Global member of the Code cast within the Cast window.

3. Within the Cast window, click your mouse on the Cast Member Script button. Director will display the Script window.

4. Within the Script window, use the Previous Cast Member and Next Cast Member buttons to view each of the Lingo scripts in the Code cast.

By now, you should have a good understanding of the logic behind the *Smac-Man* game. You will find that using Director to edit an existing game is nearly impossible unless you first understand how the game works.

DETECTING KEYBOARD EVENTS

At first glance, Director seems to be designed for programming with the mouse, because of all the simplified mouse event handlers. You have no need to worry, however, because Director makes detecting keyboard events just as easy as mouse clicks. Although Director makes a variety of keyboard event–detection methods available, you really only need one for most types of games. To add the code to the Smac-Man behavior that detects keyboard events and moves Smac-Man accordingly, perform the following steps:

1. Within the Cast window, click your mouse on the Smac-Man member. Director will update the Cast window.

2. Within the Cast window, click your mouse on the Cast Member Script button. Director will display the Script window, as shown in Figure 9.6.

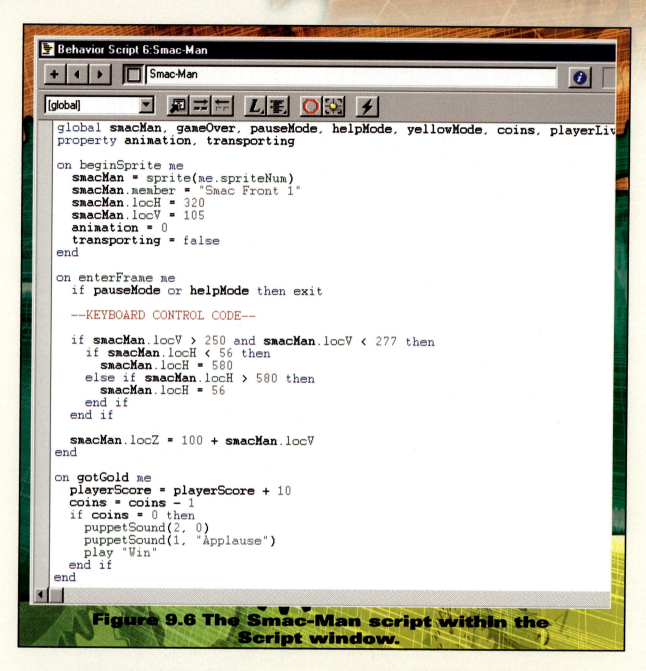

```
Behavior Script 6:Smac-Man
+  ◄  ►   □  Smac-Man                                    i

[global]  ▼    ⊞ ⇄ ⊟   L ⊟   O ⊡   ⚡

global smacMan, gameOver, pauseMode, helpMode, yellowMode, coins, playerLiv
property animation, transporting

on beginSprite me
  smacMan = sprite(me.spriteNum)
  smacMan.member = "Smac Front 1"
  smacMan.locH = 320
  smacMan.locV = 105
  animation = 0
  transporting = false
end

on enterFrame me
  if pauseMode or helpMode then exit

  --KEYBOARD CONTROL CODE--

  if smacMan.locV > 250 and smacMan.locV < 277 then
    if smacMan.locH < 56 then
      smacMan.locH = 580
    else if smacMan.locH > 580 then
      smacMan.locH = 56
    end if
  end if

  smacMan.locZ = 100 + smacMan.locV
end

on gotGold me
  playerScore = playerScore + 10
  coins = coins - 1
  if coins = 0 then
    puppetSound(2, 0)
    puppetSound(1, "Applause")
    play "Win"
  end if
end
```

Figure 9.6 The Smac-Man script within the Script window.

3.   Within the Script window, replace —*KEYBOARD CONTROL CODE*— with the following code:

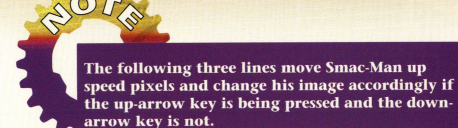

The following three lines move Smac-Man up speed pixels and change his image accordingly if the up-arrow key is being pressed and the down-arrow key is not.

```
if keyPressed(126) and not keyPressed(125) then
    smacMan.locV = smacMan.locV - speed
    smacMan.member = "Smac Back 1"
```

The following three lines move Smac-Man down speed pixels and change his image accordingly if the down-arrow key is being pressed and the up-arrow key is not.

```
else if keyPressed(125) and not keyPressed(126) then
    smacMan.locV = smacMan.locV + speed
    smacMan.member = "Smac Front 1"
```

The following three lines move Smac-Man left speed pixels and change his image accordingly if the left-arrow key is being pressed and the right-arrow key is not.

```
else if keyPressed(123) and not keyPressed(124) then
    smacMan.locH = smacMan.locH - speed
    smacMan.member = "Smac Left 1"
```

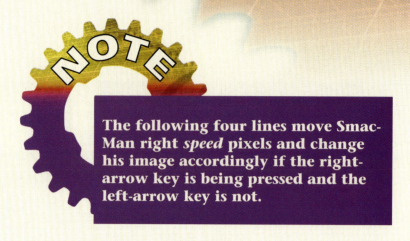

NOTE

The following four lines move Smac-Man right *speed* pixels and change his image accordingly if the right-arrow key is being pressed and the left-arrow key is not.

```
else if keyPressed(124) and not keyPressed(123) then
    smacMan.locH = smacMan.locH + speed
    smacMan.member = "Smac Right 1"
end if
```

4. Within the Toolbar, click your mouse on the Script Window button. Director will close the Script window.

5. Within the Toolbar, click your mouse on the Play button. Director will preview your game within the Stage window. You should be able to move Smac-Man around the screen in any direction you wish, as shown in Figure 9.7.

Figure 9.7 Moving Smac-Man around within the Stage window.

6. Within the Toolbar, click your mouse on the Rewind button. Director will return your game to its original state within the Stage window.

Now that you can control Smac-Man's movement around the screen, you must limit his movement for the *Smac-Man* game to make sense. The game starts getting more complicated when you try do decide on the most error-proof, efficient way to confine Smac-Man's movement.

CONFINING SMAC-MAN'S MOVEMENT

To prevent Smac-Man from walking into a wall, the *Smac-Man* game checks before each movement to make sure that Smac-Man will not move off the background image's pathways. All the pathways are colored green, so the *Smac-Man* game needs only to check whether the point on the background image to where Smac-Man will move contains a green pixel. If the pixel is not green, Smac-Man knows he has run into a wall. To add the code to the Smac-Man behavior that prevents Smac-Man from moving outside of the background image's green pathways, perform the following steps:

1. Within the Cast window, click your mouse on the Smac-Man member. Director will update the Cast window.

2. Within the Cast window, click your mouse on the Cast Member Script button. Director will display the Script window.

3. Within the Script window, replace the keyboard control code you typed earlier with the following code:

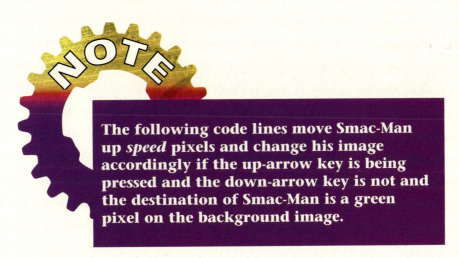

The following code lines move Smac-Man up *speed* pixels and change his image accordingly if the up-arrow key is being pressed and the down-arrow key is not and the destination of Smac-Man is a green pixel on the background image.

```
if keyPressed(126) and not keyPressed(125) then
  if member("Background").image.getPixel(smacMan.locH, \
  smacMan.locV - speed) = rgb(0, 255, 0) then
    smacMan.locV = smacMan.locV - speed
    smacMan.member = "Smac Back 1"
  end if
```

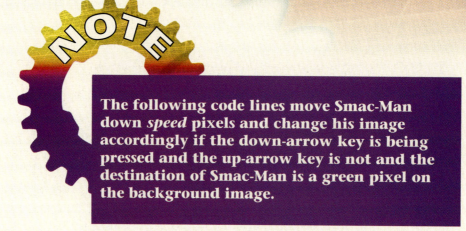

The following code lines move Smac-Man down *speed* pixels and change his image accordingly if the down-arrow key is being pressed and the up-arrow key is not and the destination of Smac-Man is a green pixel on the background image.

```
else if keyPressed(125) and not keyPressed(126) then
  if member("Background").image.getPixel(smacMan.locH, \
  smacMan.locV + speed) = rgb(0, 255, 0) then
    smacMan.locV = smacMan.locV + speed
    smacMan.member = "Smac Front 1"
  end if
```

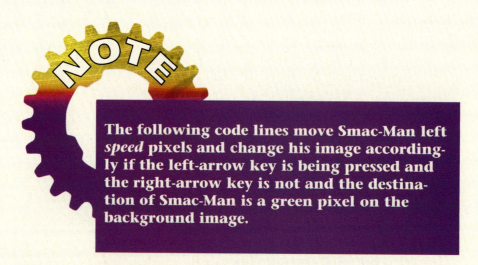

The following code lines move Smac-Man left *speed* pixels and change his image accordingly if the left-arrow key is being pressed and the right-arrow key is not and the destination of Smac-Man is a green pixel on the background image.

```
else if keyPressed(123) and not keyPressed(124) then
  if member("Background").image.getPixel(smacMan.locH - speed, \
  smacMan.locV) = rgb(0, 255, 0) then
    smacMan.locH = smacMan.locH - speed
    smacMan.member = "Smac Left 1"
  end if
```

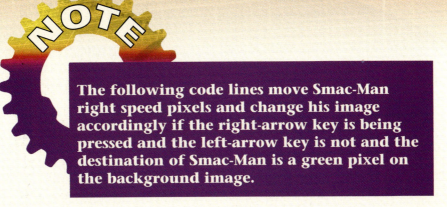

The following code lines move Smac-Man right speed pixels and change his image accordingly if the right-arrow key is being pressed and the left-arrow key is not and the destination of Smac-Man is a green pixel on the background image.

```
else if keyPressed(124) and not keyPressed(123) then
  if member("Background").image.getPixel(smacMan.locH + speed, \
  smacMan.locV) = rgb(0, 255, 0) then
    smacMan.locH = smacMan.locH + speed
    smacMan.member = "Smac Right 1"
  end if
end if
```

4. Within the Toolbar, click your mouse on the Script Window button. Director will close the Script window.

5. Within the Toolbar, click your mouse on the Play button. Director will preview your game within the Stage window. You should be able to move Smac-Man around, but only within the background image's pathways, as shown in Figure 9.8.

Figure 9.8 Moving Smac-Man through the pathways within the Stage window.

6. Within the Toolbar, click your mouse on the Rewind button. Director will return your game to its original state within the Stage window.

Currently, the color of the Stage is blue. You can tell this because the background image's pathways are transparent and the Stage color shows through. Blue is a good Stage color to use to make sure the characters stay on the pathways, but a more appropriate color for the street would be black. To set the Stage color to black, perform the following steps:

1. Within the Property Inspector window, click your mouse on the Movie tab. Director will display the movie sheet.

2. Within the Property Inspector window, click your mouse on the Stage Fill Color button, and select a black swatch, as shown in Figure 9.9. Director will change the color of the Stage to black.

Figure 9.9 Changing the color of the Stage within the Property Inspector window.

Now that you can move Smac-Man around the screen but only in the specified pathways, the *Smac-Man* game is fully functional. However, Smac-Man's walking still looks a bit mechanical. By displaying only one image per direction, Smac-Man appears to slide across the screen in a mechanical, unnatural manner.

CREATING A WALKING ANIMATION

By alternating between two slightly different images as Smac-Man walks, the game could appear much more realistic. If Smac-Man is walking, he should alternate his image around once every two frames to ensure a relaxed, natural looking pace. To add the code to the Smac-Man behavior that animates Smac-Man as he walks, perform the following steps:

1. Within the Cast window, click your mouse on the Smac-Man member. Director will update the Cast window.

2. Within the Cast window, click your mouse on the Cast Member Script button. Director will display the Script window.

3. Within the Script window, replace the code you typed earlier with the following code:

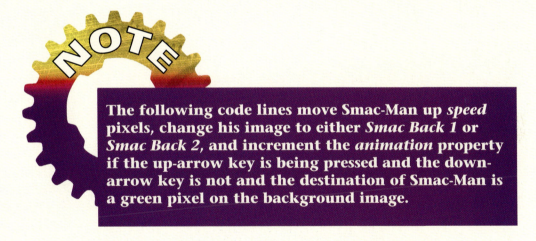

The following code lines move Smac-Man up *speed* pixels, change his image to either *Smac Back 1* or *Smac Back 2*, and increment the *animation* property if the up-arrow key is being pressed and the down-arrow key is not and the destination of Smac-Man is a green pixel on the background image.

```
if keyPressed(126) and not keyPressed(125) then
  if member("Background").image.getPixel(smacMan.locH, \
  smacMan.locV - speed) = rgb(0, 255, 0) then
    smacMan.locV = smacMan.locV - speed
    smacMan.member = "Smac Back" && integer((animation+1.5)/2)
    animation = animation + 1
  end if
```

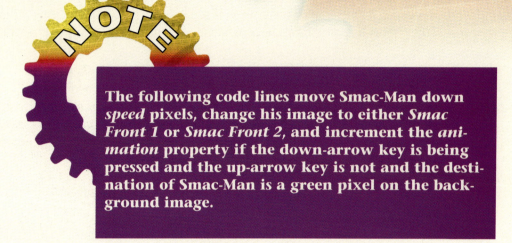

NOTE

The following code lines move Smac-Man down *speed* pixels, change his image to either *Smac Front 1* or *Smac Front 2*, and increment the *animation* property if the down-arrow key is being pressed and the up-arrow key is not and the destination of Smac-Man is a green pixel on the background image.

```
else if keyPressed(125) and not keyPressed(126) then
  if member("Background").image.getPixel(smacMan.locH, \
  smacMan.locV + speed) = rgb(0, 255, 0) then
    smacMan.locV = smacMan.locV + speed
    smacMan.member = "Smac Front" && integer((animation+1.5)/2)
    animation = animation + 1
end if
```

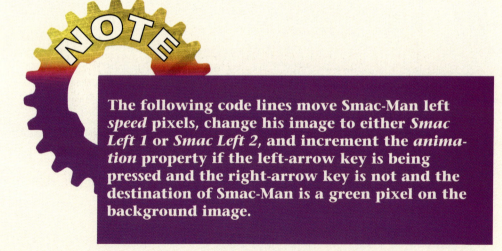

NOTE

The following code lines move Smac-Man left *speed* pixels, change his image to either *Smac Left 1* or *Smac Left 2*, and increment the *animation* property if the left-arrow key is being pressed and the right-arrow key is not and the destination of Smac-Man is a green pixel on the background image.

```
else if keyPressed(123) and not keyPressed(124) then
  if member("Background").image.getPixel(smacMan.locH - speed,\
  smacMan.locV) = rgb(0, 255, 0) then
    smacMan.locH = smacMan.locH - speed
    smacMan.member = "Smac Left" && integer((animation+1.5)/2)
    animation = animation + 1
  end if
```

NOTE

The following code lines move Smac-Man right *speed* pixels, change his image to either *Smac Right 1* or *Smac Right 2,* and increment the *animation* property if the right-arrow key is being pressed and the left-arrow key is not and the destination of Smac-Man is a green pixel on the background image.

```
else if keyPressed(124) and not keyPressed(123) then
  if member("Background").image.getPixel(smacMan.locH + speed, smacMan.locV)\
= rgb(0, 255, 0) then
    smacMan.locH = smacMan.locH + speed
    smacMan.member = "Smac Right" && integer((animation+1.5)/2)
    animation = animation + 1
  end if
```

NOTE

The following three lines reset the *animation* property to 0 if Smac-Man is not moving. While the *animation* property stays at the same value, Smac-Man's walking animation stops.

```
else
  animation = 0
end if
```

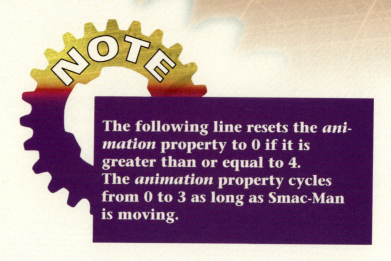

> The following line resets the *animation* property to 0 if it is greater than or equal to 4. The *animation* property cycles from 0 to 3 as long as Smac-Man is moving.

```
if animation >= 4 then animation = 0
```

4. Within the Toolbar, click your mouse on the Script Window button. Director will close the Script window.

5. Within the Toolbar, click your mouse on the Play button. Director will preview your game within the Stage window. Smac-Man should alternate images as he walks to display a walking animation, as shown in Figure 9.10.

Figure 9.10 Making Smac-Man walk within the Stage window.

6. Within the Toolbar, click your mouse on the Rewind button. Director will return your game to its original state within the Stage window.

By now Smac-Man should be fully functional. You should be able to make Smac-Man walk all around the screen, but not outside of the background image's pathways. The *Smac-Man* game is now a complete, playable game. However, if you feel the need to experiment with keyboard control a bit more, you should try adding a few secret cheat commands to the *Smac-Man* game.

ADDING A SECRET CHEAT COMMAND

Cheat commands are not only a fun addition, but also a useful tool for testing various aspects of games. Originally, programmers added cheat commands simply to get around easier in their games. For example, if a programmer couldn't beat his or her game, but wanted to make sure the ending sequence worked correctly, he or she would simply enter a cheat command and skip to the ending scene. To add a secret cheat command to the *Smac-Man* game, perform the following steps:

1. Within the Cast window, click your mouse on the Global member. Director will update the Cast window.

2. Within the Cast window, click your mouse on the Cast Member Script button. Director will display the Script window, as shown in Figure 9.11.

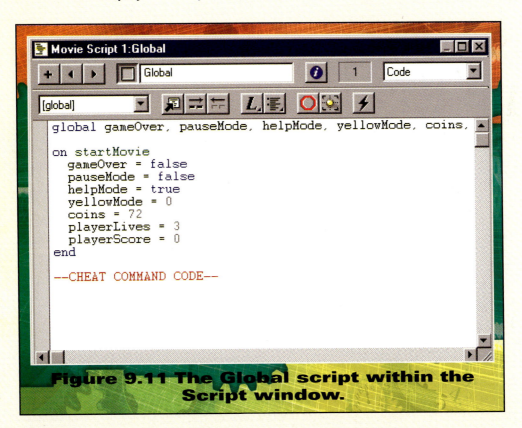

Figure 9.11 The Global script within the Script window.

3. Within the Script window, replace —*CHEAT COMMAND CODE*— with the following code:

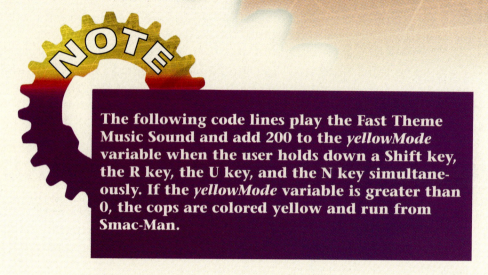

The following code lines play the Fast Theme Music Sound and add 200 to the *yellowMode* variable when the user holds down a Shift key, the R key, the U key, and the N key simultaneously. If the *yellowMode* variable is greater than 0, the cops are colored yellow and run from Smac-Man.

```
on keyDown
   if the shiftDown and keyPressed("r") and keyPressed("u") and \
   keyPressed("n") then
      puppetSound(2, "Fast Theme Music")
      yellowMode = yellowMode + 200
   end if
end
```

4.   Within the Toolbar, click your mouse on the Script Window button. Director will close the Script window.

5.   Within the Toolbar, click your mouse on the Play button. Director will preview your game within the Stage window. You should be able to make the cops run from Smac-Man whenever you hold down a Shift key, the R key, the U key, and the N key simultaneously.

6.   Within the Toolbar, click your mouse on the Rewind button. Director will return your game to its original state within the Stage window.

To keep uninvited players from stumbling onto your secret cheat commands, you can make them as complicated as you wish. For instance, many games make cheat commands available only during specific areas of the game. Others require you to complete certain tasks before the cheat commands become active. If you wanted, you could require the user to hold down every key on the keyboard to activate the cheat commands. It's all up to you.

APPLYING YOUR SKILLS

Now that you have the skills required to utilize keyboard control, your games' features can be much easier to access. Any game with more than a couple major commands would be ridiculously hard to play without at least some degree of keyboard control. Often, character movement is just easier with the arrow keys instead of the mouse. The user does not have to worry about keeping a steady hand or accidentally knocking the mouse. For simple point-and-click games, the keyboard is usually not essential, but for more complex games, it is a necessity.

Chapter 10
The *Great Erudini*: Animating with Film Loops

"There comes a time when the mind takes a higher plane of knowledge but can never prove how it got there." —Albert Einstein

Chapter

10

- Approaching the *Great Erudini* Game

- Opening the *Great Erudini* Game's Template

- Understanding the *Great Erudini* Game

- Setting Up an Animation Sequence

- Converting the Animation into a Film Loop

- Displaying the Film-Loop Animation

- Editing the Film-Loop Animation

- Applying Your Skills

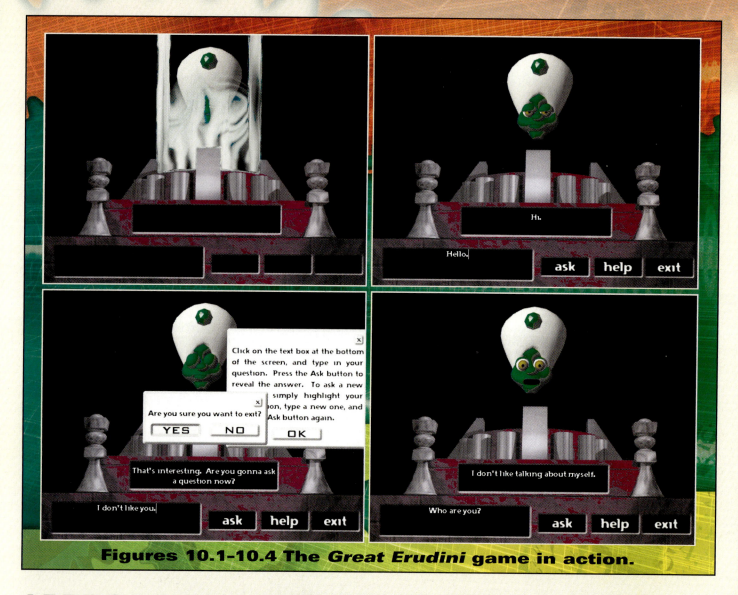

Figures 10.1–10.4 The *Great Erudini* game in action.

APPROACHING THE *GREAT ERUDINI* GAME

Fortune-teller games can be a source of great entertainment to all sorts of people. Unlike old-fashioned fortune-teller games, computer games can actually base their responses on input data and can therefore be much more believable. Despite the *Great Erudini* game's realistic responses, probably the most noticeable feature of the game is its cartoon-animation sequences. The most convenient way to deal with animation sequences is through the use of film loops. A *film loop* is simply a collection of frames in one or more sprite channels that you can treat like any other graphical cast member. The *Great Erudini* game will teach you how to create, manipulate, and edit film loops.

OPENING THE *GREAT ERUDINI* GAME'S TEMPLATE

On this book's companion CD-ROM is a partially completed version of the *Great Erudini* game that you will use to learn about animating with film loops. This template will allow you to use Director as a learning tool. To open the *Great Erudini* game's template in Director and save a copy to your hard drive, perform the following steps:

1. If the companion CD-ROM is not currently in your CD drive, then insert it in your CD-ROM drive now.

2. Within Director, in the Toolbar, click your mouse on the Open button. Director will display the Open dialog box.

3. Within the Open dialog box, click your mouse on the Look In drop-down list, and select your CD drive. Director will display the contents of your CD drive.

4. Within the Open dialog box, double-click your mouse on the *Great Erudini* folder. Director will display the contents of the *Great Erudini* folder.

5. Within the Open dialog box, click your mouse on the *greaterudinitemplate.dir* file. Director will update the Open dialog box.

6. Within the Open dialog box, click your mouse on the OK button. Director will open the *greaterudinitemplate.dir* file.

7. Click your mouse on the File menu, and select the Save As option. Director will display the Save Movie dialog box.

8. Within the Save Movie dialog box, click your mouse on the Save In drop-down list, and select your primary hard drive. Director will display the contents of your primary hard drive.

9. Within the Save Movie dialog box, double-click your mouse on the *Director Games* folder you created in Chapter 2, "Using Director." Director will display the contents of the *Director Games* folder.

10. Within the Save Movie dialog box, in the File Name text field, type **mygreaterudini.dir**, and press the Enter key. Director will save the *Great Erudini* game's template as a file named "mygreaterudini.dir."

As you create more and more games in Director, you will develop your own system of organization. For the purpose of clarity, however, you will keep all your edited template files in a single folder.

UNDERSTANDING THE *GREAT ERUDINI* GAME

To create the illusion of artificial intelligence, the *Great Erudini* game checks the user's input question for various words and responds accordingly. To add to the game's entertainment value, the Great Erudini character often changes facial expressions based on a number of conditions. Because the *Great Erudini* game makes use of film loops, animating the Great Erudini character is a relatively simple task. To view the various Lingo scripts in the Code cast, perform the following steps:

1. Within the Cast window, click your mouse on the Choose Cast button, and select the Code option. Director will display the Code cast within the Cast window. The Code cast contains 14 Lingo scripts, as shown in Table 10.1.

Table 10.1 The 14 Lingo scripts of the Code cast and their descriptions.

Script Name	Description
Global	Stores the global variables *question*, *lastQuestion*, *answer*, and *faceTimer*, and the *askQuestion* function.
Generic Button	Makes its associated sprite behave as a button complete with specified image, cursor, and sound options.
Wait	Keeps the *Great Erudini* game looping on one frame until otherwise specified.
End Game	Ends the *Great Erudini* game when the game exits its associated frame.
Default Invisible	Sets its associated sprite's *visible* property to false when the sprite begins.
Floating Head	Randomly moves the Great Erudini around and regulates his facial expressions.
Ask Button	Calls the *askQuestion* function when the user clicks on its associated sprite.
Drag Help Window	Moves the help window sprites when the user drags its associated sprite.
Drag Exit Window	Moves the exit window sprites when the user drags its associated sprite.
Open Help Window	Sets the *visible* property of the help window sprites to true when the user clicks on its associated sprite.
Open Exit Window	Sets the *visible* property of the exit window sprites to true when the user clicks on its associated sprite.
Close Help Window	Sets the *visible* property of the help window sprites to false when the user clicks on its associated sprite.
Close Exit Window	Sets the *visible* property of the exit window sprites to false when the user clicks on its associated sprite.
Yes Button	Plays game's Exit frame when the user clicks on its associated sprite.

Chapter 10 The *Great Erudini*
Animating with Film Loops

2. Within the Cast window, click your mouse on the Global member. Director will update the Cast window, as shown in Figure 10.5.

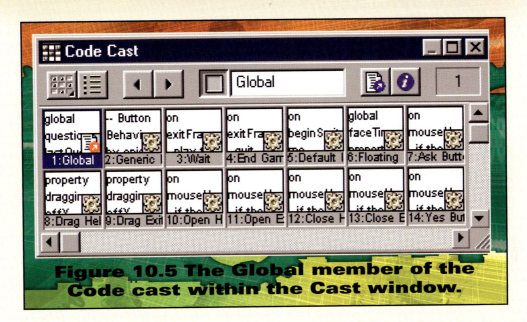

Figure 10.5 The Global member of the Code cast within the Cast window.

3. Within the Cast window, click your mouse on the Cast Member Script button. Director will display the Script window.

4. Within the Script window, use the Previous Cast Member and Next Cast Member buttons to view each of the Lingo scripts in the Code cast.

By now, you should have a good understanding of the logic behind the *Great Erudini* game. You will find that using Director to edit an existing game is nearly impossible unless you first understand how the game works.

SETTING UP AN ANIMATION SEQUENCE

Before you create a film loop, you must first set up your entire animation within the Score. Once you convert a Score animation into a film loop, you cannot directly edit it. Therefore, you should be fairly sure you like the animation the way it is before converting it into a film loop. To set up the animation sequence for the Spinning Head film loop, perform the following steps:

1. Within the Cast window, click your mouse on the Choose Cast button, and select the Animations option, as shown in Figure 10.6. Director will display the Animations cast within the Cast window.

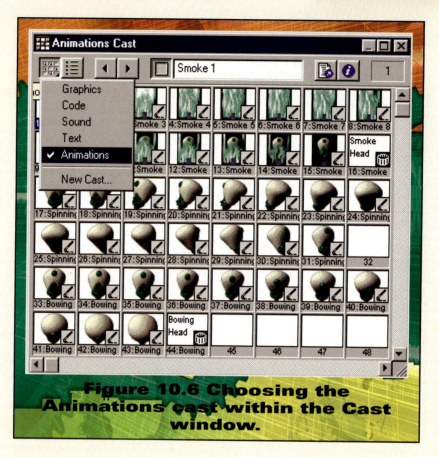

Figure 10.6 Choosing the Animations cast within the Cast window.

2. Within the Cast window, click your mouse on the Spinning 1 member, hold down the Shift key, and click your mouse on the Spinning 15 member. Director will select cast members 17 through 31 within the Cast window.

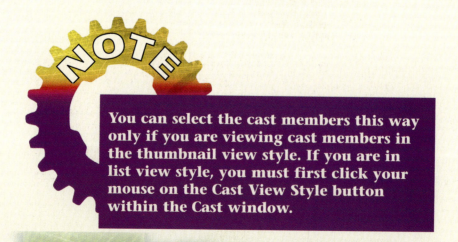

You can select the cast members this way only if you are viewing cast members in the thumbnail view style. If you are in list view style, you must first click your mouse on the Cast View Style button within the Cast window.

3. Within the Score window, click your mouse on cell 1 of channel 3. Director will select cell 1 of channel 3 within the Stage window.

4. Click your mouse on the Modify menu, and select the Cast to Time option. Director will insert an animation sequence into cells 1 through 15 of channel 3, as shown in Figure 10.7.

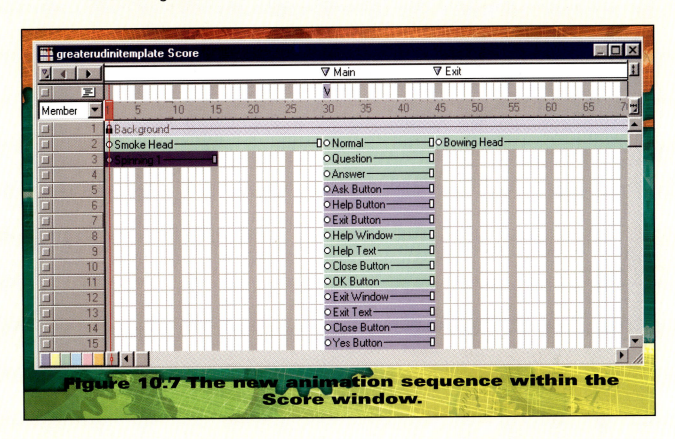

Figure 10.7 The new animation sequence within the Score window.

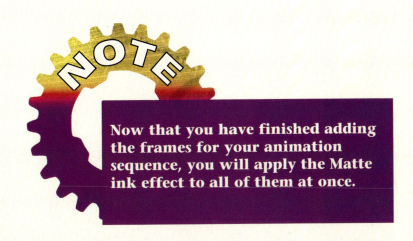

Now that you have finished adding the frames for your animation sequence, you will apply the Matte ink effect to all of them at once.

5.   Within the Score window, click your mouse on cell 1 of channel 3, press and hold the Shift key, and click your mouse on cell 15 of channel 3. Director will select cells 1 through 15 of channel 3.

6.   Within the Property Inspector window, click your mouse on the Ink drop-down list, and select the Matte option. Director will remove the background rectangles from all the frames of your animation sequence.

7.   Within the Toolbar, click your mouse on the Play button. Director will preview your game within the Stage window. Make sure your animation sequence is working properly. You should see the Great Erudini's head make one complete rotation at the beginning of the game.

8.   Within the Toolbar, click your mouse on the Rewind button. Director will return your game to its original state within the Stage window.

You should now have a complete animation sequence built within the Score. The animation should take up 15 frames and end with an image similar to the beginning image. The beginning and ending frames should match so that when you convert the animation sequence into a film loop, it will loop smoothly as long as you wish.

CONVERTING THE ANIMATION INTO A FILM LOOP

Animating within the Score should be nothing new to you. What makes film loops unique is their ability to behave just like other graphical sprites in most cases. For example, you can move, resize, apply behaviors, and change the cast members of film-loop sprites without any problem. Film loops do, however, lose some degree of functionality. Among other disadvantages, you cannot apply ink effects, rotate, or skew film loops. For the most part, however, you will have no need to apply extra effects to film loops. To convert your animation sequence into a film loop, perform the f ollowing steps:

1.   If cells 1 through 15 of channel 3 are not still selected, then within the Score window, click your mouse on cell 1 of channel 3, hold down the Shift key, and click your mouse on cell 15 of channel 3. Director will select cells 1 through 15 of channel 3, as shown in Figure 10.8.

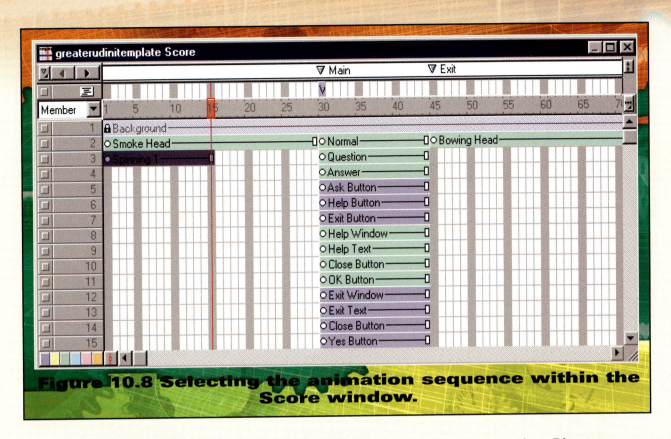

Figure 10.8 Selecting the animation sequence within the Score window.

2. Click your mouse on the Insert menu, and select the Film Loop option. Director will display the Create Film Loop dialog box.

3. Within the Create Film Loop dialog box, in the Name field, type **Spinning Head**, and press the Enter key. Director will convert cells 1 through 15 of channel 3 into a film loop cast member named "Spinning Head."

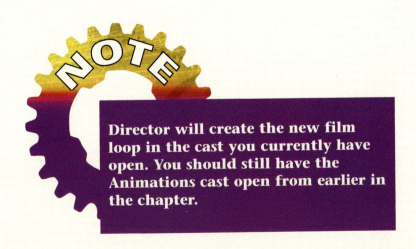

NOTE

Director will create the new film loop in the cast you currently have open. You should still have the Animations cast open from earlier in the chapter.

4. Click your mouse on the Edit menu, and select the Clear Sprites option. Director will delete your animation sequence from cells 1 through 15 of channel 3.

By now, the Spinning Head film loop should be fully functional. Now that you have a complete film-loop animation in your Animations cast, you should find a way to use it. You can either place the film loop directly on the Score like the Smoke Head and Bowing Head film loops, or you can change an existing sprite's cast member through Lingo.

DISPLAYING THE FILM-LOOP ANIMATION

The simplest way to make use of the Spinning Head film loop in the *Great Erudini* game is through Lingo. At the appropriate times, you should change the Great Erudini's cast member to the Spinning Head film loop, just as if you were changing it to any other graphical cast member. To display the Spinning Head film loop at the appropriate times through Lingo, perform the following steps:

1. Within the Cast window, click your mouse on the Choose Cast button, and select the Code option. Director will display the Code cast within the Cast window.

2. Within the Cast window, click your mouse on the Global member. Director will update the Cast window.

3. Within the Cast window, click your mouse on the Cast Member Script button. Director will display the Script window, as shown in Figure 10.9.

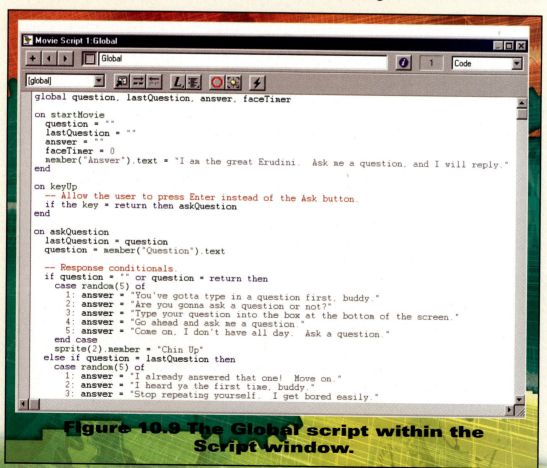

```
global question, lastQuestion, answer, faceTimer

on startMovie
  question = ""
  lastQuestion = ""
  answer = ""
  faceTimer = 0
  member("Answer").text = "I am the great Erudini.  Ask me a question, and I will reply."
end

on keyUp
  -- Allow the user to press Enter instead of the Ask button.
  if the key = return then askQuestion
end

on askQuestion
  lastQuestion = question
  question = member("Question").text

  -- Response conditionals.
  if question = "" or question = return then
    case random(5) of
      1: answer = "You've gotta type in a question first, buddy."
      2: answer = "Are you gonna ask a question or not?"
      3: answer = "Type your question into the box at the bottom of the screen."
      4: answer = "Go ahead and ask me a question."
      5: answer = "Come on, I don't have all day.  Ask a question."
    end case
    sprite(2).member = "Chin Up"
  else if question = lastQuestion then
    case random(5) of
      1: answer = "I already answered that one!  Move on."
      2: answer = "I heard ya the first time, buddy."
      3: answer = "Stop repeating yourself.  I get bored easily."
```

Figure 10.9 The Global script within the Script window.

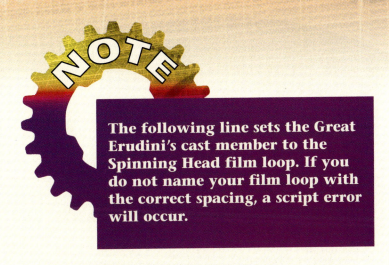

NOTE

The following line sets the Great Erudini's cast member to the Spinning Head film loop. If you do not name your film loop with the correct spacing, a script error will occur.

4. Within the Script window, replace —*GREETING MEMBER CODE*—, —*WHAT MEMBER CODE*—, and —*WHO MEMBER CODE*— with the following code:

```
sprite(2).member = "Spinning Head"
```

5. Within the Toolbar, click your mouse on the Script Window button. Director will close the Script window.

6. Within the Toolbar, click your mouse on the Play button. Director will preview your game within the Stage window. The Spinning Head film loop should play when you type "hello" or "what?" or "who?" into the question field.

7. Within the Toolbar, click your mouse on the Rewind button. Director will return your game to its original state within the Stage window.

By now, the *Great Erudini* game should be fully functional. The Great Erudini's head should spin when you greet him and when you ask "what" or "who" questions. If you want to change the Spinning Head film loop, however, you need to re-create it almost from the beginning.

EDITING THE FILM-LOOP ANIMATION

To edit the Spinning Head film loop, you must first extract all its frames back into the Score and delete the Spinning Head cast member. Once the frames are back in the Score, you can edit them as you wish, but you must convert them back into a film loop when you are finished with the new animation sequence. To edit the Spinning Head film loop by adding another sprite channel, perform the following steps:

1. Within the Cast window, click your mouse on the Choose Cast button, and select the Animations option. Director will display the Animations cast within the Cast window.

2. Within the Cast window, click your mouse on the Spinning Head member. Director will update the Cast window.

3. Click your mouse on the Edit menu, and select the Copy Cast Members option. Director will copy the Spinning Head member into memory.

4. Within the Score window, click your mouse on cell 1 of channel 3. Director will select cell 1 of channel 3 within the Score window.

5. Click your mouse on the Edit menu, and select the Paste Sprites option. Director will paste the frames of the Spinning Head film loop into cells 1 through 15 of channel 3.

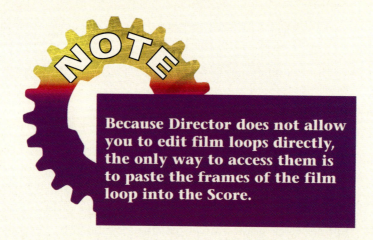

NOTE

Because Director does not allow you to edit film loops directly, the only way to access them is to paste the frames of the film loop into the Score.

6. Within the Score window, click your mouse on cell 2 of channel 4. Director will select cell 2 of channel 4 within the Score window.

7. Click your mouse on the Edit menu, and select the Paste Sprites option. Director will paste the frames of the Spinning Head film loop into cells 2 through 16 of channel 4, as shown in Figure 10.10.

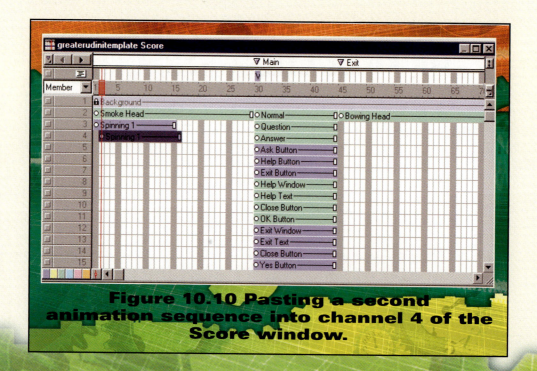

Figure 10.10 Pasting a second animation sequence into channel 4 of the Score window.

8. Within the Property Inspector window, click your mouse on the Ink drop-down list and select the Blend option. Director will allow you to edit the *blend* properties of the sprites in cells 2 through 16 of channel 4.

9. Within the Property Inspector window, click your mouse on the Blend drop-down list and select the 50 option. Director will set the visibility of the sprites in cells 2 through 16 of channel 4 to 50 percent.

10. Within the Score window, click your mouse on cell 16 of channel 4. Director will select cell 16 of channel 4 within the Score window.

11. Click your mouse on the Edit menu, and select the Cut Sprites option. Director will delete cell 16 of channel 4 and copy it into memory.

12. Within the Score window, click your mouse on cell 1 of channel 4. Director will select cell 1 of channel 4 within the Score window, as shown in Figure 10.11.

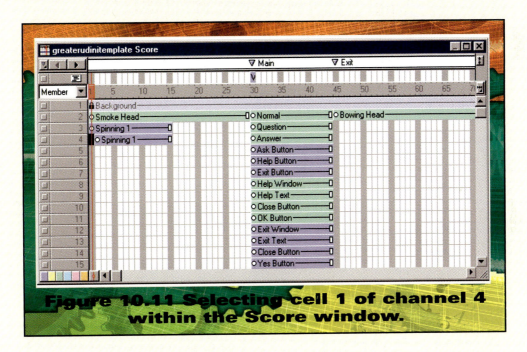

Figure 10.11 Selecting cell 1 of channel 4 within the Score window.

13. Click your mouse on the Edit menu, and select the Paste Sprites option. Director will paste the last frame of the translucent animation sequence into cell 1 of channel 4.

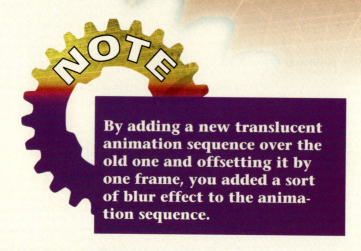

By adding a new translucent animation sequence over the old one and offsetting it by one frame, you added a sort of blur effect to the animation sequence.

14. Within the Cast window, click your mouse on the Spinning Head member. Director will update the Cast window.

15. Click your mouse on the Edit menu, and select the Clear Cast Members option. Director will delete the Spinning Head member.

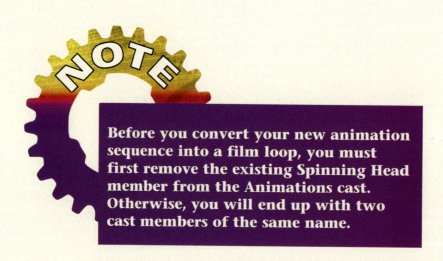

Before you convert your new animation sequence into a film loop, you must first remove the existing Spinning Head member from the Animations cast. Otherwise, you will end up with two cast members of the same name.

16. Within the Score window, click your mouse on cell one of channel 3, hold down the Shift key, and click your mouse on cell 15 of channel 4. Director will select cells 1 through 15 of channels 3 and 4, as shown in Figure 10.12.

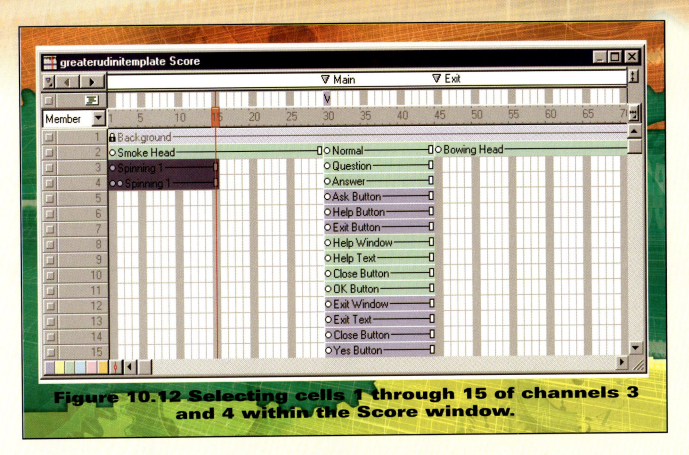

Figure 10.12 Selecting cells 1 through 15 of channels 3 and 4 within the Score window.

17. Click your mouse on the Insert menu, and select the Film Loop option. Director will display the Create Film Loop dialog box.

18. Within the Create Film Loop dialog box, in the Name field, type **Spinning Head**, and press the Enter key. Director will convert cells 1 through 15 of channels 3 and 4 into a film-loop cast member named "Spinning Head."

19. Click your mouse on the Edit menu, and select the Clear Sprites option. Director will delete your original animation sequence from cells 1 through 15 of channels 3 and 4.

20. Within the Toolbar, click your mouse on the Play button. Director will preview your game within the Stage window. The Great Erudini's head should now appear to blur a bit as it spins.

21. Within the Toolbar, click your mouse on the Rewind button. Director will return your game to its original state within the Stage window.

Not only can film loops include multiple sprite channels, but they can also include the sound channels. You could tell the Spinning Head film loop to play a noise every time the head spins around. Don't forget that while you cannot apply ink effects directly to film loops, you can apply them to the various sprites inside of them. Film loops allow a great deal of customization.

APPLYING YOUR SKILLS

Now that you have the skills required to create complex animation with film loops, you should be able to easily add animations to your Director games. Film-loop animations can contribute a great deal to the overall appearance of your game. For instance, you can make a character appear to really walk by simply creating a short film loop. Or perhaps you would like a lengthy animation to loop at the beginning of your game, but don't want to waste Score space. Film loops often come in quite handy.

Chapter 11
Old-Fashioned Pinball:
Applying Realistic Physics

"All that is not eternal is eternally out of date." —C.S. Lewis

Chapter

11

- Approaching the *Old-Fashioned Pinball* Game

- Opening the *Old-Fashioned Pinball* Game's Template

- Understanding the *Old-Fashioned Pinball* Game

- Creating Moveable Objects

- Applying Gravity and Friction to the Objects

- Applying Magnetism to the Objects

- Changing the Magnetic Attraction of the Objects

- Applying Your Skills

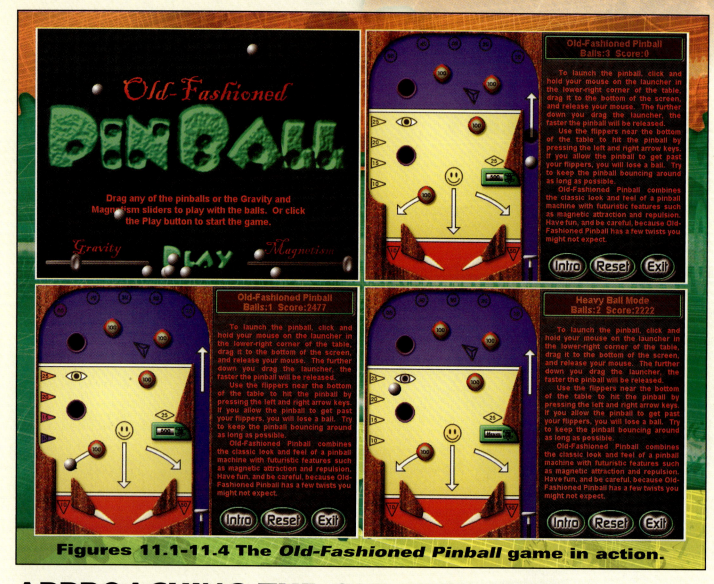

Figures 11.1-11.4 The *Old-Fashioned Pinball* game in action.

APPROACHING THE *OLD-FASHIONED PINBALL* GAME

In today's world of first-person shooters, flight simulators, and cinematic role-playing games, realistic physics are a necessity. If a game lacks a certain physical element such as friction or its gravity is slightly off, the players will notice. Unrealistic movement can drastically lower the believability of your game. To make users forget that your game is just a matrix of color-changing dots, you should apply the basic principles of physics to your games. The *Old-Fashioned Pinball* game will teach you how to create objects with velocity properties that are affected by gravity, friction, and magnetism.

OPENING THE *OLD-FASHIONED PINBALL* GAME'S TEMPLATE

On the companion CD-ROM is a partially completed version of the *Old-Fashioned Pinball* game that you will use to learn about applying realistic physics. This template will allow you to use Director as a learning tool. To open the *Old-Fashioned Pinball* game's template in Director and save a copy to your hard drive, perform the following steps:

1. If the companion CD-ROM is not currently in your CD drive, then insert it in your CD-ROM drive now.

2. Within Director, in the Toolbar, click your mouse on the Open button. Director will display the Open dialog box.

3. Within the Open dialog box, click your mouse on the Look In drop-down list, and select your CD drive. Director will display the contents of your CD drive.

4. Within the Open dialog box, double-click your mouse on the *Old-Fashioned Pinball* folder. Director will display the contents of the *Old-Fashioned Pinball* folder.

5. Within the Open dialog box, click your mouse on the *old-fashionedpinballtemplate.dir* file. Director will update the Open dialog box.

6. Within the Open dialog box, click your mouse on the OK button. Director will open the *old-fashionedpinballtemplate.dir* file.

7. Click your mouse on the File menu, and select the Save As option. Director will display the Save Movie dialog box.

8. Within the Save Movie dialog box, click your mouse on the Save In drop-down list, and select your primary hard drive. Director will display the contents of your primary hard drive.

9. Within the Save Movie dialog box, double-click your mouse on the *Director Games* folder you created in Chapter 2, "Using Director." Director will display the contents of the *Director Games* folder.

10. Within the Save Movie dialog box, in the File Name text field, type **myold-fashionedpinball.dir**, and press the Enter key. Director will save the *Old-Fashioned Pinball* game's template as a file named "myold-fashionedpinball.dir."

As you create more and more games in Director, you will develop your own system of organization. For the purpose of clarity, however, you will keep all your edited template files in a single folder.

UNDERSTANDING THE *OLD-FASHIONED PINBALL* GAME

While the body of the *Old-Fashioned Pinball* game does incorporate basic physics into the pinball's motion, it is not as clear an example of physics as the game's introduction screen. To make the pinball behave correctly, the game sometimes compromises the scientific accuracy of its movement. For example, making the pinball roll along the smooth edges of the table's border is no simple task. The computer does not see any curved surfaces when it looks at the Border bitmap, only an arrangement of colored squares. Without a few shortcuts, believable pinball motion would be nearly impossible. To view the various Lingo scripts in the Code cast, perform the following steps:

1. Within the Cast window, click your mouse on the Choose Cast button, and select the Code option. Director will display the Code cast within the Cast window. The Code cast contains 24 Lingo scripts, as shown in Table 11.1.

Table 11.1 The 24 Lingo scripts of the Code cast and their descriptions.

Script Name	Description
Global	Stores global variables, such as *gravity*, *friction*, and *magnetism*, and the global function *resetGame*.
Generic Button	Makes its associated sprite behave as a button complete with specified image, cursor, and sound options.
Wait	Keeps the *Old-Fashioned Pinball* game looping on one frame until otherwise specified.
Game	Updates the player's score information and keeps the *Old-Fashioned Pinball* game looping on one frame until otherwise specified.
Introduction Ball	Allows the user to drag and throw its associated sprite around the screen while it moves based on gravity and magnetism.
Ball	Sets its associated sprite's *visible* property to false when the sprite interacts with various obstacles as it moves its associated sprite around the screen based on gravity and friction.
Launcher	Allows the user to drag its associated sprite down a few pixels to send the pinball flying out of the launching chamber.
Left Flipper	Controls its associated sprite's *rotation* property based on whether the left-arrow key is being pressed.
Right Flipper	Controls its associated sprite's *rotation* property based on whether the right-arrow key is being pressed.
Bumper	Allows its associated sprite to interact with the pinball when the pinball touches its associated sprite or one of the magnetism modes is activated.
Bumper Overlay	Makes its associated sprite visible when the pinball touches its associated sprite or magnetism is currently affecting the pinball. Otherwise, makes its associated sprite's *blend* property gradually approach zero.
Trapper	Allows its associated sprite to keep the pinball still for 25 to 50 frames when the pinball touches its associated sprite. Then, sends the pinball flying in a random direction.

Table 11.1 The 24 Lingo scripts of the Code cast and their descriptions. (cont.)

Script Name	Description
Trapper Overlay	Makes its associated sprite invisible when the pinball does not touch its associated sprite. Otherwise, makes its associated sprite's *blend* property gradually approach 100.
Lotto	Allows its associated sprite to keep the pinball still for 50 to 70 frames when the pinball touches its associated sprite. Then, chooses a random pinball action and sends the pinball flying in an appropriate direction.
Lotto Overlay	Makes its associated sprite visible when the pinball touches its associated sprite. Otherwise, makes its associated sprite invisible.
Decal	Makes its associated sprite visible and awards the player a specified number of points when the pinball touches its associated sprite.
Fade Out	Makes its associated sprite's *blend* property gradually approach zero by decrements of five.
Move to Front	Sets its associated sprite's *locZ* property to 1,000 when the sprite begins.
Gravity Slider	Allows the player to control the introduction's *gravity* variable by dragging its associated sprite.
Magnetism Slider	Allows the player to control the introduction's *magnetism* variable by dragging its associated sprite.
Play Button	Resets the game's sprites and variables and plays the game's Game frame when the user clicks on its associated sprite.
Intro Button	Resets the movies and plays the game's Intro frame when the user clicks on its associated sprite.
Reset Button	Resets the game when the user clicks on its associated sprite.
Exit Button	Exits the game when the user clicks on its associated sprite.

2. Within the Cast window, click your mouse on the Global member. Director will update the Cast window, as shown in Figure 11.5.

Figure 11.5 The Global member of the Code cast within the Cast window.

3. Within the Cast window, click your mouse on the Cast Member Script button. Director will display the Script window.

4. Within the Script window, use the Previous Cast Member and Next Cast Member buttons to view each of the Lingo scripts in the Code cast.

By now, you should have a good understanding of the logic behind the *Old-Fashioned Pinball* game. You will find that using Director to edit an existing game is nearly impossible unless you first understand how the game works.

CREATING MOVEABLE OBJECTS

Generally, any object that can move on a two-dimensional plane should contain four basic properties. The *x* and *y* properties hold the object's horizontal and vertical locations in memory. You should usually work with the *x* and *y* properties instead of directly with the built-in *locH* and *locV* properties, because *locH* and *locV* can only hold integer values. Integer X and Y coordinates can result in inaccurate and unnatural movement. You will use the *vx* and *vy* properties to indirectly modify *x* and *y*. The *vx* and *vy* properties store the horizontal and vertical velocities of the object. Each frame, you will change the horizontal location of the object by *vx* pixels and the vertical location by *vy* pixels to give the illusion of movement. To add the code to the Introduction Ball behavior that uses velocity properties to make the introduction screen's pinballs moveable, perform the following steps:

1. Within the Cast window, click your mouse on the Introduction Ball member. Director will update the Cast window.

2. Within the Cast window, click your mouse on the Cast Member Script button. Director will display the Script window, as shown in Figure 11.6.

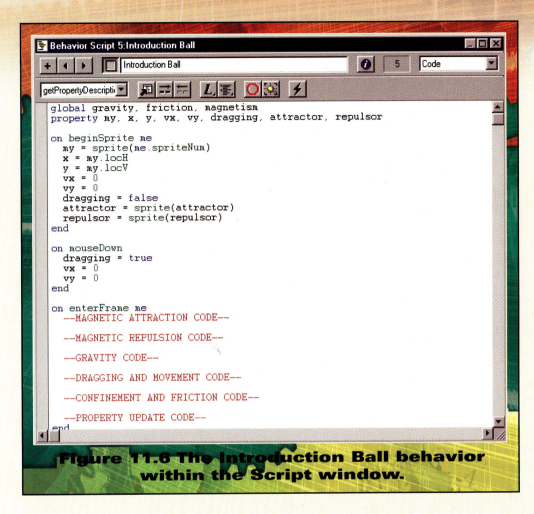

```
Behavior Script 5:Introduction Ball

+  ◄  ►    □ Introduction Ball                        ❶  5   Code   ▼

getPropertyDescripti▼  🔲 ⇥ ⇤   L≣   ◯●  ⚡

global gravity, friction, magnetism
property my, x, y, vx, vy, dragging, attractor, repulsor

on beginSprite me
  my = sprite(me.spriteNum)
  x = my.locH
  y = my.locV
  vx = 0
  vy = 0
  dragging = false
  attractor = sprite(attractor)
  repulsor = sprite(repulsor)
end

on mouseDown
  dragging = true
  vx = 0
  vy = 0
end

on enterFrame me
  --MAGNETIC ATTRACTION CODE--

  --MAGNETIC REPULSION CODE--

  --GRAVITY CODE--

  --DRAGGING AND MOVEMENT CODE--

  --CONFINEMENT AND FRICTION CODE--

  --PROPERTY UPDATE CODE--
end
```

Figure 11.6 The Introduction Ball behavior within the Script window.

3. Within the Script window, replace —*PROPERTY UPDATE CODE*— with the following code:

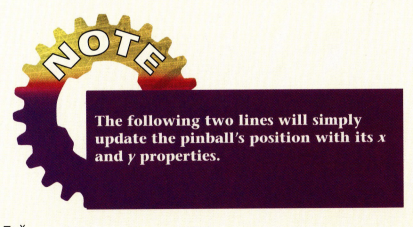

The following two lines will simply update the pinball's position with its *x* and *y* properties.

```
my.locH = x
my.locV = y
```

4. Within the Script window, replace —DRAGGING AND MOVEMENT CODE— with the following code:

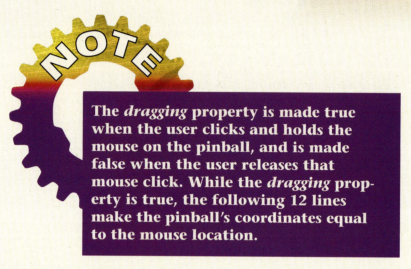

The *dragging* property is made true when the user clicks and holds the mouse on the pinball, and is made false when the user releases that mouse click. While the *dragging* property is true, the following 12 lines make the pinball's coordinates equal to the mouse location.

```
if dragging then
  if the mouseUp then
    dragging = false
    vx = the mouseH - x
    vy = the mouseV - y
  else
    x = the mouseH
    y = the mouseV
    vx = 0
    vy = 0
  end if
end if
```

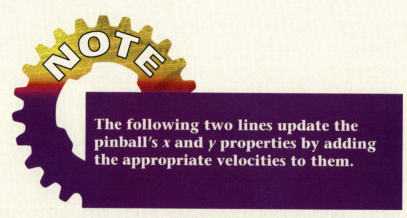

The following two lines update the pinball's *x* and *y* properties by adding the appropriate velocities to them.

```
x = x + vx
y = y + vy
```

5. Within the Toolbar, click your mouse on the Script Window button. Director will close the Script window.

6. Within the Toolbar, click your mouse on the Play button. Director will preview your game within the Stage window. You should be able to drag and throw the pinballs off screen, as shown in Figure 11.7.

Figure 11.7 Dragging and throwing the pinballs within the Stage window.

7. Within the Toolbar, click your mouse on the Rewind button. Director will return your game to its original state within the Stage window.

Now that you have applied the basic principles of motion to the pinballs, they will move much like objects do in the real world. The law of inertia states that when an object is set into motion, it will continue at a constant velocity unless acted upon by external forces. For example, gravity will change an object's vertical velocity and friction will slow and eventually stop the object in motion.

APPLYING GRAVITY AND FRICTION TO THE OBJECTS

To keep the introduction screen interesting, you must keep the user from moving the pinballs off screen. The most entertaining way to achieve this goal is to have the pinballs bounce back when they hit one of the screen's edges. Making an object bounce is perhaps more simple than you would imagine. When an object hits a horizontal or vertical boundary, its appropriate velocity should reverse. To make a realistic bounce, however, you must also slow the object down a bit when it hits a boundary. The less bouncy an object is, the more you should slow it down when it hits a boundary. Gravity and friction help to make the object's movement and boundary collisions appear more natural. To add the code to the Introduction Ball behavior that applies gravity and friction to the pinballs and keeps them within the screen's boundaries, perform the following steps:

1. Within the Cast window, click your mouse on the Introduction Ball member. Director will update the Cast window.

2. Within the Cast window, click your mouse on the Cast Member Script button. Director will display the Script window.

3. Within the Script window, replace —*GRAVITY CODE*— with the following code:

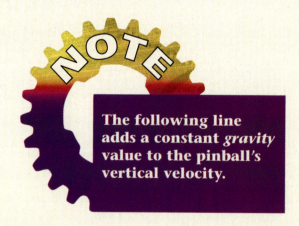

NOTE

The following line adds a constant *gravity* value to the pinball's vertical velocity.

```
vy = vy + gravity
```

4. Within the Script window, replace —*CONFINEMENT AND FRICTION CODE*— with the following code:

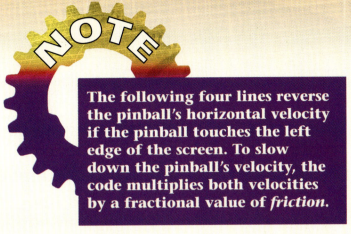

The following four lines reverse the pinball's horizontal velocity if the pinball touches the left edge of the screen. To slow down the pinball's velocity, the code multiplies both velocities by a fractional value of *friction*.

```
if x-my.width/2 < 0 then
  x = my.width/2
  vx = -vx*friction
  vy = vy*friction
```

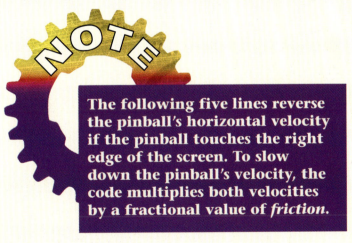

The following five lines reverse the pinball's horizontal velocity if the pinball touches the right edge of the screen. To slow down the pinball's velocity, the code multiplies both velocities by a fractional value of *friction*.

```
else if x+my.width/2 > 640 then
  x = 640-my.width/2
  vx = -vx*friction
  vy = vy*friction
end if
```

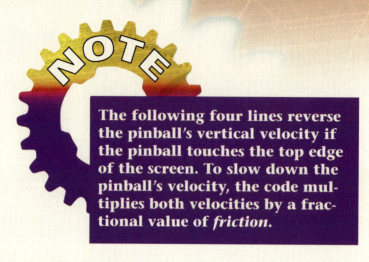

The following four lines reverse the pinball's vertical velocity if the pinball touches the top edge of the screen. To slow down the pinball's velocity, the code multiplies both velocities by a fractional value of *friction*.

```
if y-my.height/2 < 0 then
    y = my.height/2
    vx = vx*friction
    vy = -vy*friction
```

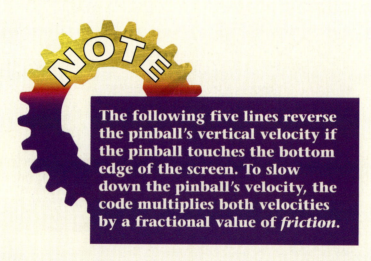

The following five lines reverse the pinball's vertical velocity if the pinball touches the bottom edge of the screen. To slow down the pinball's velocity, the code multiplies both velocities by a fractional value of *friction*.

```
else if y+my.height/2 > 480 then
    y = 480-my.height/2
    vx = vx*friction
    vy = -vy*friction
end if
```

5. Within the Toolbar, click your mouse on the Script Window button. Director will close the Script window.

6. Within the Toolbar, click your mouse on the Play button. Director will preview your game within the Stage window. The pinballs should be able to bounce around the screen freely without any magnetic interference from other balls, as shown in Figure 11.8.

Figure 11.8 Allowing the balls to bounce around within the Stage window.

7.   Within the Toolbar, click your mouse on the Rewind button. Director will return your game to its original state within the Stage window.

By now, the introduction screen's pinballs should have all they need to behave like real, physical objects. You will rarely need to go beyond basic physics principles such as inertia, gravity, and friction to make your games realistic. Sometimes, however, your game might need just a bit more than basic motion. To change an object's motion in any way, you need only to edit the object's velocity properties.

APPLYING MAGNETISM TO THE OBJECTS

Magnetism and gravity behave in basically the same manner. Because gravity works on a much larger scale, however, it is not as easy to observe. When people witness an object falling, they think of it as moving down. A more accurate description would say that the object is moving toward the earth. Planets and other objects of great mass attract particles in much the same way as a magnet. But magnets do not always attract each other. If the poles of two magnets are lined up, the magnets will repel each other. Each of the introduction screen's pinballs will repel one ball and attract another. To add the code to the Introduction Ball behavior that magnetizes the pinballs, perform the following steps:

1. Within the Cast window, click your mouse on the Introduction Ball member. Director will update the Cast window.

2. Within the Cast window, click your mouse on the Cast Member Script button. Director will display the Script window, as shown in Figure 11.9.

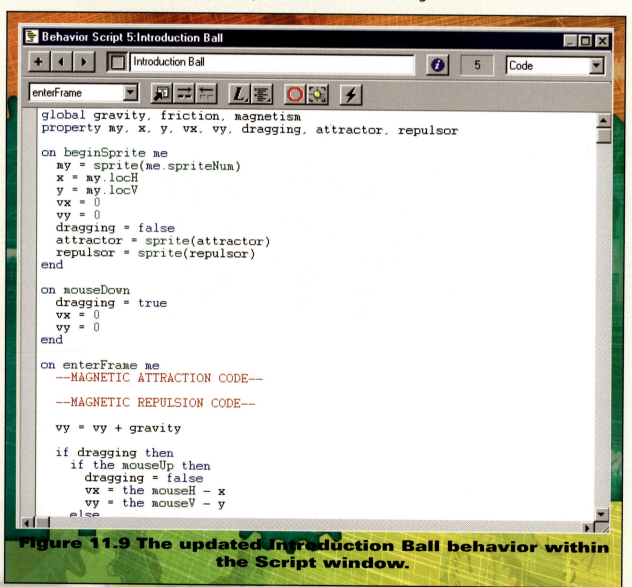

Figure 11.9 The updated Introduction Ball behavior within the Script window.

3. Within the Script window, replace —*MAGNETIC ATTRACTION CODE*— with the following code:

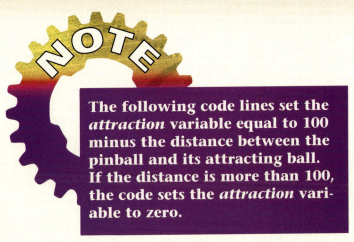

The following code lines set the *attraction* variable equal to 100 minus the distance between the pinball and its attracting ball. If the distance is more than 100, the code sets the *attraction* variable to zero.

```
attraction = 100 - sqrt(power(x-attractor.locH, 2) + power(y-\
attractor.locV, 2))
if attraction < 0 then attraction = 0
```

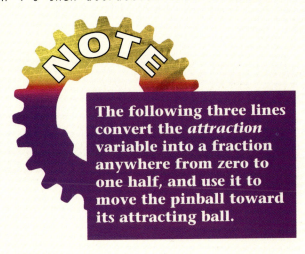

The following three lines convert the *attraction* variable into a fraction anywhere from zero to one half, and use it to move the pinball toward its attracting ball.

```
attraction = attraction/200
vx = vx + (attractor.locH - x)*attraction*magnetism
vy = vy + (attractor.locV - y)*attraction*magnetism
```

4. Within the Script window, replace —*MAGNETIC REPULSION CODE*— with the following code:

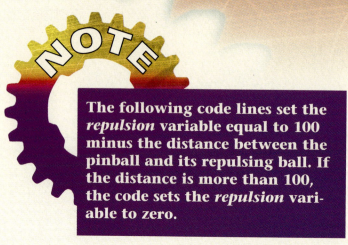

The following code lines set the *repulsion* variable equal to 100 minus the distance between the pinball and its repulsing ball. If the distance is more than 100, the code sets the *repulsion* variable to zero.

```
repulsion = 100 - sqrt(power(x-repulsor.locH, 2) + power(y-repulsor.locV,\
2))
if repulsion < 0 then repulsion = 0
```

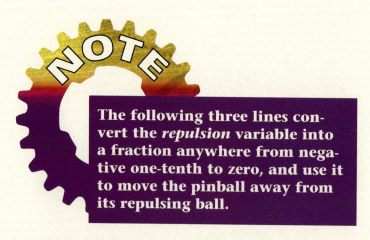

The following three lines convert the *repulsion* variable into a fraction anywhere from negative one-tenth to zero, and use it to move the pinball away from its repulsing ball.

```
repulsion = -repulsion/1000
vx = vx + (repulsor.locH - x)*repulsion*magnetism
vy = vy + (repulsor.locV - y)*repulsion*magnetism
```

5. Within the Toolbar, click your mouse on the Script Window button. Director will close the Script window.

6. Within the Toolbar, click your mouse on the Play button. Director will preview your game within the Stage window. Each pinball should gravitate toward a certain ball and away from another.

7. Within the Toolbar, click your mouse on the Rewind button. Director will return your game to its original state within the Stage window.

Currently, each pinball will be attracted to the ball one channel ahead of it in the Score, and repulsed by the ball five channels ahead of it. Each ball will chase another ball, and no two balls are attracted to one another. If you were to change the *attractor* and *repulsor* properties of each of the pinballs, they would behave quite differently.

CHANGING THE MAGNETIC ATTRACTION OF THE OBJECTS

Because the Introduction ball specifies two of its properties in a *getPropertyDescriptionList* handler, these properties act as parameters for the behavior. You can change their initial values at any time through the Property Inspector window. More importantly, you can apply the same behavior to several sprites that behave differently from one another. For example, the pinball in sprite channel 6 is attracted to the ball in channel 7, but none of the other balls are. To edit the Introduction Ball behavior's parameters for the introduction screen's pinballs, perform the following steps:

1. Within the Score window, click your mouse on cell 14 of channel 6, press and hold the Shift key, and click your mouse on cell 1 of channel 15. Director will select cells 1 through 14 of channels 6 through 15, as shown in Figure 11.10.

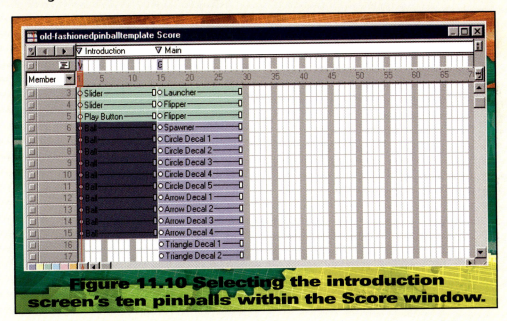

Figure 11.10 Selecting the introduction screen's ten pinballs within the Score window.

2. Within the Property Inspector window, click your mouse on the Behavior tab. Director will display the Behavior sheet.

3. Within the Property Inspector window, click your mouse on the Introduction Ball behavior. Director will update the Property Inspector window.

4. Within the Property Inspector window, click your mouse on the Parameters button. Director will display the Parameters dialog box.

5. Within the Parameters dialog box, type **15** into the Attracting Ball field. Director will set each of the pinballs to be attracted to the ball in channel 15.

6. Within the Parameters dialog box, type **15** into the Repulsing Ball field. Director will set each of the pinballs to be repulsed by the ball in channel 15. However, the attraction will outweigh the repulsion.

7. Within the Parameters dialog box, click your mouse on the OK button. Director will update the parameters of the Introduction Ball behavior for the introduction screen's pinballs.

8. Within the Toolbar, click your mouse on the Play button. Director will preview your game within the Stage window. Each pinball should gravitate toward the ball near the middle of the screen. Try dragging that ball around to attract the other balls, as shown in Figure 11.11.

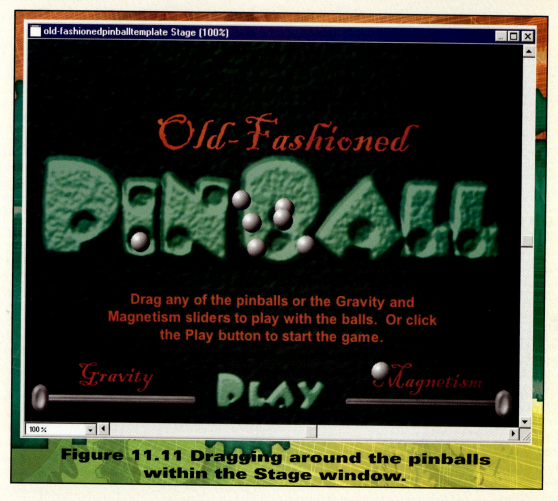

Figure 11.11 Dragging around the pinballs within the Stage window.

9. Within the Toolbar, click your mouse on the Rewind button. Director will return your game to its original state within the Stage window.

By now, you should have a basic understanding of how to apply magnetic attraction and repulsion to moveable objects. By varying the strength of an object's magnetism and the area affected by it, you can customize the magnetism for your own purposes. You might find more uses than you think for such a variation on moveable objects.

APPLYING YOUR SKILLS

Now that you have the skills required to apply realistic physics to objects in your games, their overall appearance and gameplay should improve greatly. Almost any game you design with moving characters will require at least some degree of realistic physics. Whether you are making a car drive, a ball bounce, or a character run, you must remember basic physics principles such as inertia, gravity, and friction.

Chapter 12
Backyard Brawl: Creating Dynamic Characters

"You may not realize it when it happens, but a kick in the teeth may be the best thing in the world for you." —Walt Disney

Chapter

12

- Approaching the *Backyard Brawl* Game

- Opening the *Backyard Brawl* Game's Template

- Understanding the *Backyard Brawl* Game

- Assigning Characters to the Fighters

- Inflicting Damage on the Fighters

- Activating Bot Control for the Fighters

- Indicating Fighter Pain with Ink Effects

- Applying Your Skills

Figures 12.1–12.4 The *Backyard Brawl* game in action.

APPROACHING THE *BACKYARD BRAWL* GAME

Most complex games involve at least a few main characters. These characters should be able to perform several different tasks to keep the game interesting. Therefore, each character should have several different images to indicate changes in the character's position. These images act as frames in an animation. When you change a character's image through Lingo code, you create a sort of dynamic animation. The *Backyard Brawl* game will teach you how to create characters that change and interact based on their properties.

OPENING THE *BACKYARD BRAWL* GAME'S TEMPLATE

On the companion CD-ROM is a partially completed version of the *Backyard Brawl* game that you will use to learn about creating dynamic characters. This template will allow you to use Director as a learning tool. To open the *Backyard Brawl* game's template in Director and save a copy to your hard drive, perform the following steps:

1. If the companion CD-ROM is not currently in your CD drive, then insert it in your CD-ROM drive now.

2. Within Director, in the Toolbar, click your mouse on the Open button. Director will display the Open dialog box.

3. Within the Open dialog box, click your mouse on the Look In drop-down list, and select your CD drive. Director will display the contents of your CD drive.

4. Within the Open dialog box, double-click your mouse on the *Backyard Brawl* folder. Director will display the contents of the *Backyard Brawl* folder.

5. Within the Open dialog box, click your mouse on the *backyardbrawltemplate.dir* file. Director will update the Open dialog box.

6. Within the Open dialog box, click your mouse on the OK button. Director will open the *backyardbrawltemplate.dir* file.

7. Click your mouse on the File menu, and select the Save As option. Director will display the Save Movie dialog box.

8. Within the Save Movie dialog box, click your mouse on the Save In drop-down list, and select your primary hard drive. Director will display the contents of your primary hard drive.

9. Within the Save Movie dialog box, double-click your mouse on the *Director Games* folder you created in Chapter 2, "Using Director." Director will display the contents of the *Director Games* folder.

10. Within the Save Movie dialog box, in the File Name text field, type **mybackyardbrawl.dir**, and press the Enter key. Director will save the *Backyard Brawl* game's template as a file named "mybackyardbrawl.dir."

As you create more and more games in Director, you will develop your own system of organization. For the purpose of clarity, however, you will keep all your edited template files in a single folder.

UNDERSTANDING THE *BACKYARD BRAWL* GAME

The *Backyard Brawl* game consists mainly of two characters that can fight in a variety of ways. In the introduction screen, before a fight has begun, the user must choose how many of the two fighters are user-controlled, and how the fighters will look and behave. Just before each fight begins, the *Backyard*

Brawl game sets fighter properties such as *speed*, *strength*, and *weight* based on the two characters chosen by the user. To make the fighters inflict damage on one another, the *Backyard Brawl* game checks to see if a fighter is facing his opponent, touching his opponent, and currently attacking. If all three conditions are met, the fighter's opponent will react. To view the various Lingo scripts in the Code cast, perform the following steps:

1. Within the Cast window, click your mouse on the Choose Cast button, and select the Code option. Director will display the Code cast within the Cast window. The Code cast contains 26 Lingo scripts, as Table 12.1 briefly describes.

Table 12.1 The 26 Lingo scripts of the Code cast and their descriptions.

Script Name	Description
Global	Initializes all the local variables such as *one*, *two*, and *characters* and allows the user to cheat.
Generic Button	Makes its associated sprite behave as a button complete with specified image, cursor, and sound options.
Wait	Keeps the *Backyard Brawl* game looping on one frame until otherwise specified.
Game	Checks for a character's death and keeps the *Backyard Brawl* game looping on one frame until otherwise specified.
Default Blank	Sets its associated sprite's cast member text to a blank string.
Fade In	Increases its associated sprite's visibility by 5 each frame if the sprite is translucent.
Fighter	Handles the animations and properties necessary for a fighting character.
Damage	Handles collisions and deaths of fighting characters.
Bot Control	Controls a fighting character by manipulating its properties if the appropriate fighting mode is chosen.
Player 1 Control	Allows the user to control a fighting character by manipulating its properties if the appropriate fighting mode is chosen.
Player 2 Control	Allows a second user to control a fighting character by manipulating its properties if the appropriate fighting mode is chosen.
Fighter Mask	Follows the position and mimics the animation of its fighting character. Because its associated sprite is in Matte ink style, it can be used for collision detection.
Fighter Shadow	Follows the horizontal position of its fighting character and changes the properties of its associated sprite based on its fighting character's vertical position.
Left Health Bar	Displays the health of the first fighter by changing the width of its associated sprite.
Right Health Bar	Displays the health of the second fighter by changing the width of its associated sprite.
Alert Text Fade	Displays the value of the *alertText* variable by changing the cast member of its associated sprite and then gradually fades into the background.

Table 12.1 The 26 Lingo scripts of the Code cast and their descriptions. (cont.)

Script Name	Description
Alert Text Smaller	Slightly decreases the size of its associated sprite when the *alertText* variable changes, then resets the *alertText* variable.
Hand	Randomly moves its associated sprite onto the screen holding a random weapon.
Weapon	Handles collisions with fighters and rotates its associated sprite back and forth while a fighter is holding it.
Fight Mode	Changes its associated sprite's cast member text and sets a fighting mode when the user clicks on its associated sprite.
Status Text	Changes its associated sprite's cast member text to give the user instruction while he or she is choosing a fighter.
Character Face	Chooses the appropriate fighting character when the user clicks on its associated sprite.
Fight Button	Resets the game and plays the game's Game frame when the user clicks on its associated sprite.
Help Button	Plays game's Help frame when the user clicks on its associated sprite.
Help Exit Button	Plays game's Main frame when the user clicks on its associated sprite.
Quit Button	Ends the game when the user clicks on its associated sprite.

2. Within the Cast window, click your mouse on the Global member. Director will update the Cast window, as shown in Figure 12.5.

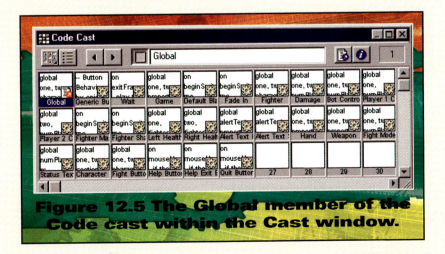

Figure 12.5 The Global member of the Code cast within the Cast window.

3. Within the Cast window, click your mouse on the Cast Member Script button. Director will display the Script window.

4. Within the Script window, use the Previous Cast Member and Next Cast Member buttons to view each of the Lingo scripts in the Code cast.

By now, you should have a good understanding of the logic behind the *Backyard Brawl* game. You will find that using Director to edit an existing game is nearly impossible unless you first understand how the game works.

ASSIGNING CHARACTERS TO THE FIGHTERS

At the very beginning of the *Backyard Brawl* game, the user selects two characters to fight each other. When the user finalizes his or her selection by clicking on the Fight button, the *Backyard Brawl* game must store the chosen characters in two global variables. The code that actually initializes the fighters uses these two variables to decide how the characters should look and behave. To add the code to the Fight Button behavior that assigns character names to the first and second fighters, perform the following steps:

1. Within the Cast window, click your mouse on the Fight Button member. Director will update the Cast window.

2. Within the Cast window, click your mouse on the Cast Member Script button. Director will display the Script window, as shown in Figure 12.6.

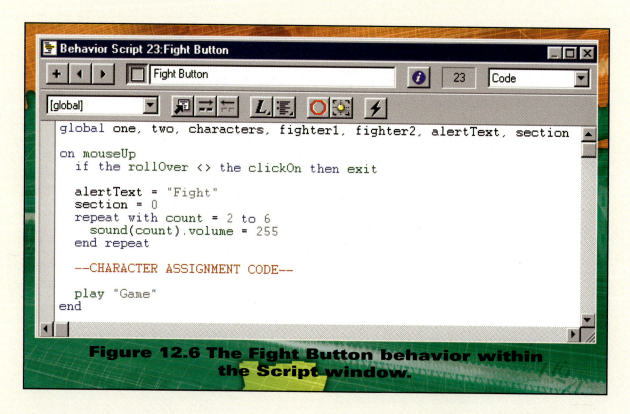

Figure 12.6 The Fight Button behavior within the Script window.

3. Within the Script window, replace —CHARACTER ASSIGNMENT CODE— with the following code:

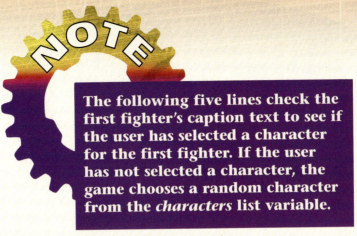

NOTE

The following five lines check the first fighter's caption text to see if the user has selected a character for the first fighter. If the user has not selected a character, the game chooses a random character from the *characters* list variable.

```
if sprite(one + 8).member.text <> "" then
   fighter1 = sprite(one + 8).member.text
else
   fighter1 = characters[random(5)]
end if
```

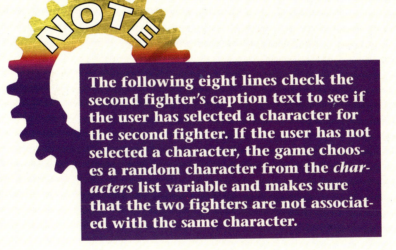

NOTE

The following eight lines check the second fighter's caption text to see if the user has selected a character for the second fighter. If the user has not selected a character, the game chooses a random character from the *characters* list variable and makes sure that the two fighters are not associated with the same character.

```
if sprite(two + 8).member.text <> "" then
   fighter2 = sprite(two + 8).member.text
else
   fighter2 = characters[random(5)]
   repeat while fighter1 = fighter2
      fighter2 = characters[random(5)]
   end repeat
end if
```

4. Within the Toolbar, click your mouse on the Script Window button. Director will close the Script window.

5. Within the Toolbar, click your mouse on the Play button. Director will preview your game within the Stage window. You should be able to select the fighting characters you want, but they will be unable to inflict damage on one another by punching and kicking.

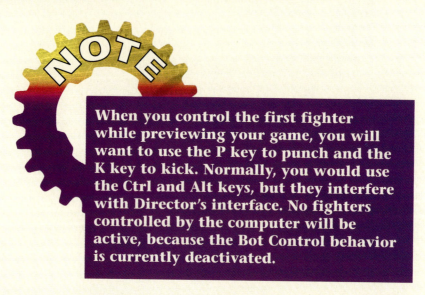

When you control the first fighter while previewing your game, you will want to use the P key to punch and the K key to kick. Normally, you would use the Ctrl and Alt keys, but they interfere with Director's interface. No fighters controlled by the computer will be active, because the Bot Control behavior is currently deactivated.

6. Within the Toolbar, click your mouse on the Rewind button. Director will return your game to its original state within the Stage window.

Now that your *Backyard Brawl* game allows the user to choose the fighting characters, you must allow the characters to actually fight. The *Backyard Brawl* game in its current state does not inflict damage on the fighters when they punch or kick one another. The simple matter of inflicting damage on the fighters is the most important aspect of the *Backyard Brawl* game, because it determines who wins and who loses.

INFLICTING DAMAGE ON THE FIGHTERS

When a fighter is facing his opponent, touching his opponent, and currently attacking, the *Backyard Brawl* game uses properties of both fighters to indicate that a successful attack has just occurred. The game removes a bit of health from the opponent based on the strength of the attacking fighter. Then, the opponent moves away from the attacking fighter based on the strength of the attack and the weight of the opponent. To add the code to the Damage behavior that handles punches and kicks, perform the following steps:

1. Within the Cast window, click your mouse on the Damage member. Director will update the Cast window.

2. Within the Cast window, click your mouse on the Cast Member Script button. Director will display the Script window, as shown in Figure 12.7.

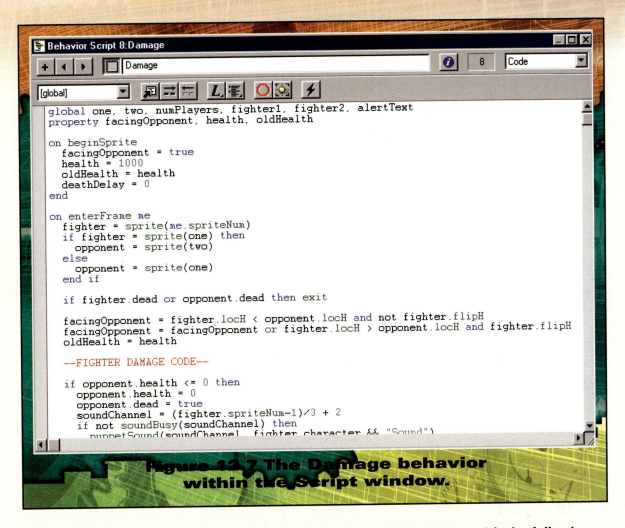

```
Behavior Script 8:Damage

[+]  [◄]  [►]   [ ] Damage                                    [i]  [8]  [Code ▼]

[global ▼]   [icons...]

global one, two, numPlayers, fighter1, fighter2, alertText
property facingOpponent, health, oldHealth

on beginSprite
  facingOpponent = true
  health = 1000
  oldHealth = health
  deathDelay = 0
end

on enterFrame me
  fighter = sprite(me.spriteNum)
  if fighter = sprite(one) then
    opponent = sprite(two)
  else
    opponent = sprite(one)
  end if

  if fighter.dead or opponent.dead then exit

  facingOpponent = fighter.locH < opponent.locH and not fighter.flipH
  facingOpponent = facingOpponent or fighter.locH > opponent.locH and fighter.flipH
  oldHealth = health

  --FIGHTER DAMAGE CODE--

  if opponent.health <= 0 then
    opponent.health = 0
    opponent.dead = true
    soundChannel = (fighter.spriteNum-1)/3 + 2
    if not soundBusy(soundChannel) then
      puppetSound(soundChannel, fighter.character && "Sound")
```

Figure 12.7 The Damage behavior within the Script window.

3. Within the Script window, replace —*FIGHTER DAMAGE CODE*— with the following code:

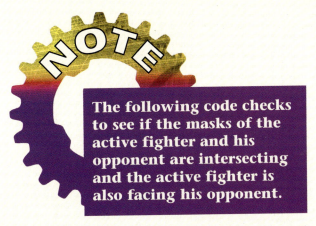

The following code checks to see if the masks of the active fighter and his opponent are intersecting and the active fighter is also facing his opponent.

```
if sprite(fighter.spriteNum-1).intersects(opponent.spriteNum-1) and \
   facingOpponent then
```

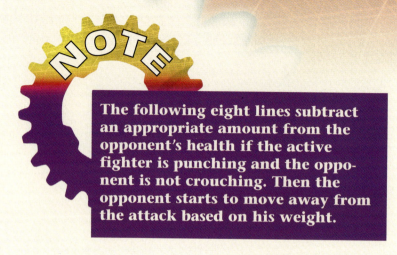

The following eight lines subtract an appropriate amount from the opponent's health if the active fighter is punching and the opponent is not crouching. Then the opponent starts to move away from the attack based on his weight.

```
if fighter.punching and not opponent.crouching then
    opponent.health = opponent.health - sprite(me.spriteNum).strength/10
    if opponent.facingOpponent then
        opponent.velocity = opponent.velocity - (10 - opponent.weight/100)
    else
        opponent.velocity = opponent.velocity + (10 - opponent.weight/100)
    end if
end if
```

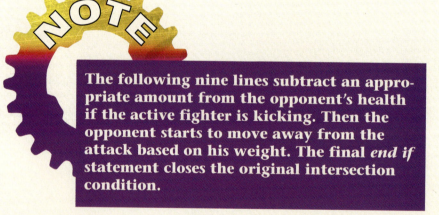

The following nine lines subtract an appropriate amount from the opponent's health if the active fighter is kicking. Then the opponent starts to move away from the attack based on his weight. The final *end if* statement closes the original intersection condition.

```
if fighter.kicking then
    opponent.health = opponent.health - sprite(me.spriteNum).strength/5
    if opponent.facingOpponent then
        opponent.velocity = opponent.velocity - (50 - opponent.weight/20)
    else
        opponent.velocity = opponent.velocity + (50 - opponent.weight/20)
    end if
  end if
end if
```

4. Within the Toolbar, click your mouse on the Script Window button. Director will close the Script window.

5. Within the Toolbar, click your mouse on the Play button. Director will preview your game within the Stage window. The fighters should be able to inflict damage on one another normally.

6. Within the Toolbar, click your mouse on the Rewind button. Director will return your game to its original state within the Stage window.

The only thing missing from the *Backyard Brawl* game at this point should be the artificial intelligence. Without good artificial intelligence for the game, the single-player mode would be boring and the bot matches, or computer against computer mode, would be impossible. So far, the artificial intelligence has been deactivated to make sure you understand the basic aspects of the game before you start playing around in it. There will be plenty of time for that later.

ACTIVATING BOT CONTROL FOR THE FIGHTERS

In games of combat, the common name for a character controlled entirely by the computer is a *bot*. Usually, bots occur in multi-player games and try to behave as much like human players as possible. The *Backyard Brawl* game is the first in this book to employ artificial intelligence that mimics complex human behavior. If you are interested in artificial intelligence, you may want to take a close look at the Bot Control behavior. To activate the Bot Control behavior, perform the following steps:

1. Within the Cast window, click your mouse on the Bot Control member. Director will update the Cast window.

2. Within the Cast window, click your mouse on the Cast Member Script button. Director will display the Script window, as shown in Figure 12.8.

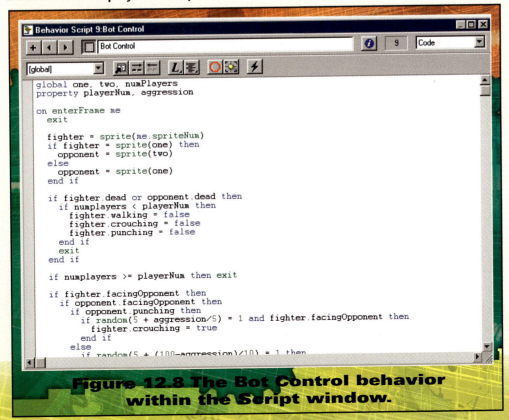

Figure 12.8 The Bot Control behavior within the Script window.

3. Within the Script window, delete *exit* from the first line of the *enterFrame* handler. The *Backyard Brawl* game will no longer ignore the *enterFrame* handler of the Bot Control behavior.

4. Within the Toolbar, click your mouse on the Script Window button. Director will close the Script window.

5. Within the Toolbar, click your mouse on the Play button. Director will preview your game within the Stage window. The *Backyard Brawl* game should be complete with artificial intelligence.

6. Within the Toolbar, click your mouse on the Rewind button. Director will return your game to its original state within the Stage window.

By now, the *Backyard Brawl* game should be fully functional. Although the game functions just fine as it is, there is always room for improvement. You could spend years adding little improvements to a perfectly good game. As a programmer, you must decide exactly when you are satisfied with your game.

INDICATING FIGHTER PAIN WITH INK EFFECTS

One effect that is somewhat reminiscent of older, arcade-style games involves the use of ink effects. By simply changing the ink effect of a graphical sprite in each frame, you will cause the sprite's image to flash rapidly by displaying altered versions of itself. To add the code to the Fighter behavior that randomly changes a fighter sprite's ink effect while the fighter is being hurt, perform the following steps:

1. Within the Cast window, click your mouse on the Fighter member. Director will update the Cast window.

2. Within the Cast window, click your mouse on the Cast Member Script button. Director will display the Script window, as shown in Figure 12.9.

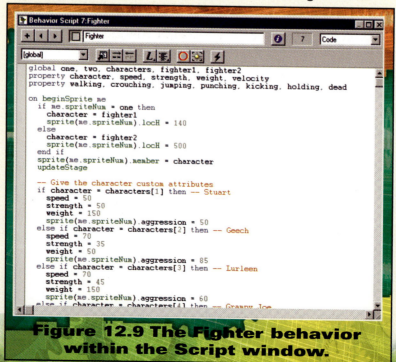

Figure 12.9 The Fighter behavior within the Script window.

3. Within the Script window, replace —*RANDOM INK CODE*— with the following code:

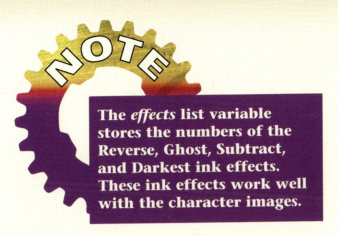

The *effects* list variable stores the numbers of the Reverse, Ghost, Subtract, and Darkest ink effects. These ink effects work well with the character images.

```
effects = [2, 3, 38, 39]
```

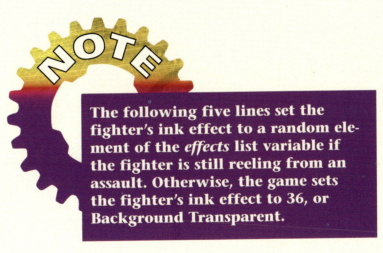

The following five lines set the fighter's ink effect to a random element of the *effects* list variable if the fighter is still reeling from an assault. Otherwise, the game sets the fighter's ink effect to 36, or Background Transparent.

```
if fighter.velocity <> 0 then
   fighter.ink = effects[random(effects.count)]
else
   fighter.ink = 36
end if
```

4. Within the Toolbar, click your mouse on the Script Window button. Director will close the Script window.

5. Within the Toolbar, click your mouse on the Play button. Director will preview your game within the Stage window. The fighters should flash randomly after each time they absorb damage, as shown in Figure 12.10.

Figure 12.10 Testing the random ink effects within the Stage window.

6. Within the Toolbar, click your mouse on the Rewind button. Director will return your game to its original state within the Stage window.

Adding translucency or ink effects can often improve the overall look of your game, but when you decide to improve a game, you will hopefully add more than just simple visual effects. In a game like *Backyard Brawl*, for example, you might decide to add extra character images to make the fighters' movement appear more fluent and natural. Or, you might decide to add entirely new fighting moves to make the game more interesting. Perhaps you would simply like to have the background image change at the start of each fight. Little improvements can sometimes make a world of difference.

APPLYING YOUR SKILLS

Now that you have the skills required to create dynamic characters, you can build more complex, realistic games. To create most types of games, you must animate many different characters in a variety of positions. You must also compare the properties of these characters to perform most major functions of the game such as detecting collisions and determining a winner. You will find that creating dynamic characters is a basic skill you will use in virtually all of the major games you create.

Chapter 13
Covert Mayhem: Animating in Three Dimensions

"Like what you do. If you don't like it, do something else."
—Paul Harvey

Chapter

13

- Approaching the *Covert Mayhem* Game

- Opening the *Covert Mayhem* Game's Template

- Understanding the *Covert Mayhem* Game

- Generating Walls in a Three-Dimensional Field

- Translating an Entity's Properties into Movement

- Checking the Map for Obstacle Collisions

- Allowing Movement Control on the Z-Axis

- Applying Your Skills

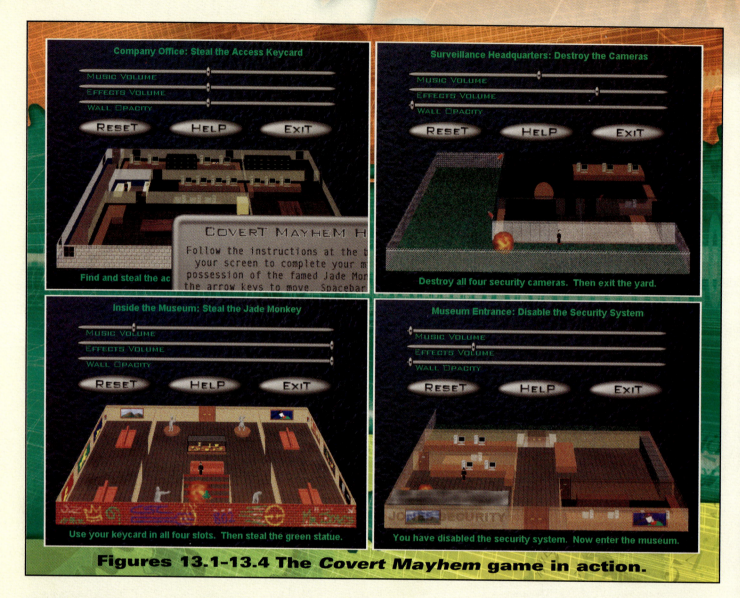

Company Office: Steal the Access Keycard

MUSIC VOLUME
EFFECTS VOLUME
WALL OPACITY

RESET HELP EXIT

COVERT MAYHEM H
Follow the instructions at the t
your screen to complete your m
possession of the famed Jade Mor
the arrow keys to move. Spacebar

Find and steal the ac

Surveillance Headquarters: Destroy the Cameras

MUSIC VOLUME
EFFECTS VOLUME
WALL OPACITY

RESET HELP EXIT

Destroy all four security cameras. Then exit the yard.

Inside the Museum: Steal the Jade Monkey

MUSIC VOLUME
EFFECTS VOLUME
WALL OPACITY

RESET HELP EXIT

Use your keycard in all four slots. Then steal the green statue.

Museum Entrance: Disable the Security System

MUSIC VOLUME
EFFECTS VOLUME
WALL OPACITY

RESET HELP EXIT

You have disabled the security system. Now enter the museum.

Figures 13.1–13.4 The *Covert Mayhem* game in action.

APPROACHING THE *COVERT MAYHEM* GAME

Three-dimensional environments are increasingly becoming the standard format for commercial games. Director does not provide a built-in three-dimensional engine, nor does it particularly lend itself to the high-intensity, full-screen animation that 3D environments require. However, you can gain a good understanding of how 3D engines work by placing two-dimensional sprites onto a plane in a three-dimensional field. The *Covert Mayhem* game will teach you how to create a pseudo-3D environment by distorting and layering graphical sprites.

OPENING THE *COVERT MAYHEM* GAME'S TEMPLATE

On the companion CD-ROM is a partially completed version of the *Covert Mayhem* game that you will use to learn about animating with film loops. This template will allow you to use Director as a learning tool. To open the *Covert Mayhem* game's template in Director and save a copy to your hard drive, perform the following steps:

1. If the companion CD-ROM is not currently in your CD drive, then insert it in your CD-ROM drive now.

2. Within Director, in the Toolbar, click your mouse on the Open button. Director will display the Open dialog box.

3. Within the Open dialog box, click your mouse on the Look In drop-down list, and select your CD drive. Director will display the contents of your CD drive.

4. Within the Open dialog box, double-click your mouse on the *Covert Mayhem* folder. Director will display the contents of the *Covert Mayhem* folder.

5. Within the Open dialog box, click your mouse on the *covertmayhemtemplate.dir* file. Director will update the Open dialog box.

6. Within the Open dialog box, click your mouse on the OK button. Director will open the *covertmayhemtemplate.dir* file.

7. Click your mouse on the File menu, and select the Save As option. Director will display the Save Movie dialog box.

8. Within the Save Movie dialog box, click your mouse on the Save In drop-down list, and select your primary hard drive. Director will display the contents of your primary hard drive.

9. Within the Save Movie dialog box, double-click your mouse on the *Director Games* folder you created in Chapter 2, "Using Director." Director will display the contents of the *Director Games* folder.

10. Within the Save Movie dialog box, in the File Name text field, type **mycovertmayhem.dir**, and press the Enter key. Director will save the *Covert Mayhem* game's template as a file named "mycovertmayhem.dir."

As you create more and more games in Director, you will develop your own system of organization. For the purpose of clarity, however, you will keep all your edited template files in a single folder.

UNDERSTANDING THE *COVERT MAYHEM* GAME

The *Covert Mayhem* game's pseudo-3D environment consists mainly of a distorted floor image covered in distorted, translucent wall images. The *quad* sprite property allows you to position a sprite's corners in any way you wish while the *locZ* property allows you to make sure everything overlaps in the correct manner.

All images such as furniture, shadows, and the character are simply two-dimensional sprites positioned to look three-dimensional and given appropriate *locZ* values. Generally, the further down on the screen a sprite is located, the higher its *width*, *height*, and *locZ* values will be. To view the various Lingo scripts in the Code cast, perform the following steps:

1. Within the Cast window, click your mouse on the Choose Cast button, and select the Code option. Director will display the Code cast within the Cast window. The Code cast contains 27 Lingo scripts, as shown in Table 13.1.

Table 13.1 The 27 Lingo scripts of the Code cast and their descriptions.

Script Name	Description
Global	Initializes global variables, such as *musicVolume*, *effectsVolume*, and *wallOpacity*.
Generic Button	Makes its associated sprite behave as a button complete with specified image, cursor, and sound options.
Wait for Click	Keeps the *Covert Mayhem* game looping on one frame until the user clicks his or her mouse.
End Game	Exits the game upon entering its associated frame.
Map	Gradually distorts its associated sprite into the shape of the map's floor.
Wall	Distorts its associated sprite into either a horizontal or vertical wall at a specified location.
Dark Room	Makes its associated sprite invisible the first time the character comes into contact with the sprite one channel ahead of it.
Entity	Handles basic characteristics of a character in a three-dimensional field such as *x*, *y*, and *z*, and basic functions such as *translateCoordinates* and *movePixel*.
Player Control	Allows the user to control its associated sprite if that sprite is also associated with the Entity behavior.
Bomb	Makes its associated sprite behave like a bomb with a timer. When the timer runs out, it plays an explosion sound and makes the Explosion bitmap one channel ahead become visible.
Explosion	Randomly chooses a new Explosion bitmap cast member each frame and gradually fades out when it is visible.
Computer	Makes its associated sprite invisible when it comes into contact with a bomb's explosion.
Help Window	Makes its associated sprite invisible when the sprite begins, and stores its associated sprite in the global *help* variable.
Move to Front	Sets its associated sprite's *locZ* property to 1000 when the sprite begins.
Set Layer	Sets its associated sprite's *locZ* property to a specified value when the sprite begins.

Table 13.1 The 27 Lingo scripts of the Code cast and their descriptions. (cont.)

Script Name	Description
Searchlight	Makes its associated sprite randomly resize and move around the screen like a searchlight.
Roach	Makes its associated sprite randomly move across the screen in the direction it is facing. Then resets the sprite to a random off-screen location and repeats the process.
Introduction Overlay	Gradually fades its associated sprite out as long as it is visible.
You Win	Randomly resizes its associated sprite by a value of -2 to 2 pixels each frame.
Ending Explosion	Randomly chooses a new Explosion bitmap cast member for each frame. Chooses a random location to make itself visible, gradually fades out, and repeats the process.
Drag Slider	Moves its associated sprite horizontally when the user drags its associated sprite.
Music Volume Slider	Uses its associated sprite's horizontal position to affect the global *musicVolume* variable.
Effects Volume Slider	Uses its associated sprite's horizontal position to affect the global *effectsVolume* variable.
Wall Opacity Slider	Uses its associated sprite's horizontal position to affect the global *wallOpacity* variable.
Reset Button	Plays the game's Reset frame when the user clicks on its associated sprite.
Help Button	Reverses the Help Window bitmap's visibility when the user clicks on its associated sprite.
Exit Button	Ends the game when the user clicks on its associated sprite.

2. Within the Cast window, click your mouse on the Global member. Director will update the Cast window, as shown in Figure 13.5.

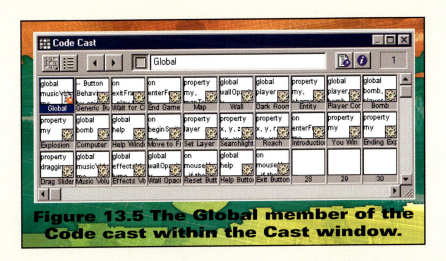

Figure 13.5 The Global member of the Code cast within the Cast window.

3. Within the Cast window, click your mouse on the Cast Member Script button. Director will display the Script window.

4. Within the Script window, use the Previous Cast Member and Next Cast Member buttons to view each of the Lingo scripts in the Code cast.

By now, you should have a good understanding of the logic behind the *Covert Mayhem* game. You will find that using Director to edit an existing game is nearly impossible unless you first understand how the game works.

GENERATING WALLS IN A THREE-DIMENSIONAL FIELD

Director does not allow you to draw three-dimensional shapes onto the Stage, so you must build them yourself out of two-dimensional images. The easiest way to create the illusion of depth is to use the *quad* sprite property to distort your images through Lingo code. To add the code to the Wall behavior that positions horizontal walls on the Stage based on behavior parameters, perform the following steps:

1. Within the Cast window, click your mouse on the Wall member. Director will update the Cast window.

2. Within the Cast window, click your mouse on the Cast Member Script button. Director will display the Script window, as shown in Figure 13.6.

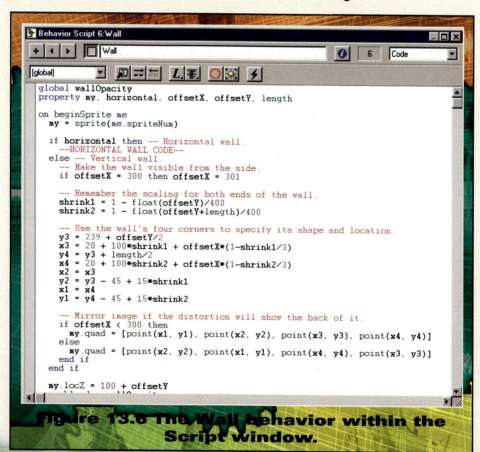

```
global wallOpacity
property my, horizontal, offsetX, offsetY, length

on beginSprite me
  my = sprite(me.spriteNum)

  if horizontal then -- Horizontal wall.
    --HORIZONTAL WALL CODE--
  else -- Vertical wall.
    -- Make the wall visible from the side.
    if offsetX = 300 then offsetX = 301

    -- Remember the scaling for both ends of the wall.
    shrink1 = 1 - float(offsetY)/400
    shrink2 = 1 - float(offsetY+length)/400

    -- Use the wall's four corners to specify its shape and location.
    y3 = 239 + offsetY/2
    x3 = 20 + 100*shrink1 + offsetX*(1-shrink1/3)
    y4 = y3 + length/2
    x4 = 20 + 100*shrink2 + offsetX*(1-shrink2/3)
    x2 = x3
    y2 = y3 - 45 + 15*shrink1
    x1 = x4
    y1 = y4 - 45 + 15*shrink2

    -- Mirror image if the distortion will show the back of it.
    if offsetX < 300 then
      my.quad = [point(x1, y1), point(x2, y2), point(x3, y3), point(x4, y4)]
    else
      my.quad = [point(x2, y2), point(x1, y1), point(x4, y4), point(x3, y3)]
    end if
  end if

  my.locZ = 100 + offsetY
```

Figure 13.6 The Wall behavior within the Script window.

3. Within the Script window, replace —*HORIZONTAL WALL CODE*— with the following code:

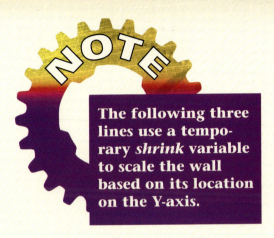

NOTE

The following three lines use a temporary *shrink* variable to scale the wall based on its location on the Y-axis.

```
shrink = 1 - float(offsetY)/400
my.width = length - length/3*shrink
my.height = 45 - 15*shrink
```

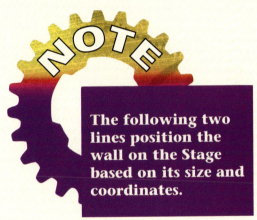

NOTE

The following two lines position the wall on the Stage based on its size and coordinates.

```
my.locH = 20 + 100*shrink + offsetX*(1-shrink/3) + my.width/2
my.locV = 239 + offsetY/2 - my.height/2
```

4. Within the Toolbar, click your mouse on the Script Window button. Director will close the Script window.

5. Within the Toolbar, click your mouse on the Play button. Director will preview your game within the Stage window. Both vertical and horizontal walls should be positioned correctly on the Stage.

6. Within the Toolbar, click your mouse on the Rewind button. Director will return your game to its original state within the Stage window.

So far, your *Covert Mayhem* game should consist of a fully constructed, three-dimensional map. Everything should appear normal except for the character. If you attempt to control the character, you will only succeed in changing the direction he is facing.

TRANSLATING AN ENTITY'S PROPERTIES INTO MOVEMENT

The Entity behavior's *x*, *y*, and *z* properties keep track of the character's position in a three-dimensional field, but do not directly affect the character's position on the Stage. You must write a special function to translate these three properties into values that are suitable for the *width*, *height*, *locH*, *locV*, and *locZ* properties of the character's sprite. To add the code to the Entity behavior that translates the *x*, *y*, and *z* properties into Stage movement, perform the following steps:

1. Within the Cast window, click your mouse on the Entity member. Director will update the Cast window.

2. Within the Cast window, click your mouse on the Cast Member Script. Director will display the Script window, as shown in Figure 13.7.

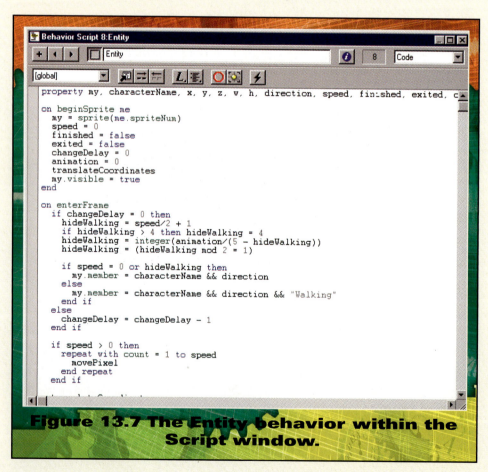

```
property my, characterName, x, y, z, w, h, direction, speed, finished, exited, c

on beginSprite me
  my = sprite(me.spriteNum)
  speed = 0
  finished = false
  exited = false
  changeDelay = 0
  animation = 0
  translateCoordinates
  my.visible = true
end

on enterFrame
  if changeDelay = 0 then
    hideWalking = speed/2 + 1
    if hideWalking > 4 then hideWalking = 4
    hideWalking = integer(animation/(5 - hideWalking))
    hideWalking = (hideWalking mod 2 = 1)

    if speed = 0 or hideWalking then
      my.member = characterName && direction
    else
      my.member = characterName && direction && "Walking"
    end if
  else
    changeDelay = changeDelay - 1
  end if

  if speed > 0 then
    repeat with count = 1 to speed
      movePixel
    end repeat
  end if
```

Figure 13.7 The Entity behavior within the Script window.

3. Within the Script window, replace —*COORDINATE TRANSLATION CODE*— with the following code:

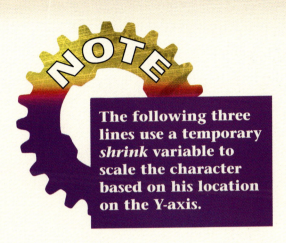

NOTE

The following three lines use a temporary *shrink* variable to scale the character based on his location on the Y-axis.

```
shrink = 1 - float(y)/400
my.width = (w*3 - w*shrink)/3
my.height = (h*3 - h*shrink)/3
```

NOTE

The following three lines position and layer the character on the Stage based on his size and coordinates.

```
my.locH = 20 + 100*shrink + x*(1-shrink/3)
my.locV = 240 + y/2 - z
my.locZ = 100 + y
```

4. Within the Toolbar, click your mouse on the Script Window button. Director will close the Script window.

5. Within the Toolbar, click your mouse on the Play button. Director will preview your game within the Stage window. You should be able to control the character's movement.

6. Within the Toolbar, click your mouse on the Rewind button. Director will return your game to its original state within the Stage window.

By now, you should be able to move the character around the screen normally. If you position the character at the far end of the map's plane, it will be two-thirds its original size. It is very important that all objects within your three-dimensional environment have the same scaling factor. This includes the map's walls and even the map itself. The width of the map's plane at the far end is two-thirds its width in the front.

CHECKING THE MAP FOR OBSTACLE COLLISIONS

The only part of your *Covert Mayhem* game left to add is the Bomb behavior's *movePixel* function. This function serves much the same purpose as the Entity behavior's *movePixel* function, but is a bit less complicated. The Bomb behavior's *movePixel* function moves the Bomb bitmap one pixel in the appropriate direction and then checks the map for obstacle collisions. If the function finds any obstacles in the map image, it quickly returns the Bomb bitmap to its original position. To add the code to the Bomb behavior that handles the Bomb bitmap's movement, perform the following steps:

1. Within the Cast window, click your mouse on the Bomb member. Director will update the Cast window.

2. Within the Cast window, click your mouse on the Cast Member Script button. Director will display the Script window, as shown in Figure 13.8.

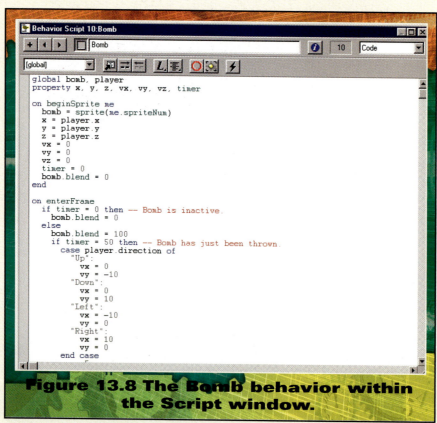

Figure 13.8 The Bomb behavior within the Script window.

3. Within the Script window, replace —*BOMB MOVEMENT CODE*— with the following code:

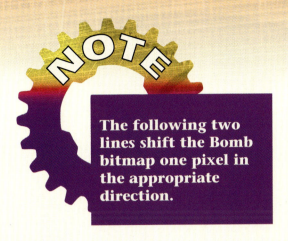

The following two lines shift the Bomb bitmap one pixel in the appropriate direction.

```
if vx <> 0 then x = x + vx/abs(vx)
if vy <> 0 then y = y + vy/abs(vy)
```

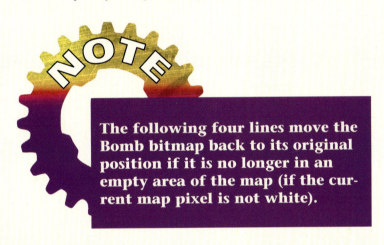

The following four lines move the Bomb bitmap back to its original position if it is no longer in an empty area of the map (if the current map pixel is not white).

```
if sprite(3).member.image.getPixel(x, y) <> rgb(255, 255, 255) then
   if vx <> 0 then x = x - vx/abs(vx)
   if vy <> 0 then y = y - vy/abs(vy)
end if
```

4. Within the Toolbar, click your mouse on the Script Window button. Director will close the Script window.

5. Within the Toolbar, click your mouse on the Play button. Director will preview your game within the Stage window. The Bomb bitmap should move normally when you throw or drop a bomb.

6. Within the Toolbar, click your mouse on the Rewind button. Director will return your game to its original state within the Stage window.

Your *Covert Mayhem* game should now be fully functional. Of course, even the finished game leaves much room for improvement. You can spend as long as you want improving a game and never be finished. You must decide when you are satisfied with your games and abandon them shortly thereafter.

ALLOWING MOVEMENT CONTROL ON THE Z-AXIS

If you really want to explore the use of three-dimensional movement, you should allow the user to control more of the character's movement. One way to fully illustrate three-dimensional motion is to allow control of movement on the Z-axis. To add the code to the Player Control behavior that allows the player to control movement on the Z-axis, perform the following steps:

1. Within the Cast window, click your mouse on the Player Control member. Director will update the Cast window.

2. Within the Cast window, click your mouse on the Cast Member Script button. Director will display the Script window, as shown in Figure 13.9.

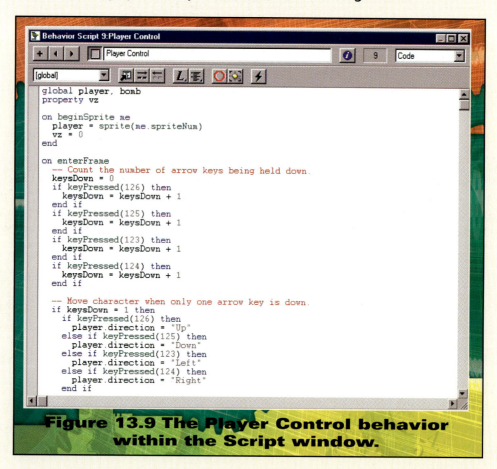

```
Behavior Script 9:Player Control

[global]

global player, bomb
property vz

on beginSprite me
  player = sprite(me.spriteNum)
  vz = 0
end

on enterFrame
  -- Count the number of arrow keys being held down.
  keysDown = 0
  if keyPressed(126) then
    keysDown = keysDown + 1
  end if
  if keyPressed(125) then
    keysDown = keysDown + 1
  end if
  if keyPressed(123) then
    keysDown = keysDown + 1
  end if
  if keyPressed(124) then
    keysDown = keysDown + 1
  end if

  -- Move character when only one arrow key is down.
  if keysDown = 1 then
    if keyPressed(126) then
      player.direction = "Up"
    else if keyPressed(125) then
      player.direction = "Down"
    else if keyPressed(123) then
      player.direction = "Left"
    else if keyPressed(124) then
      player.direction = "Right"
    end if
```

Figure 13.9 The Player Control behavior within the Script window.

3. Within the Script window, replace —*GRAVITY RESISTANCE CODE*— with the following code:

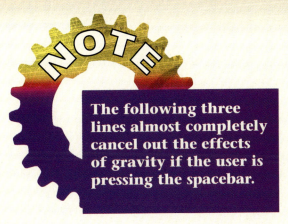

The following three lines almost completely cancel out the effects of gravity if the user is pressing the spacebar.

```
if keyPressed(" ") then
   vz = vz + 0.95
end if
```

4. Within the Toolbar, click your mouse on the Script Window button. Director will close the Script window.

5. Within the Toolbar, click your mouse on the Play button. Director will preview your game within the Stage window. The character should float through the air almost weightlessly as long as you hold down the spacebar. Notice that obstacles still restrict the character's movement no matter how high he goes, as shown in Figure 13.10.

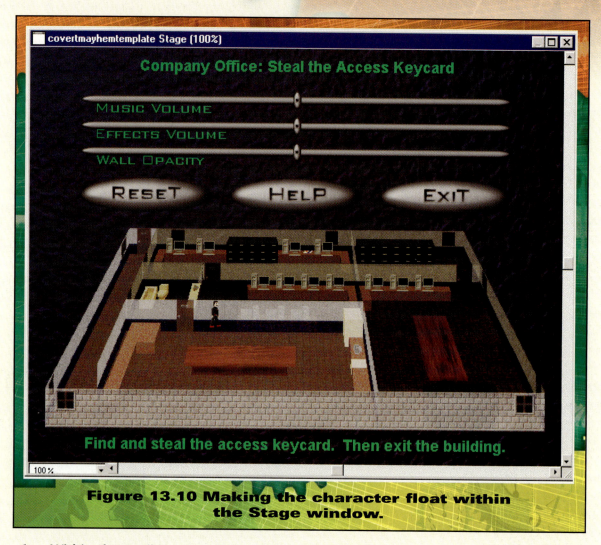

Figure 13.10 Making the character float within the Stage window.

6. Within the Toolbar, click your mouse on the Rewind button. Director will return your game to its original state within the Stage window.

Try experimenting with more changes in the character's movement. For example, you can make the character slide around the map by never setting his velocity in any direction to zero. Instead, gradually decrease velocity when the user is not holding down an arrow key. Experimentation is the best way to familiarize yourself with new programming techniques.

APPLYING YOUR SKILLS

Now that you have the skills required to animate a pseudo-3D environment, your games can offer more control to the user. With a few modifications to the map system, you can set different colors to indicate different obstacle heights so that the player can jump over certain obstacles or even climb stairs and move up ramps. Director does not limit your options. You can create an environment with as realistic three-dimensionality as you wish if you are willing to put forth the effort and your computer can handle the heavy animation.

Chapter 14
Martian Dogfight: Producing Complex Vector Graphics

"People don't start wars; governments do." —Ronald Reagan

Chapter

14

- Approaching the *Martian Dogfight* Game

- Opening the *Martian Dogfight* Game's Template

- Understanding the *Martian Dogfight* Game

- Creating a New Ship Component

- Implementing the New Ship Component

- Fine-Tuning the New Ship Component

- Editing Shape Vertices through Lingo

- Applying Your Skills

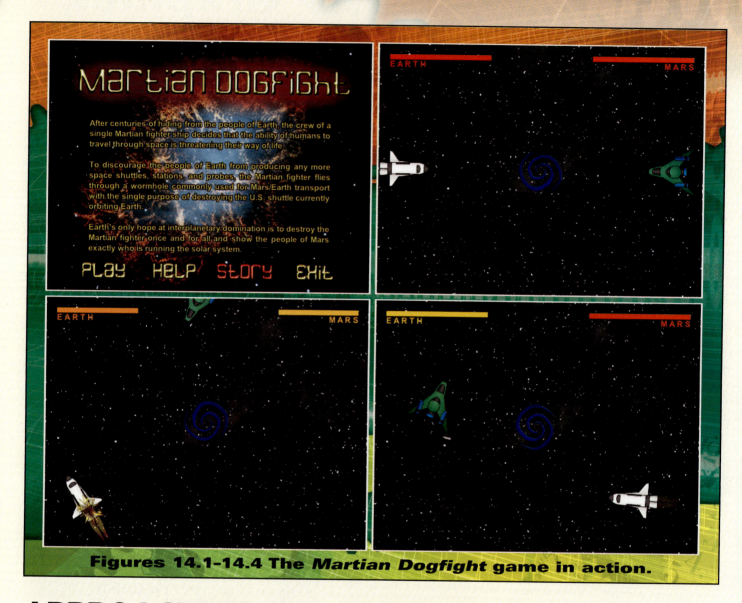

Figures 14.1–14.4 The *Martian Dogfight* game in action.

APPROACHING THE *MARTIAN DOGFIGHT* GAME

Although Director was designed with bitmap graphics in mind, it has evolved to include a variety of features to make its vector graphics extremely powerful. However, drawing complex vector graphics in Director can be quite difficult unless you know a few shortcuts to make the process easier. Many programmers believe that Director just can't produce some types of vector graphics. The truth is that you can create vector graphics as complicated and as detailed as you want if you are willing to put forth the effort. The *Martian Dogfight* game will teach you how to create a vector shape and implement it as a part of a multi-layered vector graphic.

OPENING THE *MARTIAN DOGFIGHT* GAME'S TEMPLATE

On the companion CD-ROM is a partially completed version of the *Martian Dogfight* game that you will use to learn about drawing complex vector graphics. This template will allow you to use Director as a learning tool. To open the *Martian Dogfight* game's template in Director and save a copy to your hard drive, perform the following steps:

1. If the companion CD-ROM is not currently in your CD drive, then insert it in your CD-ROM drive now.

2. Within Director, in the Toolbar, click your mouse on the Open button. Director will display the Open dialog box.

3. Within the Open dialog box, click your mouse on the Look In drop-down list, and select your CD drive. Director will display the contents of your CD drive.

4. Within the Open dialog box, double-click your mouse on the **Martian Dogfight** folder. Director will display the contents of the **Martian Dogfight** folder.

5. Within the Open dialog box, click your mouse on the **martiandogfighttemplate.dir** file. Director will update the Open dialog box.

6. Within the Open dialog box, click your mouse on the OK button. Director will open the martiandogfighttemplate.dir file.

7. Click your mouse on the File menu, and select the Save As option. Director will display the Save Movie dialog box.

8. Within the Save Movie dialog box, click your mouse on the Save In drop-down list, and select your primary hard drive. Director will display the contents of your primary hard drive.

9. Within the Save Movie dialog box, double-click your mouse on the Director Games folder you created in Chapter 2, "Using Director." Director will display the contents of the Director Games folder.

10. Within the Save Movie dialog box, in the File Name text field, type **mymartiandogfight.dir**, and press the Enter key. Director will save the **Martian Dogfight** game's template as a file named "mymartiandogfight.dir."

As you create more and more games in Director, you will develop your own system of organization. For the purpose of clarity, however, you will keep all your edited template files in a single folder.

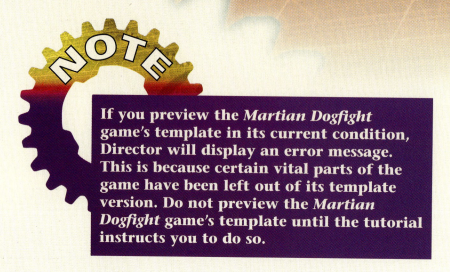

NOTE

If you preview the *Martian Dogfight* game's template in its current condition, Director will display an error message. This is because certain vital parts of the game have been left out of its template version. Do not preview the *Martian Dogfight* game's template until the tutorial instructs you to do so.

UNDERSTANDING THE *MARTIAN DOGFIGHT* GAME

Because Director allows only one fill style per vector shape cast member, you must use several sprite channels to draw a multi-layered vector graphic onto the Stage. If you want your vector graphic to move, rotate, resize, or change in any other way, you should use Lingo behaviors to group the sprite channels together as a single object rather than applying the changes to each of the sprites individually. The Ship Component behavior of the *Martian Dogfight* game keeps both sets of spaceship graphics working the way they should. To view the various Lingo scripts in the Code cast, perform the following steps:

1. Within the Cast window, click your mouse on the Choose Cast button, and select the Code option. Director will display the Code cast within the Cast window. The Code cast contains 28 Lingo scripts, as shown in Table 14.1.

Table 14.1 The 28 Lingo scripts of the Code cast and their descriptions.

Script Name	Description
Global	Stores all the global variables, such as *shuttle*, *sHealth*, and *sDelay*, and global functions, such as *resetGame*, *updateShipShrink*, and *checkCollisions*.
Generic Button	Makes its associated sprite behave as a button complete with specified image, cursor, and sound options.
Wait	Keeps the *Martian Dogfight* game looping on one frame until otherwise specified.
Reset Game	Calls the global *resetGame* function when its associated frame prepares itself.
Game	Handles major aspects of the *Martian Dogfight* game and keeps the game looping on one frame until otherwise specified.
Play Main	Plays the game's Main frame when its associated frame exits itself.

Table 14.1 The 28 Lingo scripts of the Code cast and their descriptions. (cont.)

Script Name	Description
Default Invisible	Sets its associated sprite's *visible* property to false when the sprite begins.
Ship	Moves its associated sprite in the direction of its rotation based on its *speed*, *vx*, and *vy* properties.
Ship Component	Makes its associated sprite keep its location and rotation equal to that of a specified ship.
Ship Projectile	Follows its associated ship until the user fires a projectile, then travels in the direction of the ship's rotation.
Ship Trail	Varies the visibility of its associated sprite based on the acceleration of a specified ship.
Player 1 Control	Allows the user to control its associated sprite with the arrow keys and the Enter key.
Player 2 Control	Allows the user to control its associated sprite with the S, X, Z, and C keys and the spacebar.
Gravitate to Center	Gradually moves its associated sprite toward the center of the screen.
Move to Front	Sets its associated sprite's *locZ* property to 1000 when the sprite begins.
Rotate Left	Rotates its associated sprite 15 degrees to the left upon entering each frame.
Shuttle Health Bar	Displays the health of the space shuttle by changing the width and color of its associated sprite.
Fighter Health Bar	Displays the health of the Martian fighter by changing the width and color of its associated sprite.
Explosion Animation	Randomly animates its associated sprite to make it appear as an explosion.
Explosion 1	Stores a reference to its associated sprite in the global *e1* variable.
Explosion 2	Stores a reference to its associated sprite in the global *e2* variable.
Overlay	Stores a reference to its associated sprite in the global *overlay* variable.
Title Fade	Modifies the visibility of its associated sprite to create a looping fade effect.
Introduction Text	Changes its associated sprite's cast member and position based on the mode and winner of the game.
Play Button	Plays the game's Fade In frame when the user clicks on its associated sprite.
Help Button	Sets the global *mode* variable to Help when the user clicks on its associated sprite.
Story Button	Sets the global *mode* variable to Story when the user clicks on its associated sprite.
Exit Button	Plays the game's Exit frame when the user clicks on its associated sprite.

2. Within the Cast window, click your mouse on the Global member. Director will update the Cast window as shown in Figure 14.5.

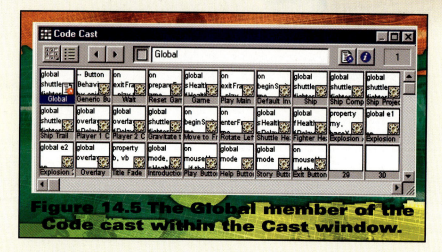

Figure 14.5 The Global member of the Code cast within the Cast window.

3. Within the Cast window, click your mouse on the Cast Member Script button. Director will display the Script window.

4. Within the Script window, use the Previous Cast Member and Next Cast Member buttons to view each of the Lingo scripts in the Code cast.

By now, you should have a good understanding of the logic behind the *Martian Dogfight* game. You will find that using Director to edit an existing game is nearly impossible unless you first understand how the game works.

CREATING A NEW SHIP COMPONENT

If you click your mouse on frame 29 of the *Martian Dogfight* game's template, you will find that the Martian fighter ship is missing its afterburner. To help you get a feel for working with vector graphics in Director, you will recreate the Fighter Trail shape and, in doing so, complete the *Martian Dogfight* game. To create a new Fighter Trail cast member in place of the old one, perform the following steps:

1. Within the Cast window, click your mouse on the Choose Cast button, and select the Graphics option. Director will display the Graphics cast within the Cast window, as shown in Figure 14.6.

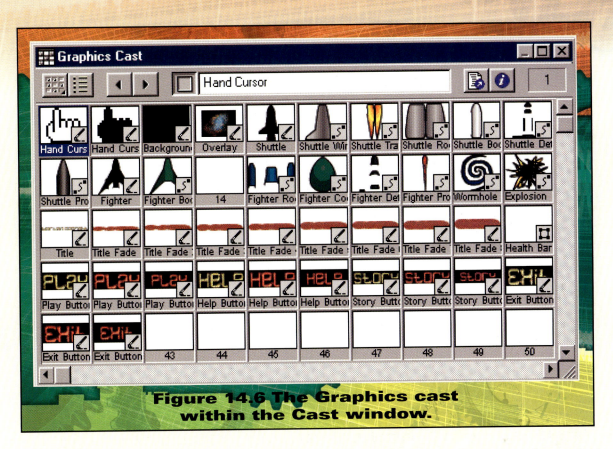

**Figure 14.6 The Graphics cast
within the Cast window.**

2. Within the Toolbar, click your mouse on the Vector Shape Window button. Director will display the Vector Shape window and add a new vector member to the Graphics cast.

3. Within the Vector Shape window, in the Cast Member Name field, type **Fighter Trail**, and press the Enter key. Director will name the bitmap you created "Fighter Trail."

4. Within the Vector Shape window, click your mouse on the Filled Round Rectangle button (see Figure 14.7). Director will select the Filled Round Rectangle tool.

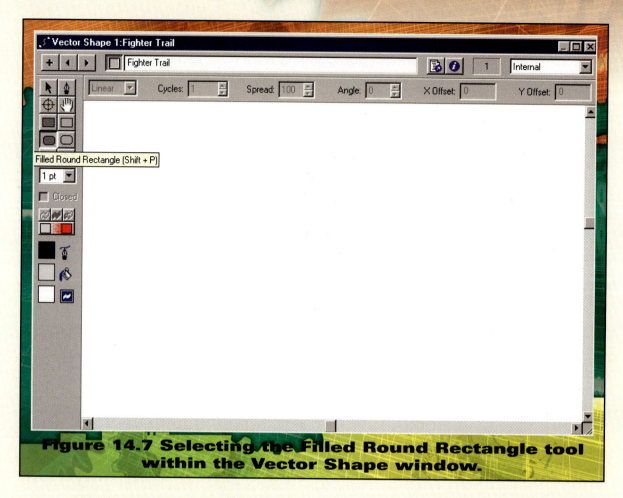

Figure 14.7 Selecting the Filled Round Rectangle tool within the Vector Shape window.

5. Within the Vector Shape window, drag your mouse around on the canvas. Director will draw a filled round rectangle based on the starting and ending points of your mouse movement.

6. Within the Vector Shape window, click your mouse on the Gradient button. Director will update the Vector Shape window.

7. Within the Vector Shape window, click your mouse on the first Gradient Color button, and select a color swatch. Director will change the first gradient fill color to whatever color you select.

8. Within the Vector Shape window, click your mouse on the second Gradient Color button, and select a color swatch. Director will change the second gradient fill color to whatever color you select, as shown in Figure 14.8.

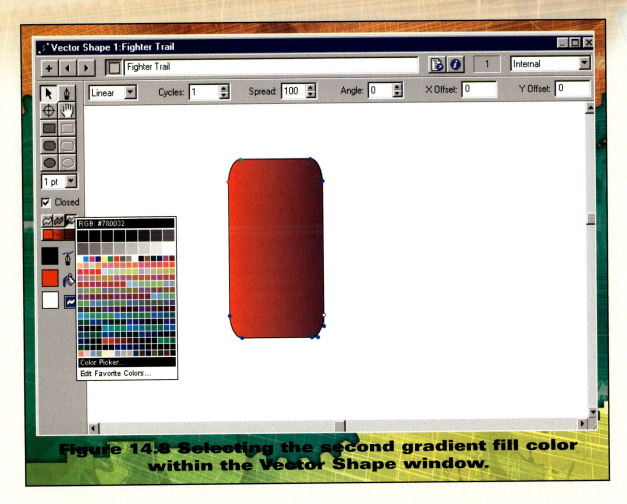

Figure 14.8 Selecting the second gradient fill color within the Vector Shape window.

9. Within the Vector Shape window, click your mouse on the Gradient Type drop-down list, and select the Radial option. Director will change the gradient fill to start in the center of your vector shape.

10. Within the Vector Shape window, in the Gradient Cycles field, type a number from one to seven and press the Enter key. Director will change the gradient fill to cycle the specified number of times within your vector shape, as shown in Figure 14.9.

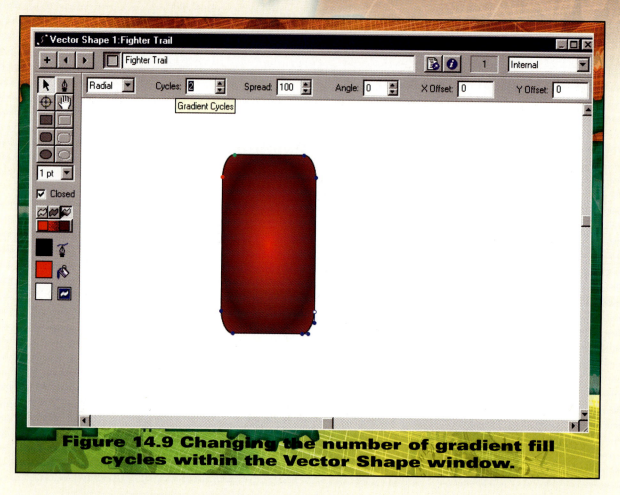

Figure 14.9 Changing the number of gradient fill cycles within the Vector Shape window.

11. Within the Toolbar, click your mouse on the Vector Shape Window button. Director will close the Vector Shape window.

Your new ship component is by no means a finished product. To get an idea of what the ship's afterburner should look like and how big it should be, you must first position it correctly within the Stage.

IMPLEMENTING THE NEW SHIP COMPONENT

To get an idea of how you should finish the new ship component, you must position it within the Stage lined up exactly with the rest of its ship. Remember that each component of a ship will have exactly the same coordinates as the rest of the ship when the game is running. To position the Fighter Trail shape within the Stage and apply its appropriate behaviors, perform the following steps:

1. Drag the Fighter Trail member from the Cast window into cell 15 of channel 12 of the Score window. Director will display the Fighter Trail shape within the Stage.

2. Within the Score window, drag cell 29 of channel 12 to frame 44. Director will extend the Fighter Trail shape to frame 44, as shown in Figure 14.10.

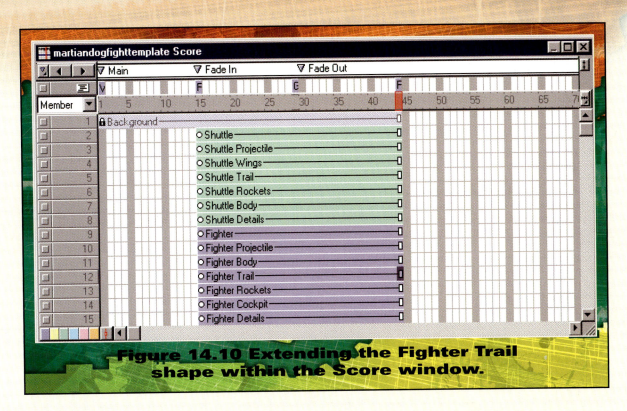

Figure 14.10 Extending the Fighter Trail shape within the Score window.

3. Within the Score window, click your mouse on cell 29 of channel 12 of the Score window. Director will update the Property Inspector window.

4. Within the Property Inspector window, click your mouse on the Ink drop-down list and select the Background Transparent option. Director will remove the white background from the Fighter Trail shape.

5. Within the Property Inspector window, in the X field, type **490**, and press the Enter key. Director will set the horizontal location of the Fighter Trail shape to 490, the same as the rest of the Martian fighter components.

6. Within the Property Inspector window, in the Y field, type **200**, and press the Enter key. Director will set the vertical location of the Fighter Trail shape to 200, the same as the rest of the Martian fighter components.

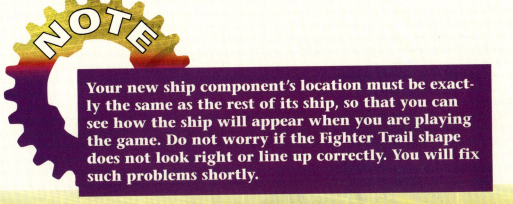

Your new ship component's location must be exactly the same as the rest of its ship, so that you can see how the ship will appear when you are playing the game. Do not worry if the Fighter Trail shape does not look right or line up correctly. You will fix such problems shortly.

7. Within the Property Inspector window, click your mouse on the Behavior tab. Director will display the Behavior sheet.

8. Within the Property Inspector window, click your mouse on the Behavior pop-up button, and select the Ship Component option. Director will display the Parameters dialog box.

9. Within the Parameters dialog box, in the Ship Number field, type **2**, and press the Enter key. Director will apply the Ship Component behavior to the Fighter Trail shape.

10. Within the Property Inspector window, click your mouse on the Behavior pop-up button, and select the Ship Trail option. Director will display the Parameters dialog box.

11. Within the Parameters dialog box, in the Ship Number field, type **2**, and press the Enter key. Director will apply the Ship Trail behavior to the Fighter Trail shape.

So far, your new ship component should be in place and fully functional within the *Martian Dogfight* game. Of course, it probably does not line up very well with the rest of the ship, and you might want to change the ship component's vector shape now that you see it set up on the Stage. You will find that editing an existing vector shape is even easier than creating one from scratch.

FINE-TUNING THE NEW SHIP COMPONENT

The reason that all the ship's components can line up so perfectly, with each having the same coordinates, is that you can specify the registration point for any new vector shape you create. A *registration point* is the point on a sprite's image that will always be at the sprite's specified coordinates within the Stage. Unless otherwise specified, the registration point will occur at the exact center of an image. To position an afterburner below the rest of its ship, for example, you would move its registration point up above its vector shape. To finish the Fighter Trail shape and line it up with the rest of its ship by specifying a registration point, perform the following steps:

1. Within the Cast window, click your mouse on the Fighter Trail member. Director will update the Cast window.

2. Click your mouse on the Edit menu, and select the Edit Cast Member option. Director will display the Vector Shape window.

3. Within the Vector Shape window, click your mouse on the Registration Point button. Director will select the Registration Point tool, as shown in Figure 14.11.

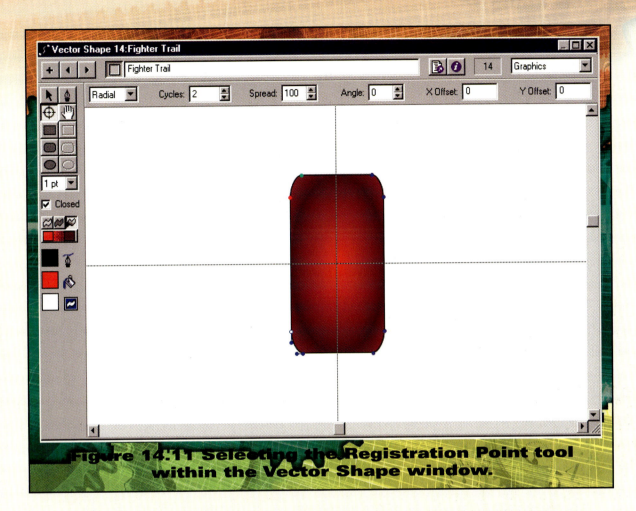

Figure 14.11 Selecting the Registration Point tool within the Vector Shape window.

4. Within the Vector Shape window, click your mouse on the vertical line of the current registration point, but somewhere above the round rectangle you drew earlier. If the Fighter Trail shape does not line up with the rest of its ship within the Stage window, change its registration point until it does.

5. Within the Vector Shape window, click your mouse on the Arrow Tool button. Director will select the Arrow tool.

6. Within the Vector Shape window, drag any of the round rectangle's eight handles around on the canvas. Director will distort the round rectangle based on the position of its handles as shown in Figure 14.12.

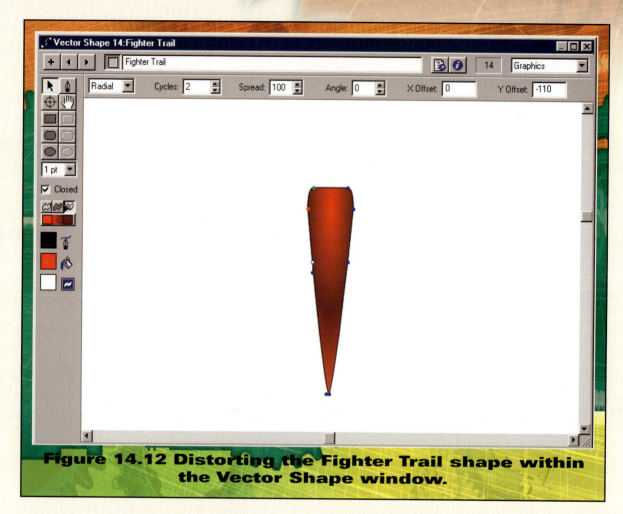

Figure 14.12 Distorting the Fighter Trail shape within the Vector Shape window.

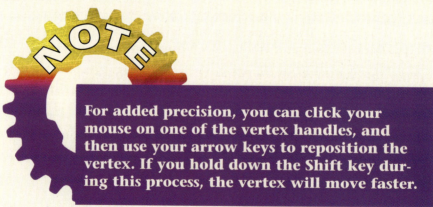

For added precision, you can click your mouse on one of the vertex handles, and then use your arrow keys to reposition the vertex. If you hold down the Shift key during this process, the vertex will move faster.

7. To add more afterburner flames, simply repeat the process of creating and distorting round rectangles until you are satisfied with your vector shape.

8. Within the Vector Shape window, in the Gradient Y Offset field, type a number somewhere around -100, and press the Enter key. Director will shift the gradient fill up around 100 pixels.

9. Within the Toolbar, click your mouse on the Vector Shape Window button. Director will close the Vector Shape window.

By now, you have completely finished your new ship component. The *Martian Dogfight* game should be fully functional. You should now have a basic feel for vector-graphics creation and manipulation. However, Director offers a completely different, and often more convenient, method of editing vector shapes.

EDITING SHAPE VERTICES THROUGH LINGO

Director does not limit vector-shape creation to the Vector Shape window. In fact, you could build a vector graphic entirely with Lingo code if you wanted to, although doing so wouldn't be very practical. Director provides you with the ability to edit vector shapes through Lingo mainly so that you can make minor edits to your vector shapes based on some occurrence in your game. To add the code to the Game behavior that gradually distorts the Wormhole cast member, perform the following steps:

1. Within the Cast window, click your mouse on the Game member. Director will update the Cast window.

2. Within the Cast window, click your mouse on the Cast Member Script button. Director will display the Script window, as shown in Figure 14.13.

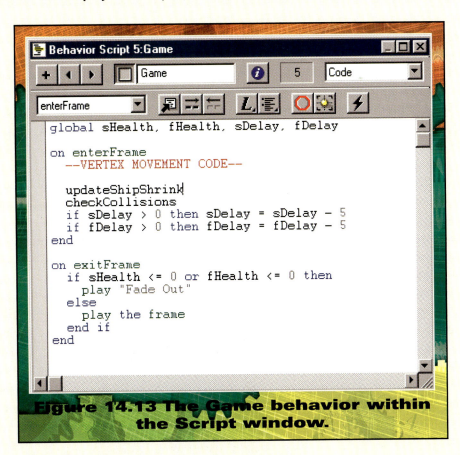

```
Behavior Script 5:Game

Game          5    Code

enterFrame

global sHealth, fHealth, sDelay, fDelay

on enterFrame
    --VERTEX MOVEMENT CODE--

    updateShipShrink
    checkCollisions
    if sDelay > 0 then sDelay = sDelay - 5
    if fDelay > 0 then fDelay = fDelay - 5
end

on exitFrame
    if sHealth <= 0 or fHealth <= 0 then
        play "Fade Out"
    else
        play the frame
    end if
end
```

Figure 14.13 The Game behavior within the Script window.

3. Within the Script window, replace —*VERTEX MOVEMENT CODE*— with the following code:

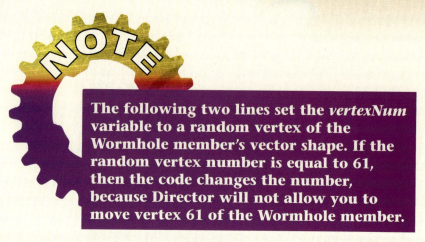

NOTE

The following two lines set the *vertexNum* variable to a random vertex of the Wormhole member's vector shape. If the random vertex number is equal to 61, then the code changes the number, because Director will not allow you to move vertex 61 of the Wormhole member.

```
vertexNum = random(member("Wormhole").vertexList.count)
if vertexNum = 61 then vertexNum = 1
```

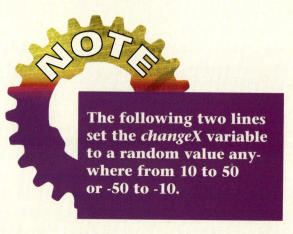

NOTE

The following two lines set the *changeX* variable to a random value anywhere from 10 to 50 or -50 to -10.

```
changeX = random(40) + 10
if random(2) = 1 then changeX = -changeX
```

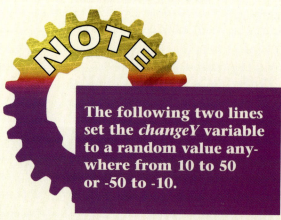

NOTE

The following two lines set the *changeY* variable to a random value anywhere from 10 to 50 or -50 to -10.

```
changeY = random(40) + 10
if random(2) = 1 then changeY = -changeY
```

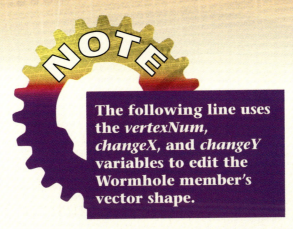

NOTE

The following line uses the *vertexNum*, *changeX*, and *changeY* variables to edit the Wormhole member's vector shape.

```
member("Wormhole").moveVertex(vertexNum, changeX, changeY)
```

4. Within the Toolbar, click your mouse on the Script Window button. Director will close the Script window.

5. Within the Toolbar, click your mouse on the Play button. Director will preview your game within the Stage window. The rotating wormhole in the center of the screen should gradually distort as the game progresses.

6. Within the Toolbar, click your mouse on the Rewind button. Director will return your game to its original state within the Stage window.

Although editing vertices of vector graphics through Lingo may seem a bit ridiculous at first, you would be surprised at how useful it can be. And Director doesn't limit you to just changing the positions of vertices. Through Lingo, you can also change a shape's registration point or even add and remove vertices and curves.

APPLYING YOUR SKILLS

Now that you have the skills required to build and manipulate complex vector graphics, you can create games with a much smaller file size than those made up of entirely bitmap, or raster, graphics. Although vector graphics are, in general, slightly slower than bitmaps, they will stay smooth no matter how you stretch, scale, or distort them. Vector graphics may not be able to replace bitmaps in every situation, but in some situations, they simply work better.

Chapter 15
Froggy:
Publishing Internet Content

"I like nonsense, it wakes up the brain cells." —Dr. Seuss

Chapter

15

- Approaching the *Froggy* Game

- Opening the *Froggy* Game

- Understanding the *Froggy* Game

- Previewing in a Web Browser

- Publishing with Custom Compression Settings

- Publishing with Custom Dimension Settings

- Publishing with a Preset Loader Game

- Applying Your Skills

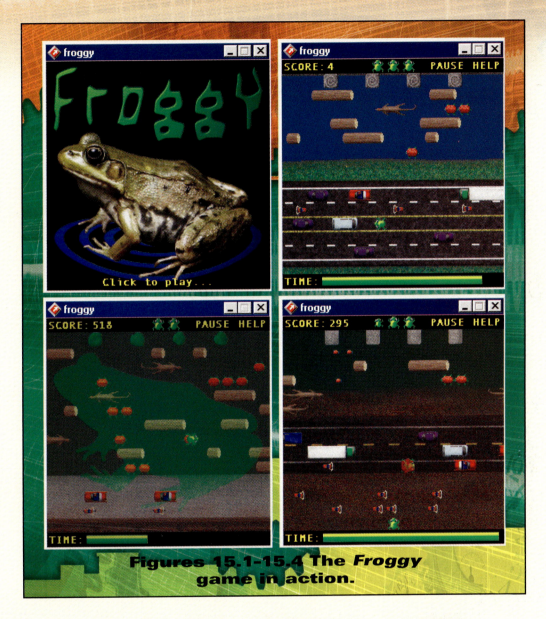

Figures 15.1–15.4 The *Froggy* game in action.

APPROACHING THE *FROGGY* GAME

When designing a game for the Internet, you must keep several things in mind. One major concern of virtually all Internet content creation is screen size. You must remember that the resolution of people's screens is often as low as 640 pixels wide and 480 pixels tall. Therefore, you must create games that fit comfortably inside an Internet browser on a computer at such a low resolution. You must also avoid including long video or audio sequences in your game as they will increase your game's file size and therefore increase the time it takes for your game to load online. The *Froggy* game will teach you how to publish your Director games as Shockwave Internet content.

OPENING THE *FROGGY* GAME

On the companion CD-ROM is a partially completed version of the *Froggy* game that you will use to learn about publishing Internet content. This template will allow you to use Director as a learning tool. To open the *Froggy* game in Director and save a copy to your hard drive, perform the following steps:

1. If the companion CD-ROM is not currently in your CD drive, then insert it in your CD-ROM drive now.

2. Within Director, in the Toolbar, click your mouse on the Open button. Director will display the Open dialog box.

3. Within the Open dialog box, click your mouse on the Look In drop-down list, and select your CD drive. Director will display the contents of your CD drive.

4. Within the Open dialog box, double-click your mouse on the *Froggy* folder. Director will display the contents of the *Froggy* folder.

5. Within the Open dialog box, click your mouse on the *froggy.dir* file. Director will update the Open dialog box.

6. Within the Open dialog box, click your mouse on the OK button. Director will open the *froggy.dir* file.

7. Click your mouse on the File menu, and select the Save As option. Director will display the Save Movie dialog box.

8. Within the Save Movie dialog box, click your mouse on the Save In drop-down list, and select your primary hard drive. Director will display the contents of your primary hard drive.

9. Within the Save Movie dialog box, double-click your mouse on the *Director Games* folder you created in Chapter 2, "Using Director." Director will display the contents of the *Director Games* folder.

10. Within the Save Movie dialog box, in the File Name text field, type **myfroggy.dir**, and press the Enter key. Director will save the *Froggy* game as a file named "myfroggy.dir."

As you create more and more games in Director, you will develop your own system of organization. For the purpose of clarity, however, you will keep all your edited files in a single folder.

UNDERSTANDING THE *FROGGY* GAME

The various obstacles in the *Froggy* game, such as cars, logs, and crocodiles, are specified by a series of text cast members. The text cast members make it easy for the programmer to edit the arrangement of obstacles on a map. Each text cast member holds all the information needed to animate one of the *Froggy* game's levels. The first character in each line of the text cast members indicates the direction in which obstacles of its corresponding row move, and whether or not that row is made up of water. The second character of each line indicates the speed at which the obstacles will move. All other characters in each line specify the type and starting position of each of the corresponding rows' obstacles. Basically, the frog must be touching an obstacle to survive in a water row, and must avoid all obstacles in land rows. To view the various Lingo scripts in the Code cast, perform the following steps:

1. Within the Cast window, click your mouse on the Choose Cast button, and select the Code option. Director will display the Code cast within the Cast window. The Code cast contains 16 Lingo scripts, as Table 15.1 briefly describes.

Table 15.1 The 16 Lingo scripts of the Code cast and their descriptions.

Script Name	Description
Global	Stores all the global variables, such as *mapNum*, *playerScore*, and *playerLives*, and global functions, such as *resetFrog* and *resetMap*.
Wait for Click	Keeps the *Froggy* game looping on one frame until the user clicks his or her mouse and then resets the game and plays the Game frame.
Game	Handles most major aspects of the *Froggy* game such as winning, losing, and restarting.
Frog	Allows the user to control the frog's movement and handles all frog animation.
Frog Dead	Replaces the Frog bitmap when the frog gets run over by a car and eventually fades away.
Frog Icon	Displays the value of the *playerLives* variable based on a specified *number* property.
Spiral	Marks one of the four targets on which the user tries to land the frog. Rotates, resizes, and fades until its cast member is replaced by the Frog bitmap to indicate that the spot is taken.
Obstacle	Animates its associated sprite based on its cast member and checks for collisions with the frog.
Click to Play	Makes its associated sprite move upwards until it is completely on the screen, then makes it blink.
Time Bar	Changes the width of its associated sprite based on its *total* and *remaining* properties.
Score Text	Displays the value of the *playerScore* variable in text form.
Fade	Creates the global *fade* variable to reference the Fade bitmap.
Text	Creates the global *text* variable to reference the text that usually appears in front of the Fade bitmap, and vertically centers that text.
Fade In	Increases its associated sprite's visibility by a specified increment if the sprite's visibility is between 1 and *maximum* percent.
Pause Button	Displays the Fade bitmap when the user releases a click on its associated sprite.
Help Button	Displays the Help text and the Fade bitmap when the user releases a click on its associated sprite.

2. Within the Cast window, click your mouse on the Global member. Director will update the Cast window, as shown in Figure 15.5.

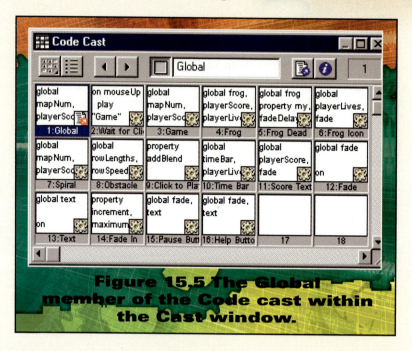

Figure 15.5 The Global member of the Code cast within the Cast window.

3. Within the Cast window, click your mouse on the Cast Member Script button. Director will display the Script window.

4. Within the Script window, use the Previous Cast Member and Next Cast Member buttons to view each of the Lingo scripts in the Code cast.

By now, you should have a good understanding of the logic behind the *Froggy* game. If you find yourself having trouble building new games, you can use pieces of the *Froggy* game to cut down on logic errors.

PREVIEWING IN A WEB BROWSER

As you build games for the Internet, you might often want to test your game in a Web browser to make sure it will work properly on the Internet. Some features of Director, such as animated mouse cursors, do not work very well in Shockwave games. Also, the time your game takes to load and the speed at which you can play it in a Web browser might be an issue. To preview a copy of the *Froggy* game in your default Web browser, perform the following steps:

1. Click your mouse on the File menu, and select the Preview in Browser option. Director will create a temporary HTML page and display it in your default Web browser.

2. When you have finished viewing the temporary version of the *Froggy* game, close your Web browser, and return to Director.

Previewing in your default Web browser is fine for a quick idea of what your game will look like online, but in order to publish a final version of your game, you should first customize your publishing settings. Most importantly, you must make sure that your game will be compressed enough to have a small file size, but not so much that quality is significantly reduced.

PUBLISHING WITH CUSTOM COMPRESSION SETTINGS

Your main concern in adjusting the compression settings for your _Froggy_ game is the image compression. JPEG compression generally makes images appear grainy and blurry and sometimes interferes with transparency. You will usually want to use standard image compression. Because sound is not a major part of the _Froggy_ game, you will want to use the highest sound compression possible. To customize your compression settings and publish a copy of the _Froggy_ game, perform the following steps:

1. Click your mouse on the File menu, and select the Publish Settings option. Director will display the Publish Settings dialog box.

2. Within the Publish Settings dialog box, click your mouse on the Default button. Director will set all publishing settings to their default values, as shown in Figure 15.6.

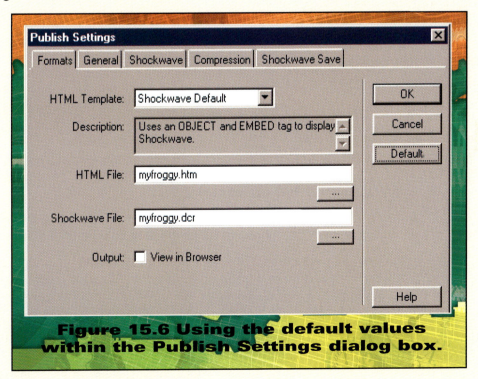

Figure 15.6 Using the default values within the Publish Settings dialog box.

3. Within the Publish Settings dialog box, click your mouse on the View in Browser check box. Director will display your new HTML page in your default browser window each time you publish a Director movie.

4. Within the Publish Settings dialog box, click your mouse on the Compression tab. Director will display the Compression sheet.

5. Within the Publish Settings dialog box, click your mouse on the Standard Image Compression radio button. Director will update the Publish Settings dialog box, as shown in Figure 15.7.

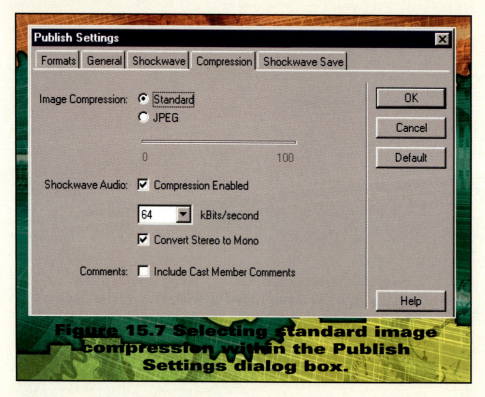

Figure 15.7 Selecting standard image compression within the Publish Settings dialog box.

6. Within the Publish Settings dialog box, click your mouse on the Shockwave Audio drop-down list, and select the 16 option. Director will set your Shockwave file's audio compression to 16 kilobits per second (Kbps).

7. Within the Publish Settings dialog box, click your mouse on the OK button. Director will remember your settings and close the Publish settings dialog box.

8. Within the Toolbar, click your mouse on the Publish button. Director will create a file named *myfroggy.dcr* and a file named *myfroggy.htm*. Because you checked the View in Browser check box earlier, Director will display the *myfroggy.htm* file in your default Web browser.

9. When you have finished viewing your published version of the *Froggy* game, close your Web browser, and return to Director.

The *myfroggy.dcr* file should be around 550KB. You may wish to edit the *myfroggy.htm* file or create your own to have more control over the presentation of your *Froggy* game. If you do not know HTML, however, or simply do not want to be bothered with it, you can use Director to generate a variety of presentation styles for your game.

PUBLISHING WITH CUSTOM DIMENSION SETTINGS

Another important part of the presentation of your *Froggy* game is its size within the Web browser. Conveniently, Director allows you to expand your game to fill the entire Web browser window, whatever size it may be. However, this option may prove most useful for larger, full-screen style games. To customize your dimension settings and publish a copy of the *Froggy* game, perform the following steps:

1. Click your mouse on the File menu, and select the Publish Settings option. Director will display the Publish Settings dialog box.

2. Within the Publish Settings dialog box, in the HTML File field, type **myfroggystretch.htm**, as shown in Figure 15.8.

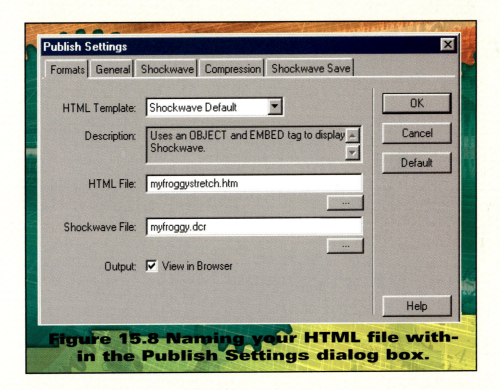

Figure 15.8 Naming your HTML file within the Publish Settings dialog box.

3. Within the Publish Settings dialog box, click your mouse on the General tab. Director will display the General sheet.

4. Within the Publish Settings dialog box, click your mouse on the Dimensions drop-down list, and select the Percentage of Browser Window option. Director will set your Shockwave game's dimensions to fill 100 percent of the browser window.

5. Within the Publish Settings dialog box, click your mouse on the Shockwave tab. Director will display the Shockwave sheet.

6. Within the Publish Settings dialog box, click your mouse on the Stretch Style drop-down list, and select the Preserve Proportions option. Director will set your Shockwave game's stretch style to preserve the *Froggy* game's original proportions.

7. Within the Publish Settings dialog box, click your mouse on the Horizontal Align drop-down list, and select Center option. Director will set your Shockwave game to be horizontally centered within the browser window.

8. Within the Publish Settings dialog box, click your mouse on the Vertical Align drop-down list, and select Center option, as shown in Figure 15.9. Director will set your Shockwave game to be vertically centered within the browser window.

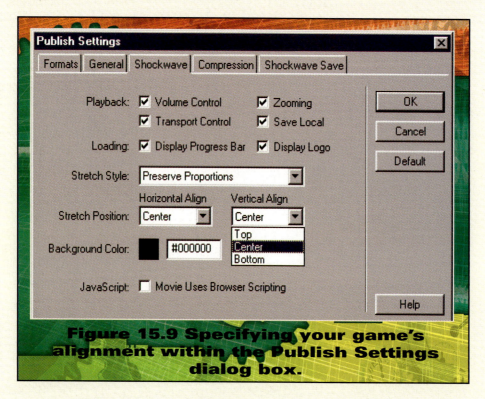

Figure 15.9 Specifying your game's alignment within the Publish Settings dialog box.

9. Within the Publish Settings dialog box, click your mouse on the OK button. Director will remember your settings and close the Publish Settings dialog box.

10. Within the Toolbar, click your mouse on the Publish button. Director will create a file named *myfroggy.dcr* and a file named *myfroggystretch.htm*. Because you checked the View in Browser check box earlier, Director will display the *myfroggystretch.htm* file in your default Web browser.

11. When you have finished viewing your published version of the *Froggy* game, close your Web browser, and return to Director.

When you view your published version of the *Froggy* game within your default Web browser, it should expand to fill up the entire window, but still maintain its original proportions. Such an enlargement would be most useful for people with their screens at an unusually high resolution that could make the *Froggy* game hard to see clearly at its original size of 256 pixels wide and 256 pixels tall.

PUBLISHING WITH A PRESET LOADER GAME

Sometimes, Shockwave games may take a long while to load. Such a delay could give your visitors time to get bored and leave your site. To avoid such a problem, you may want to use Director's preset loader game to entertain visitors as they wait. The loader game somewhat resembles the arcade classics *Pong* and *Breakout*. To publish a copy of the *Froggy* game that includes a simple loader game, perform the following steps:

1. Click your mouse on the File menu, and select the Publish Settings option. Director will display the Publish Settings dialog box.

2. Within the Publish Settings dialog box, in the HTML File field, type **myfroggy-loader.htm**.

3. Within the Publish Settings dialog box, click your mouse on the HTML Template drop-down list, and select the Loader Game option, as shown in Figure 15.10. Director will set your HTML page to include a simple game that will be active while your Shockwave game is loading.

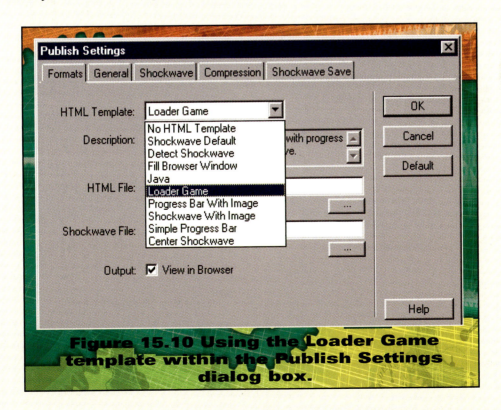

Figure 15.10 Using the Loader Game template within the Publish Settings dialog box.

4. Within the Publish Settings dialog box, click your mouse on the OK button. Director will remember your settings and close the Publish Settings dialog box.

5. Within the Toolbar, click your mouse on the Publish button. Director will create a file named *myfroggy.dcr* and a file named *myfroggyloader.htm*. Because you checked the View in Browser check box earlier, Director will display the *myfroggyloader.htm* file in your default Web browser.

6. When you have finished viewing your published version of the *Froggy* game, close your Web browser, and return to Director.

You will not see the loader game for more than a moment when you view the *myfroggyloader.htm* file in your default Web browser. The *Froggy* game will load almost instantaneously, because it is located on your local hard drive. However, you may view the *loader_game.dcr* file that Director automatically generated in your Web browser to see the simple game that visitors will be able to play as they wait for your *Froggy* game to load.

APPLYING YOUR SKILLS

Now that you have the skills required to publish Director games as Internet content, you can easily and quickly present your Director games to the entire world. There is no better place than the Internet to present your ideas and showcase your talents. If you already own a Web site, your Director games can increase traffic to your site by entertaining your visitors and giving them a reason to come back.

Chapter 16
Robo-Pong:
Exporting Digital Video

"Mechanization best serves mediocrity." —Frank Lloyd Wright

Chapter

16

- Approaching the *Robo-Pong* Game

- Opening the *Robo-Pong* Game

- Understanding the *Robo-Pong* Game

- Exporting MOV-Format Video

- Exporting AVI-Format Video

- Exporting Sequential Bitmaps

- Applying Your Skills

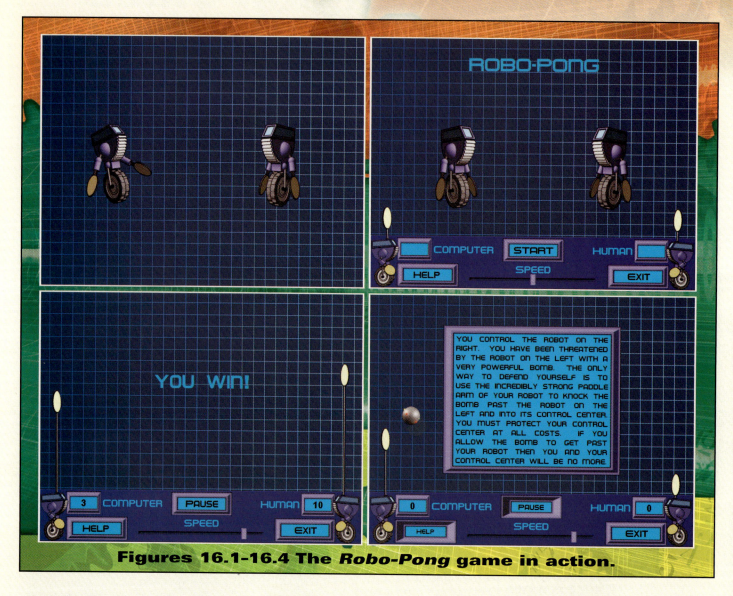

Figures 16.1–16.4 The *Robo-Pong* game in action.

APPROACHING THE *ROBO-PONG* GAME

Since the days of pixelated, two-color arcade games, pong games have remained some of the most addictive games available. Somehow, a simple bouncing ball can entertain us for hours at a time. The *Robo-Pong* game this chapter presents implements a high-tech look for the old-time game. Because of the game's simplicity, this chapter focuses less on the *Robo-Pong* game's logic, and more on its opening animation sequence. The *Robo-Pong* game will teach you how to export digital video and sequential bitmaps in a variety of ways.

OPENING THE *ROBO-PONG* GAME

On the CD-ROM that accompanies this book is the *Robo-Pong* game, which you will use to learn about exporting digital video. Unlike in most of the chapters, you will not modify the game; rather, you will simply use it to create new media files. To open the *Robo-Pong* game in Director and save a copy to your hard drive, perform the following steps:

1. If the companion CD-ROM is not currently in your CD drive, then insert it in your CD-ROM drive now.

2. Within Director, in the Toolbar, click your mouse on the Open button. Director will display the Open dialog box.

3. Within the Open dialog box, click your mouse on the Look In drop-down list, and select your CD drive. Director will display the contents of your CD drive.

4. Within the Open dialog box, double-click your mouse on the *Robo-Pong* folder. Director will display the contents of the *Robo-Pong* folder.

5. Within the Open dialog box, click your mouse on the *robo-pong.dir* file. Director will update the Open dialog box.

6. Within the Open dialog box, click your mouse on the OK button. Director will open the *robo-pong.dir* file.

7. Click your mouse on the File menu, and select the Save As option. Director will display the Save Movie dialog box.

8. Within the Save Movie dialog box, click your mouse on the Save In drop-down list, and select your primary hard drive. Director will display the contents of your primary hard drive.

9. Within the Save Movie dialog box, double-click your mouse on the *Director Games* folder you created in Chapter 2, "Using Director." Director will display the contents of the *Director Games* folder.

10. Within the Save Movie dialog box, in the File Name text field, type **myrobo-pong.dir**, and press the Enter key. Director will save the *Robo-Pong* game as a file named "myrobo-pong.dir."

As you create more and more games in Director, you will develop your own system of organization. For the purpose of clarity, however, you will keep all your edited files in a single folder.

UNDERSTANDING THE *ROBO-PONG* GAME

Although you will not be modifying the *Robo-Pong* game, you still might like to know how it works. *Robo-Pong* is a simple pong game spiced up with animations and tween effects to improve the feel of the game. In a basic pong game, when the ball hits one of the paddles, it reverses its horizontal velocity and changes its vertical velocity based on the part of the paddle it made contact with. After a set number of misses, the game declares a winner. To view the various Lingo scripts in the Code cast, perform the following steps:

1. Within the Cast window, click your mouse on the Choose Cast button, and select the Code option. Director will display the Code cast within the Cast window. The Code cast contains 22 Lingo scripts, as briefly described in Table 16.1.

Table 16.1 The 22 Lingo scripts of the Code cast and their descriptions.

Script Name	Description
Global	Initializes most of the *Robo-Pong* game's global variables.
Generic Button	Makes its associated sprite behave as a button complete with specified image, cursor, and sound options.
Wait	Keeps the *Robo-Pong* game looping on one frame until otherwise specified.
Game	Checks for ball collisions and keeps the *Robo-Pong* game looping on one frame until otherwise specified.
Show Cursor	Hides the mouse cursor, then returns it to normal while the mouse is over its associated sprite.
Ball	Handles the ball's initialization and movement.
Ball Trail	Follows the Ball bitmap, but is always a frame behind.
Computer	Controls the left paddle by following the ball.
Human	Allows the user to control the right paddle with the mouse.
Arm	Expands its associated sprite to fill in the gap between the interface and the paddle one sprite ahead.
Computer Score	Continuously updates its cast member to contain the string equivalent of the *computerScore* variable.
Human Score	Continuously updates its cast member to contain the string equivalent of the *humanScore* variable.
Speed Slider	Adjusts the *ballSpeed* variable based on mouse movements.
Start Button	Resets the scores and plays the Game frame when the user clicks on its associated sprite.
Pause Button	Sets the *pauseMode* variable to the opposite of itself and updates its button when the user clicks on its associated sprite.
Help Button	Sets the *helpMode* variable to the opposite of itself and updates its button when the user clicks on its associated sprite.
Exit Button	Sets the *exitMode* variable to the opposite of itself and updates its button when the user clicks on its associated sprite.
Window	Makes itself visible only when the *helpMode* variable or the *exitMode* variable equals true.
Help Visible	Makes itself visible only when the *helpMode* variable equals true.
Exit Visible	Makes itself visible only when the *exitMode* variable equals true.
End Game	Ends the game when the user clicks on its associated sprite.
Close Exit Window	Sets the *exitMode* variable to false when the user clicks on its associated sprite.

2. Within the Cast window, click your mouse on the Global member. Director will update the Cast window, as shown in Figure 16.5.

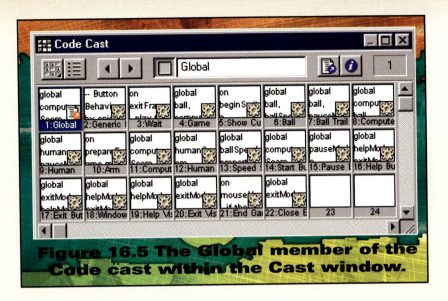

Figure 16.5 The Global member of the Code cast within the Cast window.

3. Within the Cast window, click your mouse on the Cast Member Script button. Director will display the Script window.

4. Within the Script window, use the Previous Cast Member and Next Cast Member buttons to view each of the Lingo scripts in the Code cast.

By now, you should have a good understanding of the logic behind the *Robo-Pong* game. If you find yourself having trouble building new games, you can use pieces of the *Robo-Pong* game to cut down on logic errors.

EXPORTING MOV-FORMAT VIDEO

One popular video compression format is MOV, or QuickTime, compression. Although the MOV format does not offer as many compression options as the AVI format, it allows for much easier customization of video properties such as color depth and scaling. The QuickTime format may not be as popular as AVI, but it does prove more convenient in some situations. To export a video file with the MOV format, perform the following steps:

1. Click your mouse on the File menu, and select the Export option. Director will display the Export dialog box.

2. Within the Export dialog box, click your mouse on the Format dialog box, and select the QuickTime Movie option. Director will update the Export dialog box.

3. Within the Export dialog box, click your mouse on the Export Frame Range radio button. Director will enable you to specify a frame range.

4. Within the Export dialog box, in the Begin field, type **1**, and in the End field, type **80**, as shown in Figure 16.6 Director will set the frame range to the first 80 frames of the *Robo-Pong* game.

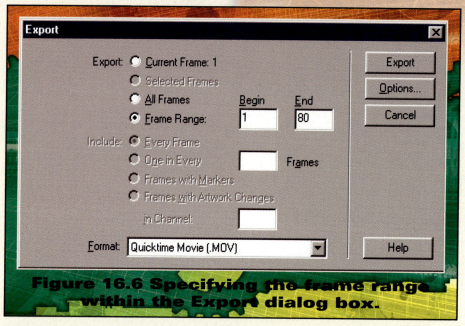

Figure 16.6 Specifying the frame range within the Export dialog box.

5. Within the Export dialog box, click your mouse on the Options button. Director will display the QuickTime Options dialog box.

6. Within the QuickTime Options dialog box, drag the Quality slider to the left until it is centered between the Low and High captions. Director will set the video file's compression quality to average.

7. Within the QuickTime Options dialog box, click your mouse on the Color Depth drop-down list, and select the Thousands option. Director will set the video file's color depth to thousands of colors.

8. Within the QuickTime Options dialog box, click your mouse on the Scale drop-down list and select the 50% option, as shown in Figure 16.7. Director will set the video file's dimensions to half of their original size.

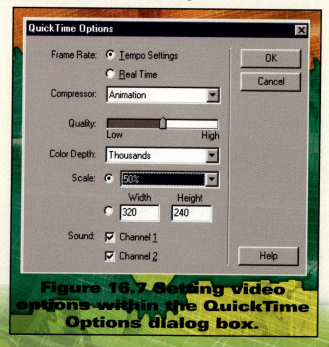

Figure 16.7 Setting video options within the QuickTime Options dialog box.

9. Within the QuickTime Options dialog box, click your mouse on the OK button. Director will remember your changes and close the QuickTime Options dialog box.

10. Within the Export dialog box, click your mouse on the Export button. Director will display the Save File(s) As dialog box.

11. Within the Save File(s) As dialog box, click your mouse on the Save In drop-down list, and select your primary hard drive. Director will display the contents of your primary hard drive.

12. Within the Save File(s) As dialog box, double-click your mouse on the *Director Games* folder you created in Chapter 2. Director will display the contents of the *Director Games* folder.

13. Within the Save File(s) As dialog box, in the File Name text field, type **robo-pong.mov**, and press the Enter key. Director will display the Ready to Export dialog box.

14. Within the Ready to Export dialog box, click your mouse on the OK button. Director will export the *Robo-Pong* game's opening animation sequence as a file named *robo-pong.mov*.

If you play the file in a QuickTime video player, you will see that it is half as big as the original animation sequence, and its quality is greatly reduced. To achieve greater quality at a reasonable file size, you should try the AVI compression format.

EXPORTING AVI-FORMAT VIDEO

AVI, or Video for Windows, compression is the standard format for PC video. The AVI format offers numerous compression options with many different compressors to choose from. You will now export the opening animation sequence using a Microsoft compressor. To export a video file with the AVI format using the Microsoft Video 1 compressor, perform the following steps:

1. Click your mouse on the File menu, and select the Export option. Director will display the Export dialog box.

2. Within the Export dialog box, click your mouse on the Format dialog box, and select the Video for Windows option. Director will update the Export dialog box.

3. Within the Export dialog box, click your mouse on the Export Frame Range radio button. Director will enable you to specify a frame range.

4. Within the Export dialog box, in the Begin field, type **1**, and in the End field, type **80**. Director will set the frame range to the first 80 frames of the *Robo-Pong* game.

5. Within the Export dialog box, click your mouse on the Options button. Director will display the Video for Windows Export Options dialog box.

6. Within the Video for Windows Export Options dialog box, in the Frame Rate field, type **20**, and press the Enter key. Director will set the video file's frame rate to 20 frames per second and close the Video for Windows Export Options dialog box.

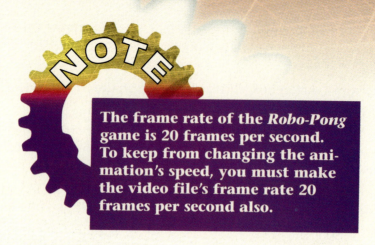

NOTE

The frame rate of the *Robo-Pong* game is 20 frames per second. To keep from changing the animation's speed, you must make the video file's frame rate 20 frames per second also.

7. Within the Export dialog box, click your mouse on the Export button. Director will display the Save File(s) As dialog box.

8. Within the Save File(s) As dialog box, click your mouse on the Save In drop-down list, and select your primary hard drive. Director will display the contents of your primary hard drive.

9. Within the Save File(s) As dialog box, double-click your mouse on the *Director Games* folder you created in Chapter 2. Director will display the contents of the *Director Games* folder.

10. Within the Save File(s) As dialog box, in the File Name text field, type **robopongmicrosoft.avi**, and press the Enter key. Director will display the Ready to Export dialog box.

11. Within the Ready to Export dialog box, click your mouse on the OK button. Director will display the Video Compression dialog box.

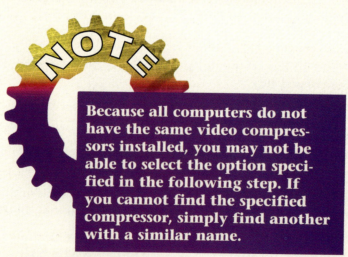

NOTE

Because all computers do not have the same video compressors installed, you may not be able to select the option specified in the following step. If you cannot find the specified compressor, simply find another with a similar name.

12. Within the Video Compression dialog box, click your mouse on the Compressor drop-down list, and select the Microsoft Video 1 option, as shown in Figure 16.8. Director will set the video compressor to Microsoft Video 1.

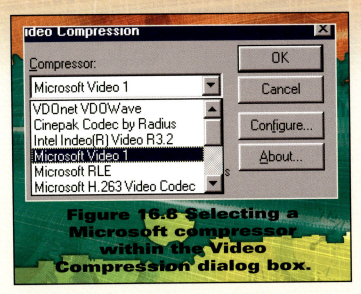

Figure 16.8 Selecting a Microsoft compressor within the Video Compression dialog box.

13. Within the Video Compression dialog box, click your mouse on the OK button. Director will export the *Robo-Pong* game's opening animation sequence as a file named *robo-pongmicrosoft.avi*.

If you play the file in a Windows video player, you will see that its quality has not changed to any measurable degree. Its file size, however, may be too large for convenience. To achieve similar quality with a much smaller file size, you should try the Intel Indeo video compressor. To export a video file with the AVI format using the Indeo Video 5.04 compressor, perform the following steps:

1. Click your mouse on the File menu, and select the Export option. Director will display the Export dialog box.

2. Within the Export dialog box, click your mouse on the Format dialog box, and select the Video for Windows option. Director will update the Export dialog box.

3. Within the Export dialog box, click your mouse on the Export Frame Range radio button. Director will enable you to specify a frame range.

4. Within the Export dialog box, in the Begin field, type **1**, and in the End field, type **80**. Director will set the frame range to the first 80 frames of the *Robo-Pong* game.

5. Within the Export dialog box, click your mouse on the Options button. Director will display the Video for Windows Export Options dialog box.

6. Within the Video for Windows Export Options dialog box, in the Frame Rate field, type **20**, and press the Enter key. Director will set the video file's frame rate to 20 frames per second and close the Video for Windows Export Options dialog box.

7. Within the Export dialog box, click your mouse on the Export button. Director will display the Save File(s) As dialog box.

8. Within the Save File(s) As dialog box, click your mouse on the Save In drop-down list, and select your primary hard drive. Director will display the contents of your primary hard drive.

9.   Within the Save File(s) As dialog box, double-click your mouse on the *Director Games* folder you created in Chapter 2. Director will display the contents of the *Director Games* folder.

10.   Within the Save File(s) As dialog box, in the File Name text field, type **robo-pongindeo.avi**, and press the Enter key. Director will display the Ready to Export dialog box.

11.   Within the Ready to Export dialog box, click your mouse on the OK button. Director will display the Video Compression dialog box.

12.   Within the Video Compression dialog box, click your mouse on the Compressor drop-down list, and select the Indeo Video option, as shown in Figure 16.9. Director will set the video compressor to Indeo Video.

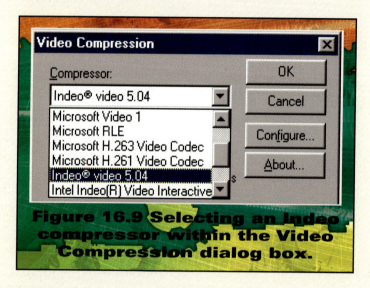

Figure 16.9 Selecting an Indeo compressor within the Video Compression dialog box.

13.   Within the Video Compression dialog box, click your mouse on the OK button. Director will export the *Robo-Pong* game's opening animation sequence as a file named *robo-pongindeo.avi*.

If you play the file in a Windows video player, you will see that although its file size is less than one-third of that of the *robo-pongmicrosoft.avi* file, its quality is only slightly reduced. When compressing video, you must always decide exactly how much quality you will sacrifice for file size.

EXPORTING SEQUENTIAL BITMAPS

Sometimes, instead of a compressed video file, you will need individual frames of a Director movie. If you export a sequence of bitmaps, they will not be compressed at all. Therefore, the bitmaps will take up a large amount of hard-drive space. You must be sure you have enough room on your hard drive before you begin exporting bitmaps. Generally, each 640×480 frame will take up around 1.2MB. To export a sequence of 16 bitmaps, perform the following steps:

1.   Click your mouse on the File menu, and select the Export option. Director will display the Export dialog box.

2. Within the Export dialog box, click your mouse on the Format dialog box, and select the DIB File Sequence option. Director will update the Export dialog box.

3. Within the Export dialog box, click your mouse on the Export Frame Range radio button. Director will enable you to specify a frame range.

4. Within the Export dialog box, in the Begin field, type **1**, and in the End field, type **80**. Director will set the frame range to the first 80 frames of the *Robo-Pong* game.

5. Within the Export dialog box, click your mouse on the Include One in Every radio button. Director will enable you to specify how many frames to skip before exporting a bitmap image.

6. Within the Export dialog box, in the Frames field, type **5**. Director will set the bitmap sequence to include one in every five frames of the *Robo-Pong* game's opening animation, as shown in Figure 16.10.

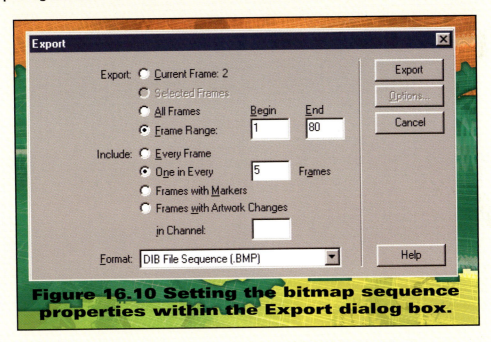

Figure 16.10 Setting the bitmap sequence properties within the Export dialog box.

7. Within the Export dialog box, click your mouse on the Export button. Director will display the Save File(s) As dialog box.

8. Within the Save File(s) As dialog box, click your mouse on the Save In drop-down list, and select your primary hard drive. Director will display the contents of your primary hard drive.

9. Within the Save File(s) As dialog box, double-click your mouse on the *Director Games* folder you created in Chapter 2. Director will display the contents of the *Director Games* folder.

10. Within the Save File(s) As dialog box, in the File Name text field, type **robo-pong.bmp**, and press the Enter key. Director will display the Ready to Export dialog box.

11. **Within the Ready to Export dialog box, click your mouse on the OK button. Director will export the *Robo-Pong* game's opening animation sequence as 16 files named *robo-pong0001.bmp, robo-pong0006.bmp, robo-pong0011.bmp*, and so on.**

The combined file size of the 16 bitmap images should be around 19MB. Through a GIF animation utility, you could load the images into one GIF animation fit for the Internet. Or, you could import them into a Flash movie. The DIB File Sequence option is convenient simply because it leaves the compression completely up to you.

APPLYING YOUR SKILLS

Now that you have the skills required to export digital video and sequential bitmaps in a variety of ways, you can use Director as a fully functional video-creation tool. If you wish to use compressed video clips in your games instead of bulky, awkward sprite animations, you can actually create the video clips right in Director. You can even create simple video clips from a few sequential photos. After all, video is easy to deal with and usually relatively small in file size.

Chapter 17
Epic-Sketch: Incorporating Flash Movies

"Before I put a sketch on paper, the whole idea is worked out mentally." —Nikola Tesla

Chapter

17

- Approaching the *Epic-Sketch* Game

- Opening the *Epic-Sketch* Game's Template

- Understanding the *Epic-Sketch* Game

- Importing the Knob Movie

- Anti-Aliasing the Screen Movie

- Adding the Background Movie

- Manipulating the Knob Movies through Lingo

- Applying Your Skills

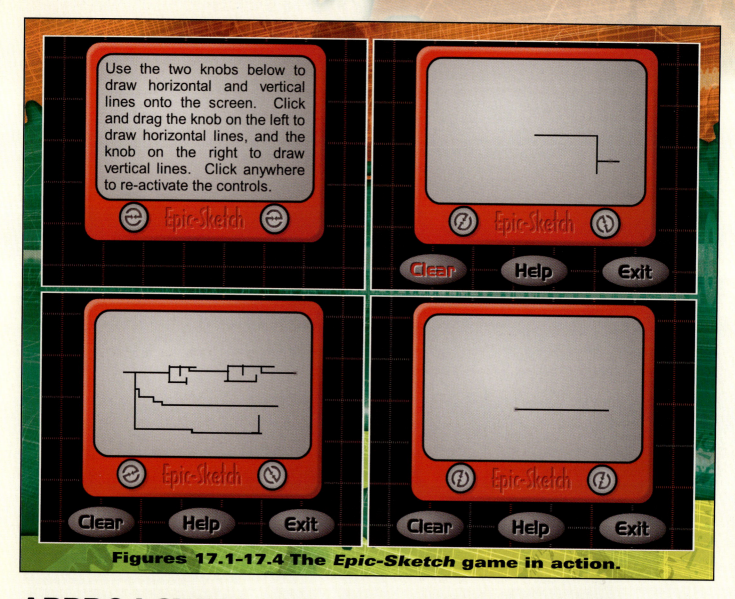

Figures 17.1-17.4 The *Epic-Sketch* game in action.

APPROACHING THE *EPIC-SKETCH* GAME

Because Flash movies are usually made up entirely of vector graphics, they are generally smaller in file size than Director movies. Programmers rarely create complex vector graphics within Director, because Director's vector graphics capabilities are somewhat limited when compared to the capabilities of Flash. To keep the file size of their games small, programmers sometimes incorporate Flash movies into their Director games. The only drawback to Director games containing Flash movies is that they often run slower than a normal Director game. The *Epic-Sketch* game will teach you how to import, implement, and manipulate Flash movies within Director.

OPENING THE *EPIC-SKETCH* GAME'S TEMPLATE

On the companion CD-ROM is a partially completed version of the *Epic-Sketch* game that you will use to learn about incorporating Flash movies. This template will allow you to use Director as a learning tool. To open the *Epic-Sketch* game's template in Director and save a copy to your hard drive, perform the following steps:

1. If the companion CD-ROM is not currently in your CD drive, then insert it in your CD-ROM drive now.

2. Within Director, in the Toolbar, click your mouse on the Open button. Director will display the Open dialog box.

3. Within the Open dialog box, click your mouse on the Look In drop-down list, and select your CD drive. Director will display the contents of your CD drive.

4. Within the Open dialog box, double-click your mouse on the *Epic-Sketch* folder. Director will display the contents of the *Epic-Sketch* folder.

5. Within the Open dialog box, click your mouse on the *epic-sketchtemplate.dir* file. Director will update the Open dialog box.

6. Within the Open dialog box, click your mouse on the OK button. Director will open the *epic-sketchtemplate.dir* file.

7. Click your mouse on the File menu, and select the Save As option. Director will display the Save Movie dialog box.

8. Within the Save Movie dialog box, click your mouse on the Save In drop-down list, and select your primary hard drive. Director will display the contents of your primary hard drive.

9. Within the Save Movie dialog box, double-click your mouse on the *Director Games* folder you created in Chapter 2, "Using Director." Director will display the contents of the *Director Games* folder.

10. Within the Save Movie dialog box, in the File Name text field, type **myepic-sketch.dir**, and press the Enter key. Director will save the *Epic-Sketch* game's template as a file named "myepic-sketch.dir."

As you create more and more games in Director, you will develop your own system of organization. For the purpose of clarity, however, you will keep all your edited template files in a single folder for now.

UNDERSTANDING THE *EPIC-SKETCH* GAME

The *Epic-Sketch* game is a fairly simple example of a Director game using only vector graphics. Based on the user's interaction with the Knob movies, the game draws a series of lines onto the screen. To create each line, the *Epic-Sketch* game puppets a new sprite channel and uses the channel to store a black rectangle of a custom size. Each new line the user draws belongs to its own sprite channel. To view the various Lingo scripts in the Code cast, perform the following steps:

1. Within the Cast window, click your mouse on the Choose Cast button, and select the Code option. Director will display the Code cast within the Cast window. The Code cast contains 10 Lingo scripts, as Table 17.1 briefly describes.

Table 17.1 The 10 Lingo scripts of the Code cast and their descriptions.

Script Name	Description
Global	Stores all the global variables, such as *dotX*, *dotY*, and *mode*, and global functions, such as *makeLine* and *clearLines*.
Generic Button	Makes its associated sprite behave as a button complete with specified image, cursor, and sound options.
Wait	Keeps the *Epic-Sketch* game looping on one frame until otherwise specified.
Wait for Click	Keeps the *Epic-Sketch* game looping on one frame until the user clicks his or her mouse. Then resets the game and plays the Game frame.
Dot	Creates and manipulates new lines based on the location of the associated sprite.
Horizontal Knob	Affects the rotation of its associated sprite and the horizontal location of the Dot shape when the user drags its associated sprite.
Vertical Knob	Affects the rotation of its associated sprite and the vertical location of the Dot shape when the user drags its associated sprite.
Clear Button	Clears the lines drawn onto the screen when the user clicks on its associated sprite.
Help Button	Hides the lines drawn onto the screen and plays game's Help frame when the user clicks on its associated sprite.
Exit Button	Ends the game when the user clicks on its associated sprite.

2. Within the Cast window, click your mouse on the Global member. Director will update the Cast window, as shown in Figure 17.5.

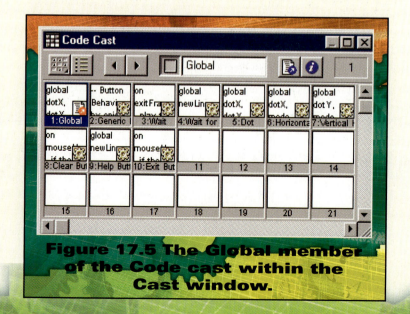

Figure 17.5 The Global member of the Code cast within the Cast window.

3. Within the Cast window, click your mouse on the Cast Member Script button. Director will display the Script window.

4. Within the Script window, use the Previous Cast Member and Next Cast Member buttons to view each of the Lingo scripts in the Code cast.

By now, you should have a good understanding of the logic behind the *Epic-Sketch* game. You will find that using Director to edit an existing game is nearly impossible unless you first understand how the game works.

IMPORTING THE KNOB MOVIE

Currently, the *Epic-Sketch* game's template contains a bitmap version of the Knob Flash movie. If you were to play the movie in its current state, you would find that the two Knobs, because they are not anti-aliased, appear quite rough and distorted when you rotate them. Flash movies in high-quality mode always appear smooth no matter how much you rotate or distort them. To replace the bitmap version of the Knob Flash movie by importing the Knob movie into the Graphics cast, perform the following steps:

1. Within the Cast window, click your mouse on the Choose Cast button, and select the Graphics option. Director will display the Graphics cast within the Cast window.

2. Within the Cast window, click your mouse on the Knob member. Director will update the Cast window, as shown in Figure 17.6.

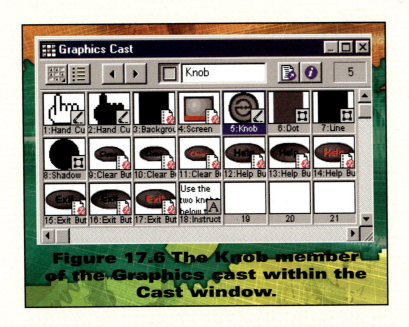

Figure 17.6 The Knob member of the Graphics cast within the Cast window.

3. Click your mouse on the Edit menu, and select the Clear Cast Members option. Director will delete the Knob member.

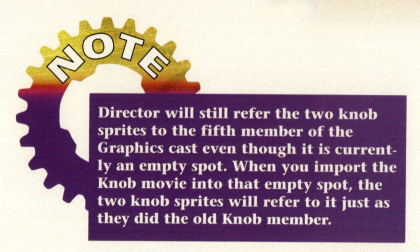

Director will still refer the two knob sprites to the fifth member of the Graphics cast even though it is currently an empty spot. When you import the Knob movie into that empty spot, the two knob sprites will refer to it just as they did the old Knob member.

4. Within the Toolbar, click your mouse on the Import button. Director will display the Import Files dialog box.

5. Within the Import Files dialog box, click your mouse on the Look In drop-down list, and select your CD drive. Director will display the contents of your CD drive.

6. Within the Import Files dialog box, double-click your mouse on the *Epic-Sketch* folder. Director will display the contents of the *Epic-Sketch* folder.

7. Within the Import Files dialog box, click your mouse on the *knob.swf* file. Director will update the Import Files dialog box.

8. Within the Import Files dialog box, click your mouse on the Import button. Director will import *knob.swf* into your game.

9. Within the Property Inspector window, click your mouse on the Member tab. Director will display the Member sheet.

10. Within the Property Inspector window, in the Name field, type **Knob**, and press the Enter key. Director will rename the movie you imported "Knob," as shown in Figure 17.7.

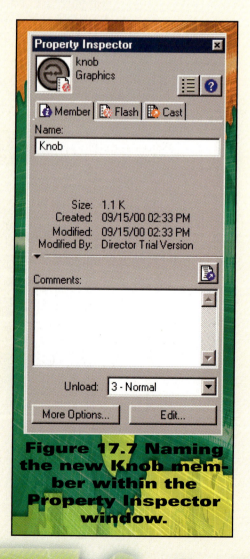

Figure 17.7 Naming the new Knob member within the Property Inspector window.

11. Within the Toolbar, click your mouse on the Play button. Director will preview your game within the Stage window. The two knobs should appear smooth as you rotate them.

12. Within the Toolbar, click your mouse on the Rewind button. Director will return your game to its original state within the Stage window.

By now, your *Epic-Sketch* game should be using a high-quality Flash version of the knob graphic. The two knobs should appear smooth throughout the course of the game. Your *Epic-Sketch* game is fully functional in its current condition, but you still can make a few improvements to the appearance of the graphics.

ANTI-ALIASING THE SCREEN MOVIE

The Screen movie is currently set to low-quality mode. Low quality means that Director will not smoothen the edges of the movie's shapes. Low-quality Flash movies generally play a bit more quickly than those in high-quality mode, but the difference in speed is not nearly as noticeable as the difference in quality. For the most part, you will want to keep all your Flash movies in high-quality mode. To set the Screen movie to high-quality mode, perform the following steps:

1. Within the Cast window, click your mouse on the Screen member. Director will update the Cast window.

2. Click your mouse on the Edit menu, and select the Edit Cast Member option. Director will display the Flash Asset Properties dialog box, as shown in Figure 17.8.

Figure 17.8 Editing the Screen member within the Flash Asset Properties dialog box.

3. Within the Flash Asset Properties dialog box, click your mouse on the Quality drop-down list, and select the High option. Director will set the display quality of the Screen movie to high.

4. Within the Flash Asset Properties dialog box, click your mouse on the OK button. Director will anti-alias the Screen movie within the Stage window.

5. Within the Toolbar, click your mouse on the Play button. Director will preview your game within the Stage window. The Screen movie should appear clean and smooth throughout the *Epic-Sketch* game.

6. Within the Toolbar, click your mouse on the Rewind button. Director will return your game to its original state within the Stage window.

Currently, every aspect of your *Epic-Sketch* game is working properly and every Flash movie is in high-quality mode. The only thing your *Epic-Sketch* game lacks is some sort of background image. One of the advantages of using Flash movies in Director is the simplicity of adding a looping animation.

ADDING THE BACKGROUND MOVIE

An animated background can add an exciting feel to any of your Director games. If your animated background is a looping Flash movie, all you need to do is place it in the Score. Director will take care of the rest. The only drawback is that an animated background might slow your game down a bit if you have a large amount of animation in the foreground. To add the Background movie to channel 1 of your *Epic-Sketch* game, perform the following steps:

1. Drag the Background member from the Cast window into cell 1 of channel 1 of the Score window. Director will display the Background movie within the Stage window.

2. Within the Score window, drag cell 14 of channel 1 to frame 44. Director will extend the Background movie to frame 44, as shown in Figure 17.9.

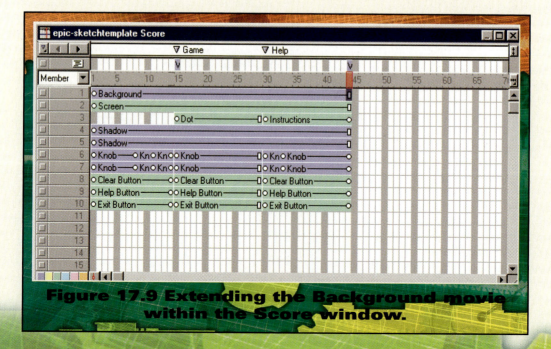

Figure 17.9 Extending the Background movie within the Score window.

3. Click your mouse on the Modify menu, and select the Lock Sprite option. Director will prevent you from accidentally modifying the Background movie.

4. Within the Toolbar, click your mouse on the Play button. Director will preview your game within the Stage window. The Background movie should loop throughout the *Epic-Sketch* game.

The background animation is subtle, so you may not notice it at first.

5. Within the Toolbar, click your mouse on the Rewind button. Director will return your game to its original state within the Stage window.

By now, your *Epic-Sketch* game should appear quite impressive and contain a good number of high-quality Flash movies. In most cases, you will treat Flash movie sprites just as if they were bitmap sprites. Sometimes, however, you might need to change certain aspects of a Flash movie through Lingo.

MANIPULATING THE KNOB MOVIES THROUGH LINGO

Most of the properties associated with graphical sprites such as *locH*, *locV*, and *rotation* also apply to Flash movies. However, Flash movies contain more aspects than ordinary bitmap graphics. Therefore, Lingo must reserve certain properties and functions specifically for Flash movies. To add code to the Horizontal Knob behavior that affects the scaling and display quality of the Knob movie, perform the following steps:

1. Within the Cast window, click your mouse on the Choose Cast button, and select the Code option. Director will display the Code cast within the Cast window.

2. Within the Cast window, click your mouse on the Horizontal Knob member. Director will update the Cast window.

3. Within the Cast window, click your mouse on the Cast Member Script button. Director will display the Script window, as shown in Figure 17.10.

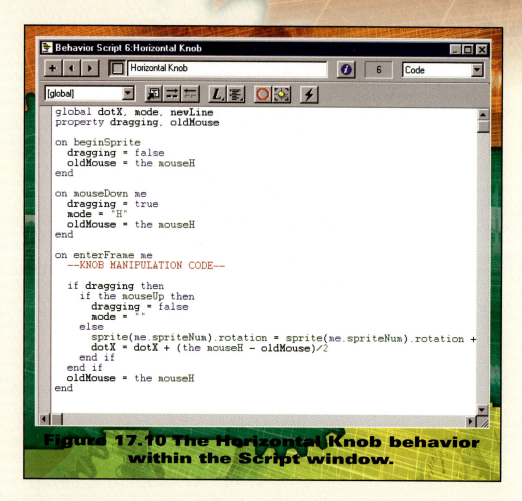

```
Behavior Script 6:Horizontal Knob

+   ◄   ►   ☐ Horizontal Knob              ℹ   6   Code

[global]        ▼   🗗 🗠 🗠   L 🗏   O 🌑   ⚡

global dotX, mode, newLine
property dragging, oldMouse

on beginSprite
  dragging = false
  oldMouse = the mouseH
end

on mouseDown me
  dragging = true
  mode = "H"
  oldMouse = the mouseH
end

on enterFrame me
  --KNOB MANIPULATION CODE--

  if dragging then
    if the mouseUp then
      dragging = false
      mode = ""
    else
      sprite(me.spriteNum).rotation = sprite(me.spriteNum).rotation +
      dotX = dotX + (the mouseH - oldMouse)/2
    end if
  end if
  oldMouse = the mouseH
end
```

Figure 17.10 The Horizontal Knob behavior within the Script window.

4.   Within the Script window, replace —KNOB MANIPULATION CODE— with the following code.

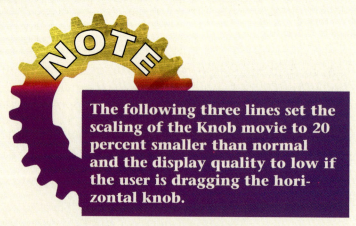

NOTE

The following three lines set the scaling of the Knob movie to 20 percent smaller than normal and the display quality to low if the user is dragging the horizontal knob.

```
if dragging then
  sprite(me.spriteNum).viewScale = 120
  sprite(me.spriteNum).quality = #low
```

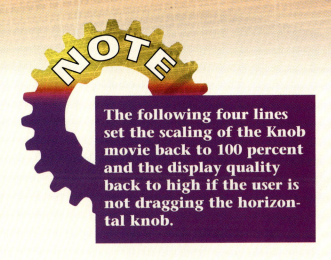

NOTE

The following four lines set the scaling of the Knob movie back to 100 percent and the display quality back to high if the user is not dragging the horizontal knob.

```
else

    sprite(me.spriteNum).viewScale = 100
    sprite(me.spriteNum).quality = #high
end if
```

5. Within the Toolbar, click your mouse on the Script Window button. Director will close the Script window.

6. Within the Toolbar, click your mouse on the Play button. Director will preview your game within the Stage window. The knob on the left side of the Stage should decrease in size and switch to low-quality mode when you click your mouse on it.

7. Within the Toolbar, click your mouse on the Rewind button. Director will return your game to its original state within the Stage window.

You can affect Flash movies in a wide variety of ways directly through Lingo. Most of the time, however, you will have no need to. Flash movies are generally most useful simply as still images or looping animations.

APPLYING YOUR SKILLS

Now that you have the skills required to incorporate Flash movies into your Director games, your games can have a whole new look and feel to them. Because the vector graphics of Flash movies are usually anti-aliased, the Flash graphics you import into your games can have a clean, smooth look. You may not always choose to incorporate Flash movies into your Director games, but if you own a copy of Flash, you'll be glad to have the option.

Conclusion

- Congratulations
- Online Director Resources
- Online Game-Development Resources

CONGRATULATIONS

You have completed the entire book. By now, you should have the skills necessary for every major aspect of game development. You should be able to create Shockwave games for the Internet without much trouble at all. Moreover, you will find that once you know how to create games in Director, you can also build a variety of other applications. As Director's popularity grows, your skills will only increase in value.

As you build more games and applications in Director, you will develop your skills further. The best way to learn the details and quirks of a piece of software is to use it frequently. If you find yourself stuck and you don't know what to do, just try something and see if it works. If it doesn't, try something else. As long as you save backup copies of your games, you can't go wrong with experimentation.

You may not have realized that your skills in Director can actually translate to other programming languages. Of course, you will have to learn the syntax of the new languages and become familiar with their interfaces, but the basic programming logic will remain the same. Learning to think like a computer is generally the most challenging part of learning to program. Once you have the logic down, you should be all right.

ONLINE DIRECTOR RESOURCES

Macromedia Director Support Center

http://www.macromedia.com/support/director/

Macromedia's official Director support site offers a wide variety of information on Director, various tutorials, and free downloads of Director Xtras and plug-ins. The tutorials are organized into several different topics ranging from "The Basics" to "Top TechNotes." Registered users of Director can also obtain advice from certified Macromedia personnel. The Macromedia Director Support Center is the site to visit if you are looking for official information from the people who know Director best.

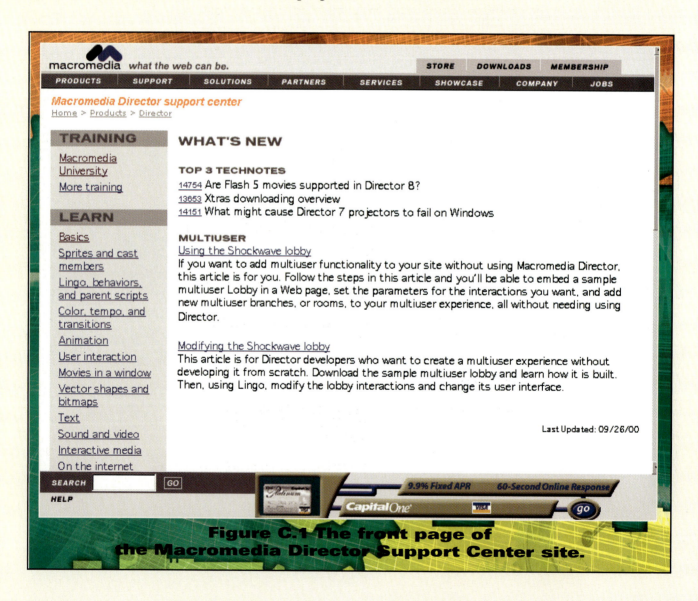

Figure C.1 The front page of the Macromedia Director Support Center site.

Director Online User Group

http://www.director-online.com/

The Director Online User Group, otherwise known as *DOUG*, is an online community of Lingo programmers complete with an extensive collection of articles written by DOUG members. An online forum allows you to post questions about Director or simply browse through the questions others have asked. DOUG also offers a wide variety of links and plug-ins to help you get more out of Director.

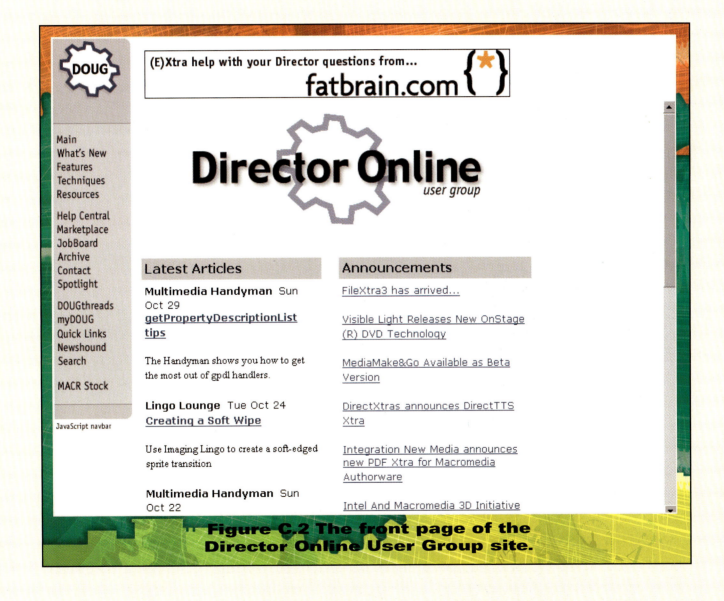

Figure C.2 The front page of the Director Online User Group site.

Director Intelligence Agency

http://www.director8.com/

The Director Intelligence Agency, or DIA, offers one of the most extensive, well-organized Director libraries available. Of course there is a catch. The DIA requires that you pay a membership fee for total access to the site. However, even if you don't want to register, you can still access the "Declassified" area, which contains a comprehensive library of Director information, resources, and categorized links to other Web sites. The "Game Resources" section contains several categories of online tutorials about Lingo game programming. Even if you don't want to pay for membership, the DIA is well worth a visit.

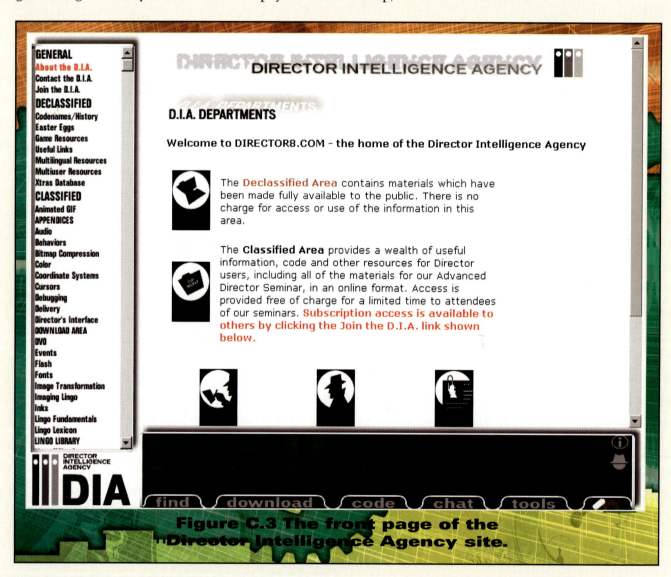

Figure C.3 The front page of the Director Intelligence Agency site.

UpdateStage

http://www.updatestage.com/

UpdateStage is an online newspaper centered on Director news and Lingo programming tips. You can browse through its archive of back issues, search its database of downloadable Xtras, or even see a complete list of all the known "quirks," or bugs, in Director. Being knowledgeable of Director's shortcomings can make debugging your Director games a much easier task.

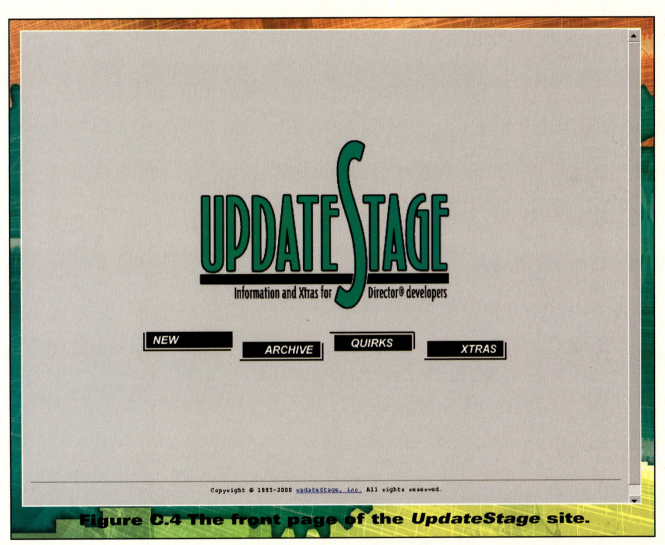

Figure C.4 The front page of the *UpdateStage* site.

Behaviors Online

http://www.behaviors.com/

Visit Behaviors Online if you want advanced help with Lingo scripting. Behaviors Online offers scripting tips and seminars, tools for behavior development, and even a searchable database of pre-built behaviors and Xtras. If you can't find the information you need, you can ask someone in the Lingo chat lounge.

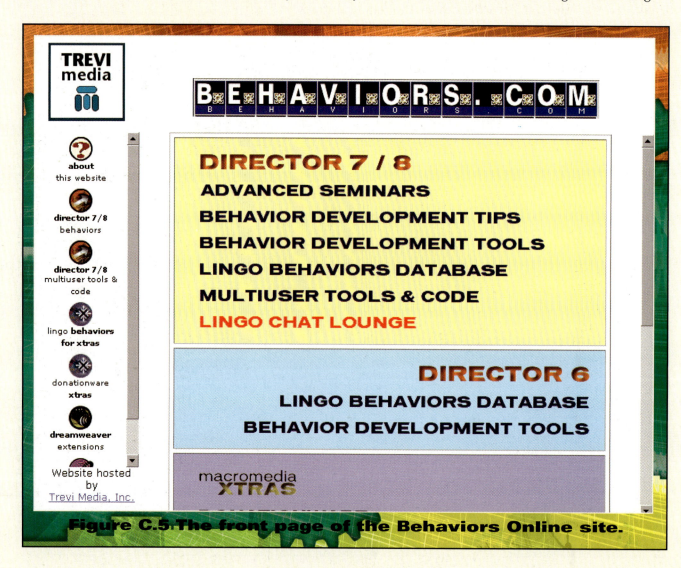

Figure C.5 The front page of the Behaviors Online site.

RobotDuck Shockwave Games

http://www.robotduck.com/

The RobotDuck site uses simple yet entertaining sample movies to teach you specific programming skills. By exploring RobotDuck's Learning Library, you can develop skills essential to game development from the basics all the way up to advanced techniques. If you get bored with the tutorials, you can play around in RobotDuck's Games Arcade or Experiment Lab.

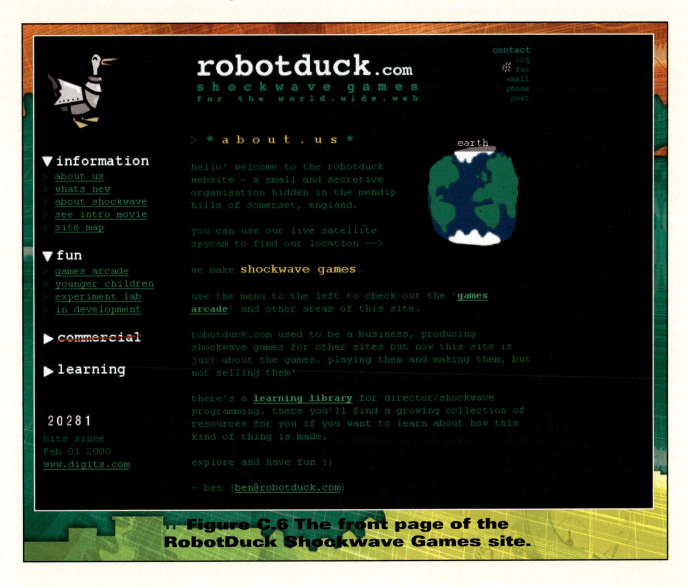

Figure C.6 The front page of the RobotDuck Shockwave Games site.

MediaMacros

http://www.mediamacros.com/

The MediaMacros site contains searchable libraries of Lingo behaviors and allows you to submit your own behaviors. Another unique feature is MediaMacro's Learning Arcade. You can play dozens of Shockwave games and then, if you like, download their source files and see how they were made. The Learning Arcade lets you learn Lingo while playing some very addictive arcade games. MediaMacros also offers a variety of other resources, but you will most likely want to spend your time in the Learning Arcade.

Figure C.7 The front page of the MediaMacros site.

Grommett

http://www.grommett.com/

Grommett is an online magazine about multimedia in general. Because Director is such a popular multimedia development tool, most of the site focuses on Lingo programming. Although the magazine is mostly geared toward teachers and professional developers, its tutorials are generally quite simple and easy to understand.

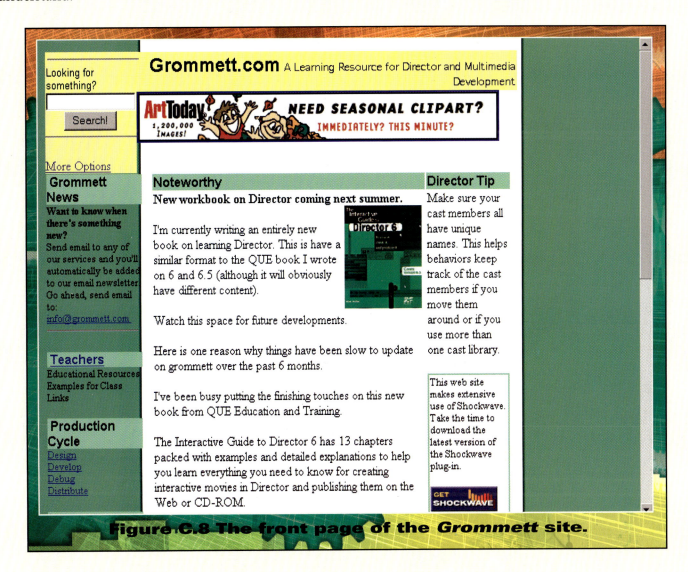

Figure C.8 The front page of the *Grommett* site.

Macromedia Director Game Development
From Concept to Creation

Director Web

http://www.mcli.dist.maricopa.edu/director/

Director Web has been around since 1994, and in that time, it has compiled several searchable databases full of useful items like "Tips 'n' Scripts," "XStuff," and "Net Resources." If you want to catch up on the *Direct-L* newsletter, Director Web offers an archive of digests all the way back to 1995. Another helpful resource is its list of external applications that allow you to do things like create screen savers with Director or change the icon of your Projector files. If you are looking for searchable libraries of Director content, you should visit Director Web immediately.

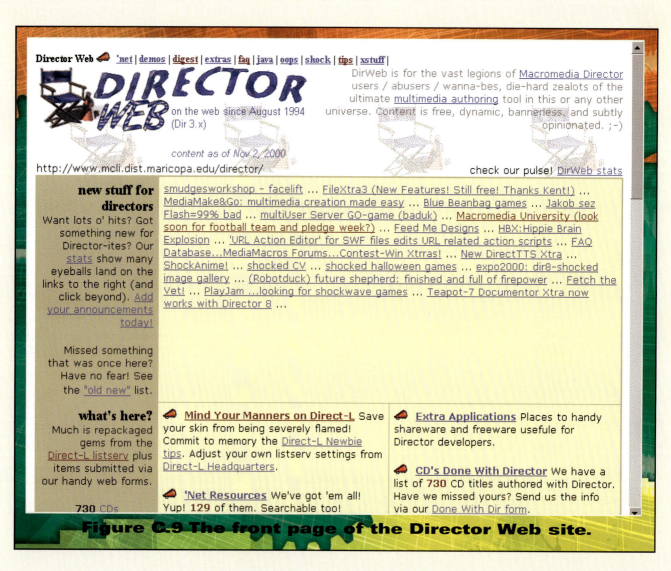

Figure C.9 The front page of the Director Web site.

Lingo User's Journal

http://www.penworks.com/LUJ/

The *Lingo User's Journal* is an online newsletter that contains Lingo source code and programming tips. If you want a subscription to the *Lingo User's Journal*, you have to pay for it, but the site also offers free Lingo code and a free trial issue. However, you will probably not find the site very useful unless you subscribe to the *Lingo User's Journal*.

[Home | Current Products | Upcoming Products | MMedia Tips | Ordering | E-mail]

Welcome to Dr. Diego's F.A.Q.
about Macromedia Director and Lingo

Dashing Dr. Diego, the daring digital sleuth who tracks down answers to the hard questions. A multi-man of mystery who keeps us all informed...

What you will find here are tips and techniques
for programmers using Macromedia Director's
Lingo and XObjects.

Index of Director/Lingo Questions

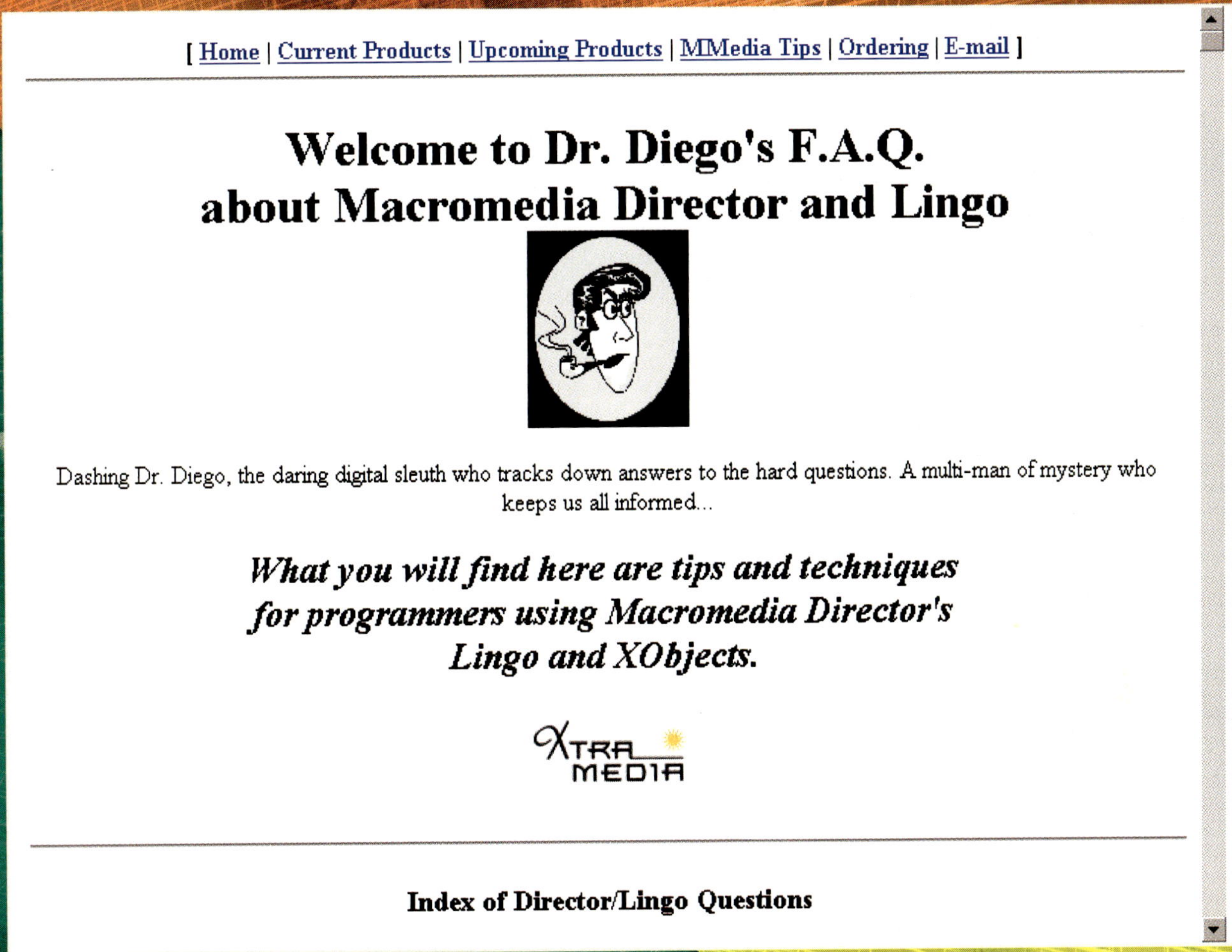

Figure C.10 The front page of the *Lingo User's Journal* site.

CleverMedia Development Resources

http://www.clevermedia.com/resources/

The CleverMedia Development Resources site consists of links to resources such as "Tips, Tricks, and Techniques," "Questions and Answers," and of course "Behaviors, Xtras, and Scripts." If you need specific questions about Director answered, then CleverMedia's Director Community Resource, or DCR, can be very useful. The rest of the CleverMedia site offers dozens of playable arcade games made in both Director and Flash.

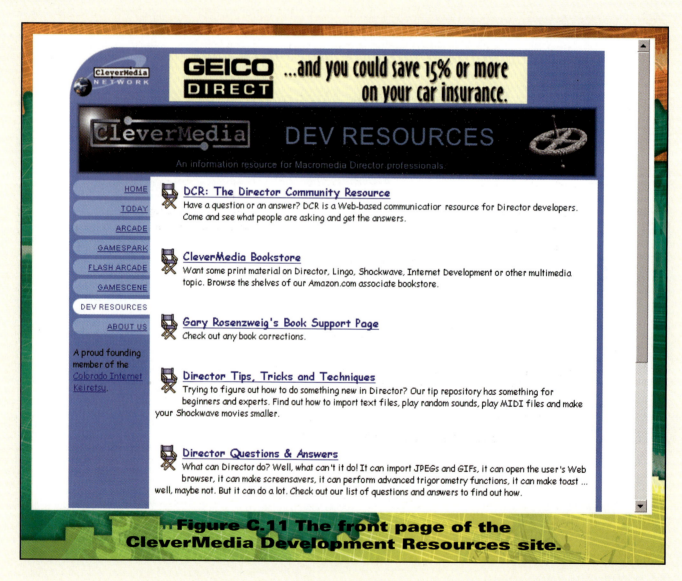

Figure C.11 The front page of the CleverMedia Development Resources site.

Director Solutions

http://space.tin.it/internet/gchoo/

The Director Solutions site consists of three main sections: "Books," "Tech," and "Designs." One of the major components of the "Tech" sections is its *Lingo Programmer's MCI Reference Guide*. The Director Solutions site also contains information on instructional books and several articles about various aspects of multimedia design.

Figure C.12 The front page of the Director Solutions site.

Director Tutorials

http://www.herts.ac.uk/lis/mmedia/directortutorial/

The Director Tutorials site contains four tutorials: "The Basics," "Animation," "Lingo," and "The Final Frontier." The site is most definitely not for advanced Director users, but can offer help to those who find themselves having trouble getting started. You should visit the Director Tutorials site if you want clear descriptions of the basic aspects of Director.

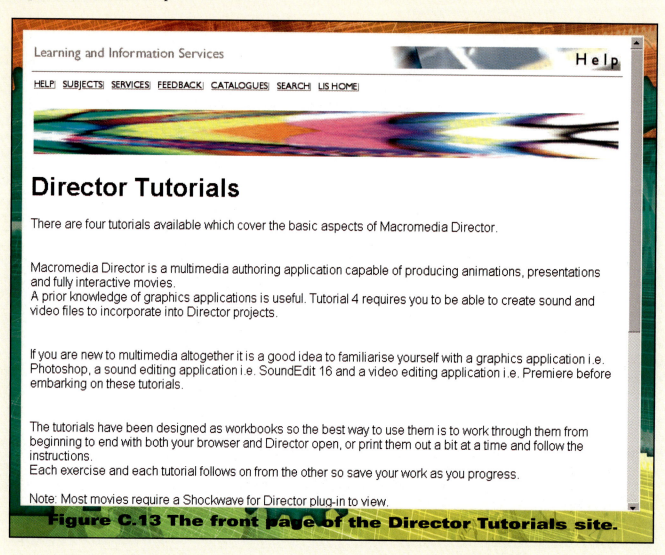

Figure C.13 The front page of the Director Tutorials site.

Dr. Diego's Lingo/Director Tips

http://www.xtramedia.com/lingoTips.shtml

Dr. Diego provides a huge list of frequently asked questions and their answers. In some cases, the answers even contain Lingo code to more thoroughly explain the Lingo concept. Because the frequently asked questions are listed in hyperlink format at the top of the page, Dr. Diego's Lingo/Director Tips site is easy to navigate.

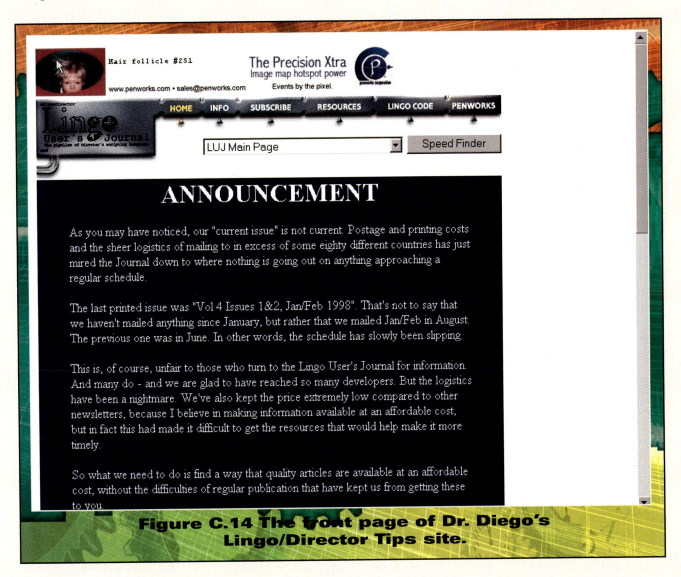

Figure C.14 The front page of Dr. Diego's Lingo/Director Tips site.

ONLINE GAME-DEVELOPMENT RESOURCES

Gamasutra

http://www.gamasutra.com/

Gamasutra differs from most game-development sites in that it not only offers production techniques but also discusses various aspects of recent games. The news articles and detailed tutorials cover virtually every aspect of game development. If you plan to develop games professionally, you can even look for job offers in your area. Joining Gamasutra is free, but most features are accessible regardless of membership.

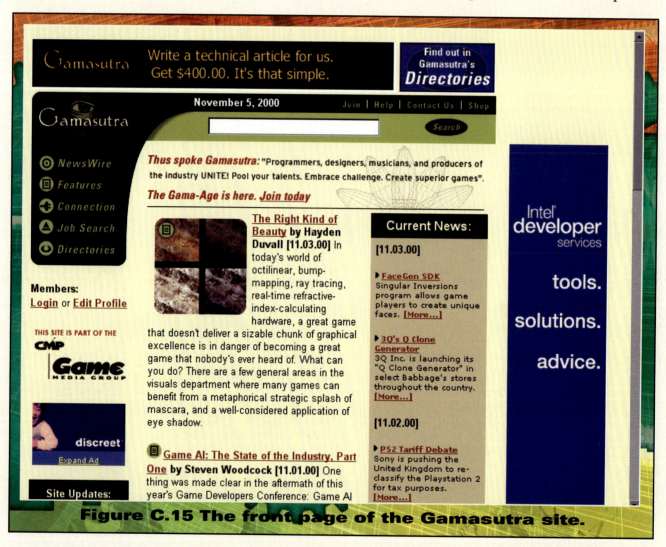

Figure C.15 The front page of the Gamasutra site.

FlipCode News and Resources

http://www.flipcode.com/

The FlipCode site is a collection of articles dealing with the latest game-development news and techniques. The site's tutorials relate mostly to advanced strategies for game design, logic, art, and programming. None of the programming examples are written in Lingo, but the FlipCode site is still universal enough to be a great help to any aspiring game developer.

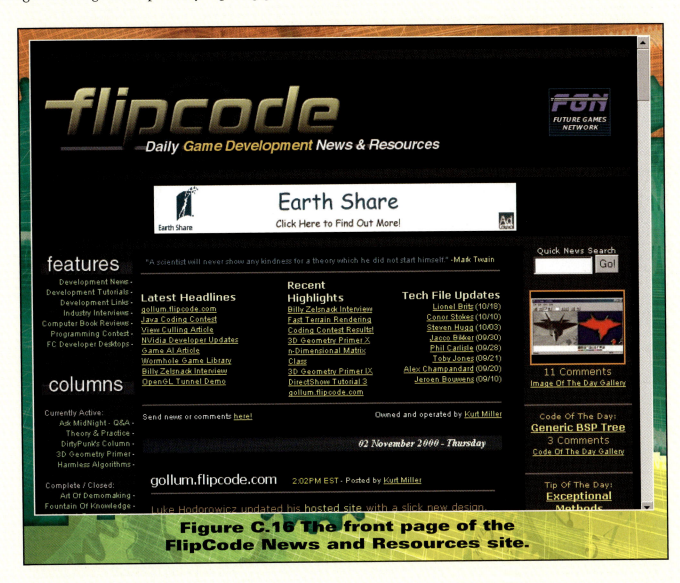

Figure C.16 The front page of the FlipCode News and Resources site.

Game Development Resources

http://www.game-developer.com/

The Game Development Resources site covers almost every part of game development from buying the correct hardware and software to producing graphics efficiently and effectively. The site offers access to archives of game source code written in various languages. The Game Development Search Engine allows you to access the information you want quickly and easily. Whether you are a professional or just a beginner, the Game Development Resources site has something for you.

Figure C.17 The front page of the Game Development Resources site.

GameDev Online

http://www.gamedev.net/

GameDev Online offers numerous features aside from standard articles about game design and industry news. The site contains a chat center, several game-development contests, interviews with game developers, a message board, and even ongoing projects to which visitors of the site can contribute. Another unusual feature of the site is its extensive *Game Dictionary*, which covers not only game terms but also influential titles and developers.

Figure C.18 The front page of the GameDev Online site.

Game Development Central
http://www.gdcentral.com/

Game Development Central is a series of tutorials designed mainly for novice game developers. The site covers topics like "How Do Games Work?," "How Do I Get Started?," and "Selling a Game." The articles are all very basic in their descriptions of the game-development process, but can offer clear information to those who find themselves confused by other development resources.

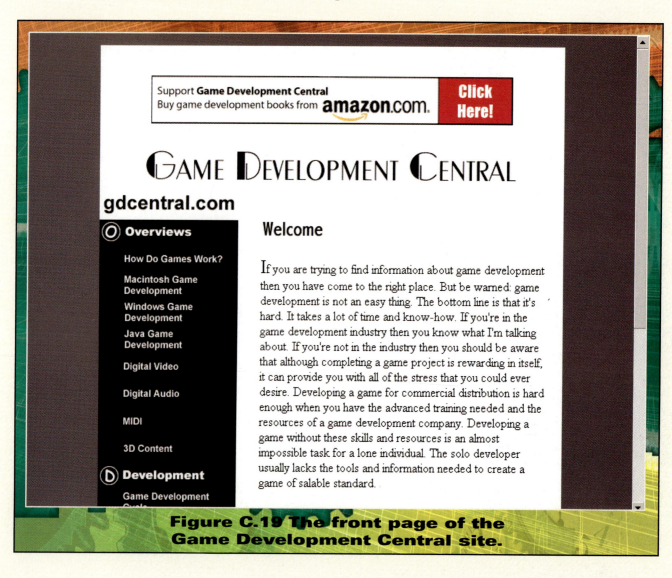

Figure C.19 The front page of the Game Development Central site.

Appendix

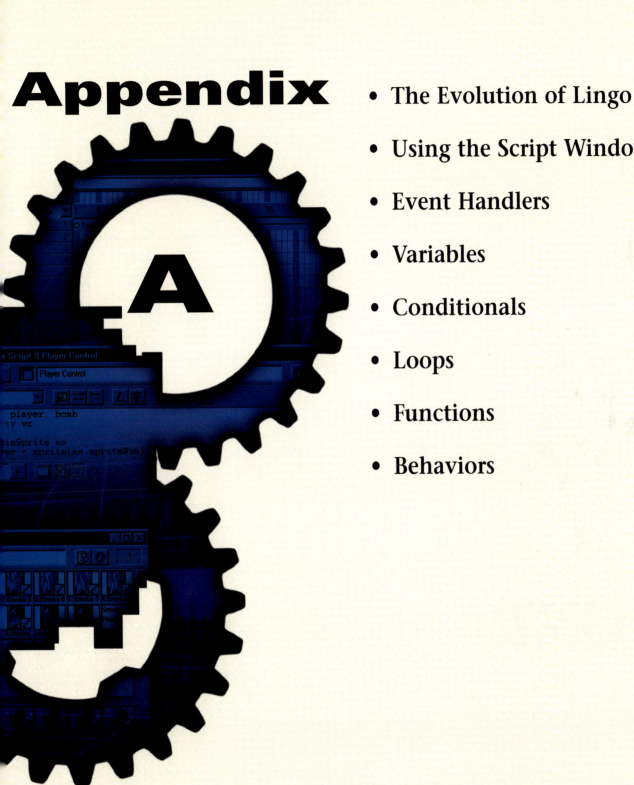

- The Evolution of Lingo

- Using the Script Window

- Event Handlers

- Variables

- Conditionals

- Loops

- Functions

- Behaviors

THE EVOLUTION OF LINGO

Lingo's original designers wanted the language to have a very plain-English, common-sense feel to it. They constructed a programming language that used real words instead of mathematical symbols as often as possible. The goal was to let programmers tell the computer what to do almost in their own words. And for years, Lingo programmers typed phrases like

```
set the rotation of sprite 5 to 90
```

instead of shorter, more mathematical phrases like

```
sprite(5).rotation = 90
```

Eventually Lingo's designers realized that trying to tell the computer what to do in plain English is simply not convenient. They developed an alternative syntax that more closely resembled other programming languages such as C++ and BASIC. A statement as confusing as

```
set stringVariable to word 2 to 5 of line 8 of the text of the member of sprite 2
```

could now be translated to

```
stringVariable = sprite(2).member.text.line[8].word[2..5]
```

Lingo still includes the option to type commands in the old verbose syntax, but most programmers feel more comfortable with the new dot syntax. The dot syntax makes code organization more obvious and, therefore, less prone to errors. Computers think in terms of mathematical operations, and so should programmers.

USING THE SCRIPT WINDOW

Director's Script window makes programming as convenient as possible. The Script window not only color-codes text as you type, but also provides methods of automatic code generation that can benefit beginners and experts alike. In addition to the Script window's convenient text and navigation options, the window also contains a variety of tools to make debugging your scripts easier than ever before. To view the Script window within Director, perform the following steps.

1. If you do not see the Script window, then within the Toolbar, click your mouse on the Script Window button. Director will display the Script window, as shown in Figure A.1.

Figure A.1 The Script Window button within the Toolbar.

2. If you want to reposition the Script window within Director, drag its title bar to the position you desire.

3. If you wish to resize the Script window within Director, drag its lower-right corner until the window is the size you desire.

As you type into the Script window, Director will color-code your text to indicate the nature of each word you type. For example, normal text will be colored black by default, but numbers will be gray, and certain reserved keywords will be blue. These color distinctions will make typos less likely to occur, because if you misspell a reserved keyword or forget to close a quote, the color of the text will be different than you had expected. Director allows you to customize the color-coding system to make your Lingo scripts appear just the way you want them. To customize your Script window preferences, perform the following steps.

1. Click your mouse on the File menu, and then the Preferences submenu, and then select the Script option. Director will display the Script Window Preferences dialog box, as shown in Figure A.2.

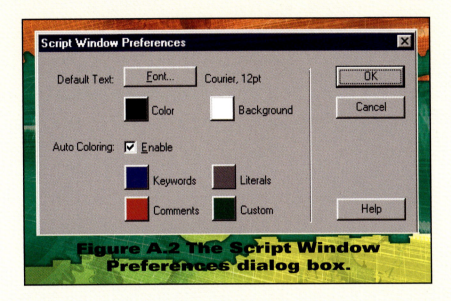

Figure A.2 The Script Window Preferences dialog box.

2. Within the Script Window Preferences dialog box, click your mouse on a color button that you would like to customize, and select a color swatch of your choice. Director will change the color of the specified script text to whatever color you select.

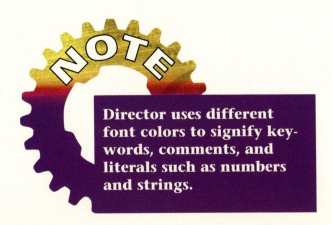

Director uses different font colors to signify keywords, comments, and literals such as numbers and strings.

3. If you want to customize the font size or face for the Script window's text, then click your mouse on the Font button. Director will display the Font dialog box.

NOTE

For a code editor, mono-spaced fonts such as Courier, Fixedsys, or Andale Mono usually work best.

4. Within the Font dialog box, customize any options that you would like to change, and then click your mouse on the OK button. Director will close the Font dialog box, and return to the Script Window Preferences dialog box.

5. Within the Script Window Preferences dialog box, click your mouse on the OK button. Director will update your text preferences within the Script window.

If you need help remembering a Lingo command, or you simply do not want to bother typing it, Director's Script window offers two extensive menu trees that can help. The Alphabetical Lingo button displays a menu that contains 29 subsections of Lingo commands organized alphabetically. Generally, the Alphabetical Lingo button is useful for when you already know the name of the command you wish to type but can't remember the exact syntax or simply do not want to type it in, as shown in Figure A.3.

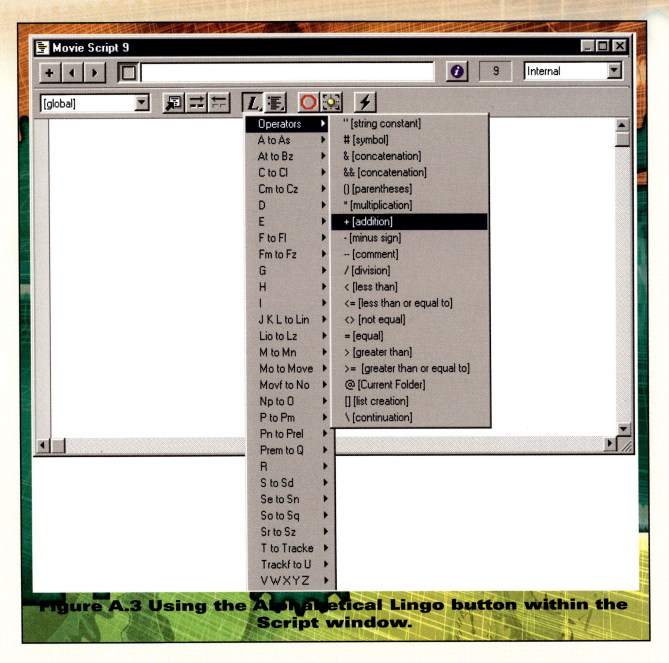

Figure A.3 Using the Alphabetical Lingo button within the Script window.

Alternatively, the Categorized Lingo button sorts Lingo commands into 38 different categories. The Categorized Lingo button is useful even if you do not have a single Lingo command memorized. You can simply move your mouse over the category you need and select an option from the submenu that Director displays, as shown in Figure A.4.

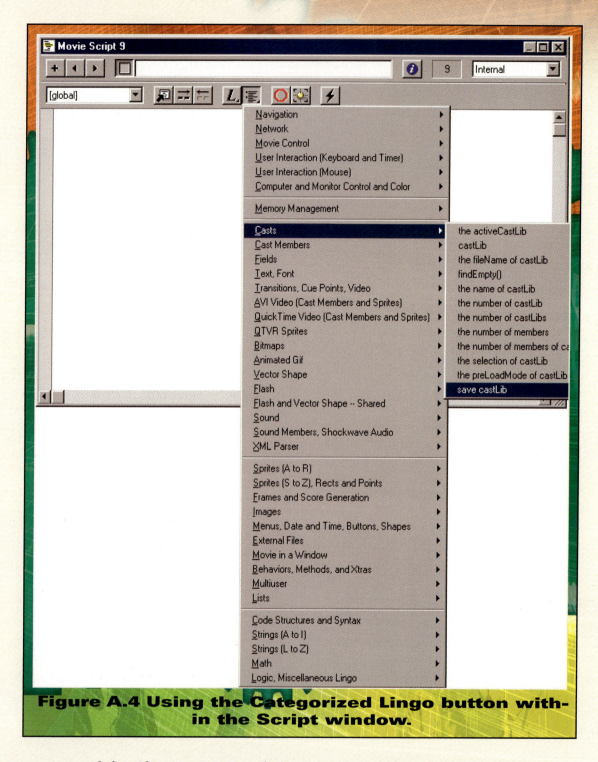

Figure A.4 Using the Categorized Lingo button within the Script window.

The Lingo menus work fine if you want to just feel your way around the language. However, to become fluent in Lingo, you should really avoid using the menus and try to memorize at least the common Lingo commands. You will find that repeatedly selecting commands from the menu trees is simply less efficient than typing them in on your own.

EVENT HANDLERS

All Lingo code executes either directly or indirectly through event handlers. An *event handler* is a predefined function that Director calls each time a certain event, such as the beginning of a frame or the clicking of a mouse, occurs. If Lingo code is not contained within or somehow linked to an event handler, Director will either ignore the code or display an error message. Every event handler begins with the word *on* and the name of the event, contains all affected Lingo commands, and then ends on another line with the word *end*, as shown in the following code:

```
on mouseDown
    beep
end
```

Some events occur only once throughout the run of the program, while others occur almost constantly, and still others may never occur at all. For a complete list of available event handlers and their descriptions, refer to Appendix B, "Lingo Quick Reference."

VARIABLES

A *variable* is a letter or word that can represent a changing value. A variable can be accessible throughout the run of a program or only in specific areas such as a single event handler, depending on how you define it. To define a global variable (one that is accessible in any of a program's scripts), you must type the global keyword, and then name the variable. Generally, a property variable is only accessible to a single Lingo script. You do not need to define variables inside of an event handler, as shown in the following code:

```
global frameCount
on enterFrame
    if frameCount = 100 then quit
end
```

To set a variable to a certain value, simply type the name of the variable, the equal sign, and then the value you want the variable to represent, as shown in the following code:

```
property number
on mouseDown
    number = 50
end
```

Local variables do not need special definitions. If you set a new variable to a value within a function or event handler, Lingo will assume that you wish to create a local variable. Local variables exist from the point that they are first assigned a value to the end of the handler in which they began, as shown in the following code:

```
global bigNumber
on enterFrame
  tempNumber = bigNumber*10
  bigNumber = bigNumber + tempNumber
end
```

Types of Variables

Integers are numbers that do not contain any decimal fractions, and are always assumed to stay that way. If you were to set an integer variable to the value of 5 divided by 2, the variable would have the value of 2, because it would ignore the decimal remainder. You can convert any number into an integer value, as shown in the following code:

```
if integer(2.5) = 2 then beep
```

Decimal numbers, commonly called *floating-point numbers*, find the exact value of all mathematical operations. The *floatPrecision* system property determines how many places past the decimal appear when the floating-point value is output. Incidentally, the *floatPrecision* system property has an integer value, because Director can never output a fractional number of digits. You can convert any number into a floating-point value, as shown in the following code:

```
the floatPrecision = 3
if float(2) = 2.000 then beep
```

Text strings consist of zero or more characters organized in a specific order. A character can be anything from a letter to a symbol to a line break. The difference between the string value of *5* and the integer value of 5 is that strings have no numerical value and can, therefore, never be used in mathematical operations. You can convert any value into a string value for output, as shown in the following code:

```
if string(4+5) && "Lives" = "9 Lives" then beep
```

Boolean variables can only hold a value of *true* or *false*. You should not enclose the words *true* and *false* in quotes because they are actually predefined Lingo keywords. The *false* keyword represents a value of zero, and the *true* keyword represents a value of one. Boolean variables can prove very useful in certain situations, but are by no means required in order to make any program run correctly. However, Boolean variables generally make your code cleaner and easier to understand. The use of a Boolean variable can also shorten an *if...then* structure, as shown in the following code:

```
trueVariable = true
falseVariable = false
if trueVariable = true then beep
if trueVariable then beep
if not falseVariable then beep
```

Lists can hold any type of value including integers, strings, or more lists. A *list* is a single variable that holds zero or more values. In Lingo, values inside a list do not necessarily have to be of the same type. You can access these values by using bracket notation, as shown in the following code:

```
listVariable = [7, 8, 9, [1, 0], [1, 1], [1, 2]]
if listVariable[2] = 8 then beep
if listVariable[4] = [1, 0] then beep
if listVariable[6][2] = 2 then beep
```

Property lists contain not only values, but also property names. For instance, a *car* variable might have a *year* property, a *color* property, and a *model* property. You can treat property lists exactly the same as linear lists if you wish, or you can use dot notation to access the values of their properties, as shown in the following code:

```
car = [#year: 1957, #color: rgb(255, 0, 0), #model "Chevy"]
if car.year = 1957 then beep
if car[1] = 1957 then beep
```

Other predefined types such as color and point values generally consist of a property list with the properties already set up. Lingo defines several media types to make multimedia programming in Lingo more powerful and quite a bit easier than in many programming languages.

CONDITIONALS

A *conditional* is a structure that keeps one or several lines of code from being executed unless a specified condition is met. The condition can be in the form of a Boolean variable, mathematical equation, or group of equations. If the final value of the condition is equal to the keyword *true*, or any number other than zero, the enclosed code will execute.

Lingo provides two forms of conditional structures. The most popular and generally most useful of the two is the *if...then* structure. If the conditional affects only one line of code, then you can type the entire structure on a single line, as shown in the following code:

```
if 5 = 4 + 1 then
   beep
end if
if 5 = 4 + 1 then beep
```

To make *if...then* structures easier to use and understand, Lingo offers an optional *else* statement to be used when you want code to execute only when the preceding code did not. For example, if the integer remainder left after a variable is divided by two is not equal to zero, then Director will move on to the next condition, as shown in the following code:

```
if integerVariable mod 2 = 0 then
   integerVariable = 1
else if integerVariable = 1 then
   integerVariable = 0
else
   integerVariable = random(100)
end if
```

The *case...of* structure is useful for when you are dealing with only one variable and want to test that variable for a variety of different values. Of course, you could replace any *case...of* structure with an *if...then...else* chain, but Lingo provides the option. In certain situations, *case...of* structures are simply more convenient, as shown in the following code:

```
case stringVariable of
  "North":
    integerVariable = 1
    stringVariable = ""
  "South": integerVariable = 2
  "East":
    integerVariable = 3
    stringVariable = ""
  "West":
    integerVariable = 4
    stringVariable = ""
end case
```

LOOPS

Loops are very similar to conditionals. A *loop* executes a group of code repeatedly as long as a specified condition is met. Loops allow programmers to avoid typing similar statements over and over. A simple *repeat while* structure can prove invaluable, as shown in the following code:

```
repeat while randomNumber = integerVariable
  randomNumber = random(100)
end repeat
```

To make a loop execute a set number of times, or iterations, you must use a loop-control variable. By adding one to the loop-control variable each time the section of code executes, you can count the iterations and end the loop when the variable is no longer below a certain value. However, Lingo will handle the entire process for you if you use a *repeat...with* structure, as shown in the following code:

```
repeat with integerVariable = 1 to 20
  listVariable[integerVariable] = random(5)
end repeat
```

FUNCTIONS

A *function* is a section of code that executes only when it is specifically told to do so. All functions must have unique names, just like variables. To call a function, or cause its code to execute, simply type the function's name in the point of your program that you would like the function to run. After Lingo executes the function, it will return to the line directly after the function's call, as shown in the following code:

```
global stringVariable
on addLetter
  stringVariable = stringVariable & "B"
end on
on startMovie
  stringVariable = "A"
  addLetter
  stringVariable = stringVariable & "C"
end on
```

A *parameter*, or *argument*, is a value that is passed to a function to be used as a variable within that function. Parameters allow the programmer to create a single function that can perform a variety of tasks, as shown in the following code:

```
global stringVariable
on addLetter letter
  stringVariable = stringVariable & letter
end on
on startMovie
  stringVariable = "A"
  addLetter("B")
  stringVariable = stringVariable & "C"
end on
```

If a function returns a value, you can treat its call as if it were a variable representing that value. You can call the function normally, or you can assign or compare a variable to the function's returned value, as shown in the following code:

```
global stringVariable
on addLetter letter
  return stringVariable & letter
end on
on startMovie
  stringVariable = "A"
  stringVariable = addLetter("B") & "C"
  if addLetter("D") = "ABCD" then beep
end on
```

BEHAVIORS

A *behavior* is a Lingo script designed to alter a single sprite as opposed to the entire program. You can also assign a behavior to a frame, but certain event handlers will no longer work. You can assign one behavior to as many different sprites as you wish. You can even assign more than one behavior to a sprite. Much like functions, behaviors can accept parameters, or arguments, to be used as variables throughout the script. To create and implement a behavior that accepts parameters, perform the following steps:

1. Within the Toolbar, click your mouse on the Script Window button. Director will display the Script window.

2. Within the Script window, in the Cast Member Name text field, type **Shake**, and press the Enter key. Director will name the new script **Shake**.

3. Within the Properties window, click your mouse on the Script tab. Director will display the Script sheet.

4. Within the Properties window, click your mouse on the Script Type drop-down list, and select the Behavior option. Director will mark the Shake script as a behavior, as shown in Figure A.5.

Figure A.5 Marking the Shake script as a behavior within the Property Inspector window.

5. Within the Script window, type the following code:

```
property my, shakiness
```

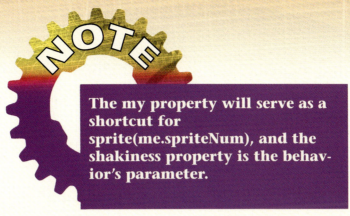

The my property will serve as a shortcut for sprite(me.spriteNum), and the shakiness property is the behavior's parameter.

```
on beginSprite me
  my = sprite(me.spriteNum)
end
```

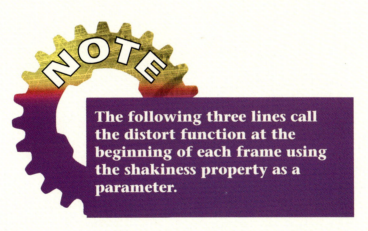

The following three lines call the distort function at the beginning of each frame using the shakiness property as a parameter.

```
on enterFrame
  distort(shakiness)
end
```

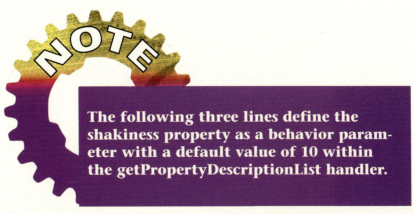

The following three lines define the shakiness property as a behavior parameter with a default value of 10 within the getPropertyDescriptionList handler.

```
on getPropertyDescriptionList
  return [#shakiness: [#comment:"Shakiness:", #format:#integer, #default:10] ]
end
```

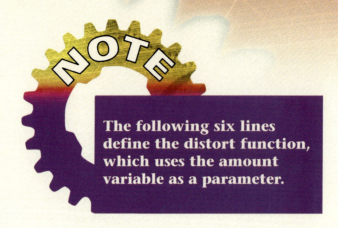

The following six lines define the distort function, which uses the amount variable as a parameter.

```
on distort amount
   my.locH = my.locH + random(amount*2 - 1) - amount
   my.locV = my.locV + random(amount*2 - 1) - amount
   my.width = my.width + random(amount*2 - 1) - amount
   my.height = my.height + random(amount*2 - 1) - amount
end
```

6. Within the Toolbar, click your mouse on the Script Window button. Director will close the Script window.

7. If you do not see the Tool Palette, then click your mouse on the Window menu, and select the Tool Palette option. Director will display the Tool Palette.

8. Within the Tool Palette, click your mouse on the Foreground Color button, and select a color swatch of your choice. Director will set the foreground color to whatever color you select.

9. Within the Tool Palette, click your mouse on the Filled Ellipse button, shown in Figure A.6. Director will select the Filled Ellipse tool.

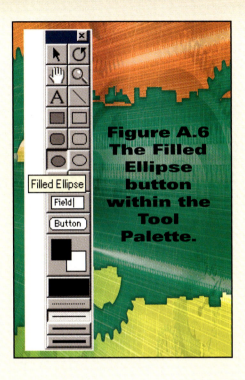

Figure A.6 The Filled Ellipse button within the Tool Palette.

10. Within the Stage window, drag your mouse around on the Stage. Director will draw a filled ellipse based on the starting and ending points of your mouse movement.

11. Within the Stage, click your mouse on the new filled ellipse. Director will update the Property Inspector window.

12. Within the Property Inspector window, click your mouse on the Behavior pop-up button, and select the Shake option. Director will display the Parameters dialog box.

13. Within the Parameters dialog box, click your mouse on the OK button. Director will apply the Shake behavior to the filled ellipse.

14. Within the Toolbar, click your mouse on the Play button. Director will preview your movie within the Stage window. Notice how the filled ellipse shakes and distorts.

15. Within the Toolbar, click your mouse on the Rewind button. Director will return your movie to its original state within the Stage window.

16. Within the Property Inspector window, click your mouse on the Parameters button. Director will display the Parameters dialog box.

17. Within the Parameters dialog box, in the Shakiness field, type **50**, and press the Enter key. Director will update the Shake behavior's parameters for the filled ellipse.

18. Within the Toolbar, click your mouse on the Play button. Director will preview your movie within the Stage window. Notice how the filled ellipse shakes and distorts much more violently than before.

19. Within the Toolbar, click your mouse on the Rewind button. Director will return your movie to its original state within the Stage window.

By now, you should be ready to start programming with Lingo. The best way to develop your programming skills is to use them. Just follow the instructions in this appendix and in the chapters in this book. If you have a question about any specific Lingo command or simply want to know more about the commands available to you, refer to Appendix B, "Lingo Quick Reference."

Appendix B
Lingo Quick Reference

Appendix

B

- Conditionals

- Events

- Lists

- Loops

- Math

- Navigation

- Sounds

- Sprites

- Strings

- Syntax

CONDITIONALS

case...of—A structure that executes code only if the specified variable matches an expression. You must close the conditional with an *end case* statement, as shown in the following code:

```
case the key of
  "1": play "Game"
  "a", "A": play "A"
  return:
    shots = shots + 1
    play "Shoot"
end case
```

If you want different code to execute only if no other conditions are met, you must add an *otherwise* statement, as shown in the following code:

```
case the key of
  "1": play "Game"
  "a", "A": play "A"
  return:
    shots = shots + 1
    play "Shoot"
  otherwise play "Exit"
end case
```

if...then—A structure that executes code only if the specified expression has a Boolean value of true. If the statement contains multiple lines of code, you must close the conditional with an *end if* statement, as shown in the following code:

```
if num = 1 then
  the floatPrecision = 5
  alert(string(pi))
end if
```

If you want different code to execute only if no other conditions are met, you must add *else* or *else if* statements, as shown in the following code:

```
if num = 1 then
  the floatPrecision = 2
  alert(string(money))
else if num = 2 then
  the floatPrecision = 0
  alert(string(dollars))
else
  the floatPrecision = -5
  alert(string(floatNum))
end if
```

EVENTS

keyPressed—A function that indicates whether or not the user is holding down a particular key. The following code makes a noise when the Enter key is down:

```
if keyPressed(return) then beep
```

on activateWindow—A handler that executes when the movie's window becomes active.

on beginSprite—A handler that executes once when a sprite first appears in the Score. Its common usage is to initialize property variables.

on deactivateWindow—A handler that executes when the movie's window becomes inactive.

on endSprite—A handler that executes once when a sprite last appears in the Score.

on enterFrame—A handler that executes at the beginning of each frame.

on exitFrame—A handler that executes at the end of each frame.

on idle—A handler that executes in a frame script or movie script when no other event is executing.

on keyDown—A handler that executes each time the user presses a key. The handler will not work in a behavior script unless it is that of an editable field.

on keyUp—A handler that executes each time the user releases a key. The handler will not work in a behavior script unless it is that of an editable field.

on mouseDown—A handler that executes each time the user presses the left mouse button.

on mouseEnter—A handler that executes each time the mouse cursor moves within the bounds of an associated object.

on mouseLeave—A handler that executes each time the mouse cursor moves outside the bounds of an associated object.

on mouseUp—A handler that executes every time the user releases the left mouse button.

on mouseWithin—A handler that executes constantly while the mouse cursor is within the bounds of an associated object.

on prepareFrame—A handler that executes just before the beginning of each frame.

on prepareMovie—A handler that executes once just before the movie begins. Its common usage is to initialize global variables.

on resizeWindow—A handler that executes when the user resizes a movie's window.

on rightMouseDown—A handler that executes each time the user presses the right mouse button.

on rightMouseUp—A handler that executes each time the user releases the right mouse button.

on startMovie—A handler that executes once at the beginning of the movie's first frame.

on stopMovie—A handler that executes once at the end of the movie's last frame.

on timeOut—A handler that executes when the mouse and keyboard are inactive for a set amount of time.

on moveWindow—A handler that executes when the user drags a movie's window to a new location.

on zoomWindow—A handler that executes when the user minimizes or maximizes a movie's window.

the clickLoc—A property that indicates the last point within the Stage clicked by the user.

the clickOn—A property that indicates the last sprite clicked by the user.

the commandDown—A property that indicates whether or not the user is holding down the Ctrl key (Command on Macintosh).

the doubleClick—A property that indicates whether or not the user has just double-clicked.

the idleHandlerPeriod—A property that indicates how many ticks may pass before the movie calls the *idle* handler.

the key—A property that indicates the character value of the last key pressed by the user.

the keyCode—A property that indicates the numerical value of the last key pressed by the user.

the keyDownScript—A property that indicates with a string value the commands to execute each time the user presses a key within the movie.

the keyUpScript—A property that indicates with a string value the commands to execute each time the user releases a key within the movie.

the mouseChar—A property that indicates the number of the character directly under the mouse cursor within a field. If the mouse cursor is not over a character, the result is -1.

the mouseDown—A property that indicates whether or not the user is holding down the left mouse button.

the mouseDownScript—A property that indicates with a string value the commands to execute each time the user presses the left mouse button within the movie.

the mouseH—A property that indicates the horizontal position of the mouse cursor within the Stage.

the mouseItem—A property that indicates the number of the item directly under the mouse cursor within a field. If the mouse cursor is not over an item, the result is -1.

the mouseLine—A property that indicates the number of the line directly under the mouse cursor within a field. If the mouse cursor is not over a line, the result is -1.

the mouseLoc—A property that indicates the position of the mouse cursor within the Stage.

the mouseMember—A property that indicates the cast member of the sprite directly under the mouse cursor within the Stage. If the mouse cursor is not over a sprite, the result is void.

the mouseUpScript—A property that indicates with a string value the commands to execute each time the user releases the left mouse button within the movie.

the mouseV—A property that indicates the vertical position of the mouse cursor within the Stage.

the mouseWord—A property that indicates the number of the word directly under the mouse cursor within a field. If the mouse cursor is not over a word, the result is -1.

the rightMouseDown—A property that indicates whether or not the user is holding down the right mouse button.

the optionDown—A property that indicates whether or not the user is holding down the Alt key (Option on Macintosh).

the rollOver—A property that indicates the sprite the mouse cursor is currently over.

the shiftDown—A property that indicates whether or not the user is holding down the Shift key.

the timeOutLength—A property that indicates how many ticks may pass before the movie calls the *timeOut* handler.

the timeOutScript—A property that indicates with a string value the commands to execute when the mouse and keyboard are inactive for a set amount of time.

LISTS

add—A function that creates a new item of a specified value in a linear list. If the list is sorted, the item is added to its proper alphanumeric position in the list. Otherwise, the item is appended, as shown in the following code:

```
sizes = ["S", "M", "L"]
sizes.add("XL")
if sizes[4] = "XL" then beep
```

addAt—A function that creates a new item of a specified value in a specified location of a linear list, as shown in the following code:

```
sizes = ["S", "M", "L"]
sizes.addAt(2, "XL")
if sizes[2] = "XL" then beep
```

addProp—A function that adds a symbol with a specified value to a property list, as shown in the following code:

```
sizes = [#S:2, #M:5, #L:10]
sizes.addProp(#XL, 20)
if sizes.XL = 20 then beep
```

append—A function that creates a new item of a specified value at the end of a linear list.

count—A list property that indicates how many items exist in a given list, as shown in the following code:

```
if [1, 2, 3, 4, 5].count = 5 then beep
```

deleteAll—A statement that removes all the items from a specified list, as shown in the following code:

```
deleteAll numList
```

deleteAt—A function that removes an item from a specified position in a list, as shown in the following code:

```
numList.deleteAt(4)
```

deleteOne—A function that removes the first occurrence of a specified value from a list, as shown in the following code:

```
propList.deleteOne("D")
```

deleteProp—A function that removes a specified symbol from a property list, as shown in the following code:

```
propList.deleteProp(#d)
```

duplicate—A function that returns a copy of a specified list, as shown in the following code:

```
newList = duplicate(oldList)
```

findPos—A function that returns the position of a specified symbol in a property list, as shown in the following code:

```
propList = [#a:"A", #b:"B", #c:"C", #d:"D"]
if propList.findPos(#c) = 3 then beep
```

getLast—A function that returns the last value in a list, as shown in the following code:

```
propList = [#a:"A", #b:"B", #c:"C", #d:"D"]
if getLast(propList) = "D" then beep
```

getOne—A function that returns the position of the first occurrence of a specified value in a linear list or the symbol of the first occurrence of a specified value in a property list, as shown in the following code:

```
charList = ["A", "B", "C", "D"]
if charList.getOne("C") = 3 then beep
propList = [#a:"A", #b:"B", #c:"C", #d:"D"]
if propList.getOne("C") = #c then beep
```

getPos—A function that returns the position of the first occurrence of a specified value in a property list, as shown in the following code:

```
propList = [#a:"A", #b:"B", #c:"C", #d:"D"]
if propList.getPos("C") = 3 then beep
```

max—A function that returns the highest value in a list or a series of numbers, as shown in the following code:

```
numList = [5, 8, 2, 3]
if max(numList) = 8 then beep
if max(5, 8, 2, 3) = 8 then beep
```

min—A function that returns the lowest value in a list or a series of numbers.

sort—A statement that sorts the items in a list alphanumerically, as shown in the following code:

```
epicList = ["e", "p", "i", "c"]
sort epicList
if epicList = ["c", "e", "i", "p"] then beep
```

LOOPS

exit repeat—A statement that tells Director to abandon the loop and execute the line following the *end repeat* statement.

next repeat—A statement that tells Director to execute the next step in the loop.

repeat while—A structure that executes code over and over as long as the specified expression has a Boolean value of true. You must close the loop with an *end repeat* statement, as shown in the following code:

```
repeat while the mouseDown
   nothing
end repeat
```

repeat with...down to—A structure that executes code over and over subtracting 1 from the loop control variable each time, as shown in the following code:

```
repeat with count = 10 down to 0
   countDown = countDown && count & ","
end repeat
```

repeat with...in—A structure that executes code over and over for each item in a list, as shown in the following code:

```
repeat with count in [10, 5, 2]
   intNum = intNum + random(count)
end repeat
```

repeat with...to—A structure that executes code over and over adding 1 to the loop control variable each time, as shown in the following code:

```
repeat with count = 1 to 5
   intNum = power(intNum, count)
end repeat
```

MATH

+ (addition)—An operator that finds the sum of two numbers in an addition problem.

/ (division)—An operator that finds the quotient of two numbers in a division problem.

* (multiplication)—An operator that finds the product of two numbers in a multiplication problem.

- (subtraction)—An operator that finds the difference of two numbers in a subtraction problem.

abs—A function that returns the absolute value (distance from zero) of a specified numerical expression.

atan—A function that returns the arctangent expressed in radians of a specified number.

cos—A function that returns the cosine of a specified angle expressed in radians.

exp—A function that returns e (the natural logarithm base) to a specified power.

float—A function that returns the decimal number value of a specified expression.

floatP—A function that indicates whether or not a specified expression is a decimal number.

integer—A function that returns the integer value of a specified expression.

integerP—A function that indicates whether or not a specified expression is an integer.

log—A function that returns the natural log (base e) of a specified numerical expression.

mod—An operator that finds the integer remainder as opposed to the quotient of two numbers in a division problem. The remainder of 5 divided by 2 is equal to 1, as shown in the following code:

```
if 5 mod 2 = 1 then beep
```

pi—A function that returns the approximate value of pi (3.14159265...).

power—A function that returns the value of a numerical expression to a specified power. The value of 2 to the third power is equal to 8, as shown in the following code:

```
if power(2, 3) = 8 then beep
```

random—A function that returns a random integer from 1 to a specified number.

sin—A function that returns the sine of a specified angle expressed in radians.

sqrt—A function that returns the square root of a specified numerical expression.

tan—A function that returns the tangent of a specified angle expressed in radians.

the floatPrecision—A property that indicates how many digits past the decimal to display of decimal numbers. If the property is set to 0, all decimal numbers round off to integers. If the property is set to a negative number, no trailing zeros will appear.

NAVIGATION

go—A statement that tells Director to move to a specified frame or marker of the movie, as shown in the following code:

```
go 20
go "Section 2"
go marker(2)
```

go next—A statement that tells Director to move to the next marker after the current frame of the movie.

go previous—A statement that tells Director to move to the previous marker before the current frame of the movie.

goToNetPage—A function that tells Director to open the default Internet browser and load a specified site, as shown in the following code:

```
goToNetPage("http://www.epicsoftware.com")
```

play—A statement that tells Director to move to a specified frame or marker of the movie and begin playing.

SOUNDS

beep—A command that plays the system beep sound.

fadeIn—A function that fades a sound channel to full volume in a specified number of milliseconds, as shown in the following code:

```
sound(2).fadeIn(5000)
```

fadeOut—A function that fades a sound channel to silence in a specified number of milliseconds.

fadeTo—A function that fades a sound channel to a specified volume in a specified number of milliseconds, as shown in the following code:

```
sound(2).fadeTo(128, 2500)
```

pan—A sound property that sets the balance between the left and right portions of a particular sound channel. The property can range anywhere from -100 (left) to 100 (right), as shown in the following code:

```
sound(1).pan = -50
sound(2).pan = 50
```

pause—A function that tells Director to stop playing but remember the position of a specified sound in a particular sound channel, as shown in the following code:

```
sound(2).pause()
```

play—A function that tells Director to start playing a specified sound in a particular sound channel, as shown in the following code:

```
sound(2).play(member("fire"))
```

puppetSound—A function that places a sound under Lingo control and tells Director to begin playing it in a specified channel, as shown in the following code:

```
puppetSound(2, "fire")
```

To tell Director to stop playing a sound, you must replace the sound's name with 0, as shown in the following code:

```
puppetSound(2, 0)
```

soundBusy—A function that indicates whether or not a specified sound channel is currently playing a sound, as shown in the following code:

```
if soundBusy(2) then puppetSound(2, 0)
```

stop—A function that tells Director to stop playing sound in a particular sound channel, as shown in the following code:

```
sound(2).stop()
```

the soundEnabled—A property that indicates whether or not sound is enabled within the movie.

volume—A sound property that sets the volume of a particular sound channel. The property can range anywhere from 0 to 256.

SPRITES

bgColor—A sprite property that indicates the background color of a particular sprite, as shown in the following code:

```
sprite(2).bgColor = rgb(64, 255, 128)
```

blend—A sprite property that indicates the visibility of a particular sprite.

bottom—A sprite property that indicates the location of the bottom edge of a particular sprite.

castLibNum—A sprite property that indicates the number of the cast that contains the cast member being used by a particular sprite.

color—A sprite property that indicates foreground color of a particular sprite.

constraint—A sprite property that indicates the sprite within whose edges a particular sprite's movement is constrained, as shown in the following code:

```
sprite(2).constraint = 3
```

editable—A sprite property that indicates whether or not the user can edit a particular field.

flipH—A sprite property that indicates whether or not a particular sprite is mirrored.

flipV—A sprite property that indicates whether or not a particular sprite is flipped.

height—A sprite property that indicates the height of a particular sprite.

hilite—A statement that tells Director to highlight a specified section of a field, as shown in the following code:

```
hilite member("Text Field").line[5].word[8]
```

ink—A sprite property that indicates the ink effect of a particular sprite. You can set the property to 0 (copy), 8 (matte), 32 (blend), or 36 (background transparent), as shown in the following code:

```
sprite(2).ink = 36
```

intersects—A function that indicates whether or not a particular sprite touches a specified sprite, as shown in the following code:

```
if sprite(2).intersects(3) then beep
```

left—A sprite property that indicates the location of the left edge of a particular sprite.

loc—A sprite property that indicates the position of a particular sprite within the Stage.

locH—A sprite property that indicates the horizontal position of a particular sprite within the Stage.

locV—A sprite property that indicates the vertical position of a particular sprite within the Stage.

locZ—A sprite property that indicates the layer of a particular sprite within the Stage. Sprites with a higher *locZ* value appear in front of other sprites. If two sprites have the same *locZ* value, their channel order determines the layer.

member—A sprite property that indicates the cast member being used by a particular sprite.

memberNum—A sprite property that indicates the number of the cast member being used by a particular sprite.

moveableSprite—A sprite property that indicates whether or not the user can drag a particular sprite across the Stage.

puppet—A sprite property that indicates whether or not a particular sprite is under Lingo control.

quad—A sprite property that indicates the coordinates of the upper-left, upper-right, lower-left, and lower-right corners of a particular sprite, as shown in the following code:

```
sprite(2).quad = [point(10, 10), point(620, 20), point(610, 450), point(40, 440)]
```

right—A sprite property that indicates the location of the right edge of a particular sprite.

rotation—A sprite property that indicates the degree of rotation of a particular sprite. The property can range from 0 to 359.

sendAllSprites—A function that sends a message to all scripts attached to all sprites within a movie, as shown in the following code:

```
sendAllSprites(#mouseDown)
sendAllSprites(#move, 2, -5)
```

sendSprite—A function that sends a message to all scripts attached to a specified sprite, as shown in the following code:

```
sendSprite(2, #mouseDown)
sendSprite(2, #move, 2, -5)
```

skew—A sprite property that indicates the degree of tilt of a particular sprite. The property can range from -90 to 90.

sprite—A function that returns the sprite associated with a specified string name or integer number.

spriteNum—A sprite property that indicates the number of a particular sprite.

top—A sprite property that indicates the location of the top edge of a particular sprite.

trails—A sprite property that indicates whether or not a particular sprite leaves a trail behind as it moves across the Stage.

visible—A sprite property that indicates whether or not a particular sprite is visible.

width—A sprite property that indicates the width of a particular sprite.

within—A function that indicates whether or not a particular sprite is completely within the edges of a specified sprite, as shown in the following code:

```
if sprite(2).within(3) then beep
```

STRINGS

& (concatenation)—An operator that concatenates two strings into one, as shown in the following code:

```
if "Button" & count = "Button5" then beep
```

&& (word concatenation)—An operator that concatenates two strings into one with a space between them, as shown in the following code:

```
if "Button" && count = "Button 5" then beep
```

backspace—A constant that represents the backspace character (Delete on Macintosh).

char—A string property that consists of a list of all the characters within the string.

chars—A function that returns a specified section of a string, as shown in the following code:

```
if chars("epic software", 6, 9) = "soft" then beep
```

charToNum—A function that returns the numerical ASCII value of a specified character.

contains—An operator that tests to see if the first string value contains the second, as shown in the following code:

```
if "epic software" contains "soft" then beep
```

delete—A statement that deletes a specified section of a string, as shown in the following code:

```
sentence = "I never said that."
delete sentence.word[2]
if sentence = "I said that." then beep
```

do—A statement that translates a string value into a Lingo statement and then executes it, as shown in the following code:

```
command = "if true then"
do command && "beep"
```

empty—A constant that represents an empty string.

item—A string property that consists of a list of all the items within the string. Items are separated by the *itemDelimiter* property.

length—A string property that indicates the length in characters of the string.

line—A string property that consists of a list of all the lines within the string.

numToChar—A function that returns the ASCII character value of a specified number.

quote—A constant that represents the quote character.

return—A constant that represents the Enter character (Return on Macintosh).

space—A constant that represents the space character.

starts—An operator that tests to see if the first string value begins with the second, as shown in the following code:

```
if "epic software" starts "epic" then beep
```

string—A function that returns the string value of a specified expression.

stringP—A function that indicates whether or not a specified expression is a string.

tab—A constant that represents the Tab character.

the itemDelimiter—A property that indicates the character used to separate items. By default, the property is equal to a comma.

word—A string property that consists of a list of all the words within the string.

SYNTAX

— (comment)—An operator that tells Director to ignore any code following it in a line. Programmers use comments to explain code or to temporarily hide lines of code to aid in debugging.

\ (continuation)—An operator that, when placed at the end of a line, tells Director that the line of code continues onto the next line. If a line of code is long enough, Director will wrap it, but that is considered bad form.

= (equal to)—An operator that tests to see if two expressions are of equal value.

> (greater than)—An operator that tests to see if the first expression is greater than the second.

>= (greater than or equal to)—An operator that tests to see if the first expression is greater than or equal to the second.

< (less than)—An operator that tests to see if the first expression is less than the second.

<= (less than or equal to)—An operator that tests to see if the first expression is less than or equal to the second.

[...] (list)—Operators that indicate a list. Several values can be placed inside of the operators separated by commas.

<> (not equal to)—An operator that tests to see if two expressions are not of equal value.

(...) (parentheses)—Operators that indicate a group of arguments or expressions.

"..." (string)—Operators that indicate a string. Several characters can be placed inside the operators.

 # (symbol)—An operator that, when placed directly before a combination of characters beginning with an alphabetical character, indicates a symbol.

abort—A command that tells Director to exit all handlers or functions without executing any more code.

alert—A statement that plays a system beep sound and displays an alert dialog box containing a specified message, as shown in the following code:

```
alert("Something is wrong with your" && problem & "!")
```

and—An operator that tests to see if two expressions are both true.

appMinimize—A command that tells Director to minimize the movie's window.

end—A command that marks the end of handlers and functions.

exit—A command that tells Director to exit the current handler or function without executing any more code.

false—A constant that represents the numerical value of 0 or the Boolean value of false.

global—A statement that defines global variables.

halt—A command that tells Director to exit all handlers or functions without executing any more code and stop the movie entirely.

ilk—A function that returns the type of a specified object, as shown in the following code:

```
if ilk([1, 2, 3, 4]) = #list then beep
if ilk("epic software") = #string then beep
if ilk(the systemDate) = #date then beep
```

me—A variable that has no predefined meaning in Director, but is commonly used by convention. The variable often refers to the object affected by the current handler, which is passed as an argument, as shown in the following code:

```
on mouseDown me
   sprite(me.spriteNum).rotation = sprite(2).rotation
end
```

not—An operator that reverses the Boolean value of an expression, as shown in the following code:

```
if not false then beep
```

nothing—A command that does absolutely nothing. The command is often useful for making Director wait while a condition is true, as shown in the following code:

```
repeat while the commandDown and the optionDown
   nothing
end repeat
```

or—An operator that tests to see if at least one of two expressions is true.

point—A function that returns the point value of specified horizontal and vertical coordinates, as shown in the following code:

```
newPoint = point(320, 240)
```

property—A statement that defines local variables.

quit—A command that tells Director to stop the movie and close its window.

restart—A command that tells Director to stop the movie and restart the computer.

return—A statement that specifies the value that a function returns, as shown in the following code:

```
on double number
   return number*2
end
```

A function with a returned value can be treated as any other expression, as shown in the following code:

```
if double(16) = 32 then beep
```

rgb—A function that returns the color value of a specified amount of red, green, and blue. The arguments can range from 0 to 255, as shown in the following code:

```
newColor = rgb(64, 255, 128)
```

shutDown—A command that tells Director to stop the movie and shut down the computer.

stopEvent—A command that tells Director not to pass an event message to subsequent locations in the message hierarchy, as shown in the following code:

```
on keyDown me
  sprite(me.spriteNum).member.text = the key
  stopEvent
end
```

symbol—A function that returns the symbol value of a specified expression.

symbolP—A function that indicates whether or not a specified expression is a symbol.

true—A constant that represents the numerical value of 1 or the Boolean value of true.

updateStage—A command that tells Director to update the Stage immediately instead of only between frames. The command is useful for movies with slow frame rates.

void—A constant that represents the absence of a value.

Appendix C
What's on the CD-ROM

Appendix

C

- Running the CD-ROM with Windows 95/98/2000/NT

- Running the CD with Linux

The CD-ROM that accompanies this book contains both binaries and source code (when available) for SDL, OpenAL, IESDK, PrettyPoly, Mesa3D, SVGALib, and source code only for Linux Kernel versions 2.2.18, 2.4.0, and 2.4.1. The CD-ROM also has all the sample files that the author used throughout the book.

RUNNING THE CD-ROM WITH WINDOWS 95/98/2000/NT

To make the CD user-friendly and take less of your disk space, no installation is required to view the CD. This means that the only files transferred to your hard disk are the ones you choose to copy or install. You can run the CD on any operating system that can view files; however, not all the programs can be installed on all operating systems.

1. Insert the CD into the CD-ROM drive and close the tray.

2. Go to My Computer or Windows Explorer and double-click the CD-ROM drive.

3. Most of the files contained on the CD can be viewed with WINZIP.

RUNNING THE CD WITH LINUX

To make the CD user-friendly and take less of your disk space, no installation is required to view the CD. This means that the only files transferred to your hard disk are the ones you choose to copy or install. You can run the CD on any operating system that can view files; however, not all the programs can be installed on all operating systems.

1. Insert the CD into the CD-ROM drive and close the tray.

2. Either make sure that automount is running or mount the CD by issuing the mount command from a shell prompt.

3. Change to the root directory of the CD, usually /mnt/cdrom.

Most of the files contained on the CD will need to be uncompressed and un-tarred with the following commands:

gunzip *filename*

tar -xvf *filename*

Glossary

A

anti-aliasing The process of smoothing an image to avoid the appearance of jagged edges due to sharp changes in the colors of pixels.

application A program involving user interaction that is usually designed for practical purposes.

argument *See* parameter.

array *See* list.

ASCII The American Standard Code for Information Interchange.

B

behavior script A Lingo script designed to alter a single sprite as opposed to the entire program.

bitmap An array of values that make up an image of one or more colors.

Boolean Having to do with a value of either true or false.

bot A character in a game that is controlled completely by the computer.

bug An error or unintentional feature inside a program.

C

cast Stores scripts, images, sounds, and other media to be used within a program.

cast member A script, image, sound, or other medium stored within a cast to be used within a program.

cell A section of a channel that holds the contents of that channel for exactly one frame.

channel A numbered row of cells that represents a single layer of a Director movie.

character A single letter, numerical digit, or symbol that could be a component of a string.

color The predefined Lingo type consisting of a red value, a green value, and a blue value that indicate a single color.

commenting The process of hiding a line of source code from the rest of the program for the purpose of clarifying unclear source code or debugging a program.

compartmentalization The process of breaking programming code up into as many small reusable parts as possible.

conditional A structure that keeps one or several lines of code from being executed unless a specified condition is met.

constant A value that is incapable of changing its worth.

D

debugging The process of running an unfinished program over and over to discover unknown problems with its code.

Director The multimedia development utility created by Macromedia designed to make programming easy.

dot syntax The new style of Lingo programming that resembles mathematical equations.

E–F

effects channels The six channels that can hold effects such as transitions, sounds, and behaviors as opposed to visual sprites.

film loop A sort of cast member that can contain multiple frames and/or sprites within itself.

Flash The multimedia development utility created by Macromedia designed to let users create Internet content with vector graphics for quick downloads.

float The predefined Lingo type indicating decimal, or floating-point, numbers.

frame A numbered column of cells that represents a single point in a Director movie.

frame rate The number of frames that a movie displays per second.

function A section of code that executes only when it is specifically told to do so.

G

game A program involving user interaction and competition of some sort that is designed for entertainment purposes.

global variable A variable that exists from the point it was first assigned a value to the end of the handler or function in which it began.

graphic A visual representation of an item either directly or indirectly made up of pixels.

I

integer The predefined Lingo type indicating numbers that do not contain any decimal fractions.

interface The layout through which the player interacts with a game.

K–L

keyframe A frame of a movie that is designated to signify a major change in a sprite channel.

linear list A list variable that contains only a list of ordered values.

Lingo The programming language used to create scripts within Director.

list A single variable that holds zero or more values within itself.

local variable A variable that exists from the point it was first assigned a value to the end of the handler or function in which it began.

loop A structure that makes a group of code execute repeatedly as long as a specified condition is met.

M

mask An image used to indicate specific characteristics of corresponding points in an associated image.

member *See* cast member.

movie script A Lingo script designed to alter the entire program as opposed to a single sprite.

O

opacity The amount of visibility a visual item conveys.

opaque The characteristic of a visual item to be completely visible.

P

parameter A value passed to a function or behavior to be used as an internal variable.

pixel A single dot of color within a raster image or video buffer.

player The person playing a particular game.

point The predefined Lingo type consisting of a horizontal value and a vertical value that indicate a single two-dimensional location.

program A series of ordered instructions to the computer.

programmer The person writing a particular application or game.

property list A list variable that contains not only values, but also property names.

property variable A variable that exists only within a single script or as an attribute of a specified sprite.

pseudo-3D A type of environment that consists mainly of two-dimensional images that move around in a three-dimensional field.

pseudo-code Statements written almost as sentences that represent longer, more precise sections of programming code.

puppet A sound or sprite that is under Lingo control as opposed to Score control.

R

raster graphics Graphics that work directly with pixels instead of shapes.

registration point The point on a graphic element that positioning and rotation is based upon.

rotating The process of distorting a graphic element by changing its angular orientation.

S

Score The visual display of all frames, channels, and cells within a Director movie.

script A section of Lingo code that makes up exactly one member of a cast.

Shockwave The name given to all Internet content created with Director.

skewing The process of distorting a graphic element by slanting it horizontally.

sprite A representation of a visual cast member once it has been placed on the Stage or within the Score.

sprite channel *See* channel.

Stage The visual area of a Director movie where all action takes place.

string The predefined Lingo type indicating a group of zero or more characters organized in a specific order.

T

tick One sixtieth of a second.

translucency The characteristic of a visual item to be partially visible.

transparency The characteristic of a visual item to be completely invisible.

type A classification of a value such as integer, string, color, and so on.

U–V

user The person using a particular application or game.

value Any number, section of text, or other item of a set worth.

variable Constant letter or word that can represent a changing value.

vector graphics Graphics that work with shapes instead of directly with pixels.

verbose syntax The old style of Lingo programming that resembles English sentences.

visual channels All channels that can hold visual sprites as opposed to transitions, sounds, or behaviors.

void Without any set value.

W

word wrap Characteristic of a text field that allows entire words to move to the next line when the preset width of the field would otherwise be exceeded.

Index

Macromedia Director Game Development
From Concept to Creation

3D environments, 186–187
    character movement, 196–198
    depth illusion, 190–192

A

accessing
    Cast window, 17
    Paint window, 18
    Property Inspector window, 11
    Score window, 13
    Script window, 24, 272
    Tool Palette window, 9–10
    Vector Shape window, 20
adding
    bell sounds, 67–69
    cast members to Stage, 35–38
    color to text, 10
    Paper Mask bitmap to Painter game, 56–57
    Scramble button to Scramble game, 35–38
    text to Stage, 9–10
addR property, 97
addX property, 97
addY property, 97, 99
Air Brush button, 18
Air Brush Settings dialog box, 19
airbrush effects, 62
Alphabetical Lingo button, 274–275
animations
    film loop
        displaying, 146–147
        editing, 147–151
    sequence
        converting into film loops, 144–146
        setting up, 141–144
    walking, 131–135
anti-aliasing, 18
arguments, 5, 281
Arrow Tool button, 211
attraction variables, 167
AVI format, exporting video files with, 233–236

B

Background Color button, 82
Background Color swatch, 81
Backyard Brawl game, 172
    fighters
        activating bot control for, 181–182
        assigning characters to, 176–178
        indicating pain with ink effects, 182–183
        inflicting damage on, 178–181
    Lingo scripts, 174–176
    logic of, 173–174

opening, 173
    saving to hard drive, 173
beginSprite handler, 97
behaviors
    Bomb, 194–195
    creating, 42–46
    defined, 281
    Entity, 192–193
    implementing, 281–286
    Player Control, 196–197
Behaviors Online Web site, 256
bell sound effects, 67–69
bitmaps
    graphics, creating, 18
    sequential, exporting, 236–238
Blend option, 19
blend property, 110
    creating behaviors with, 43–46
board games, 106
    game pieces
        allowing movement of, 111–114
        placing on board, 116–118
    updating, 109–111
board list variables, 110–111
boardString command, 86
Bomb behaviors, 194–195
boolean variables, 278
Borland C++, 8
bots
    bot control, activating, 181–182
    defined, 181
Brush button, 18
bugs, 6
buttons
    Air Brush, 18
    Alphabetical Lingo, 274–275
    Arrow Tool, 211
    Background Color, 82
    Brush, 18
    Cast Member Script, 35
    Cast View Style, 17
    Cast Window, 17
    Categorized Lingo, 275–276
    Choose Cast, 33
    Color, 10
    Create New Folder, 29
    Export Frame Range, 231
    Filled Ellipse, 21, 285
    Filled Rectangle, 20
    Filled Round Rectangle, 21, 205
    Foreground Color, 18
    Gradient, 21, 206
    Gradient Color, 21, 206

312

LICENSE AGREEMENT/NOTICE OF LIMITED WARRANTY

By opening the sealed disc container in this book, you agree to the following terms and conditions. If, upon reading the following license agreement and notice of limited warranty, you cannot agree to the terms and conditions set forth, return the unused book with unopened disc to the place where you purchased it for a refund.

License:
The enclosed software is copyrighted by the copyright holder(s) indicated on the software disc. You are licensed to copy the software onto a single computer for use by a single concurrent user and to a backup disk. You may not reproduce, make copies, or distribute copies or rent or lease the software in whole or in part, except with written permission of the copyright holder(s). You may transfer the enclosed disc only together with this license, and only if you destroy all other copies of the software and the transferee agrees to the terms of the license. You may not decompile, reverse assemble, or reverse engineer the software.

Notice of Limited Warranty:
The enclosed disc is warranted by Prima Publishing to be free of physical defects in materials and workmanship for a period of sixty (60) days from end user's purchase of the book/disc combination. During the sixty-day term of the limited warranty, Prima will provide a replacement disc upon the return of a defective disc.

Limited Liability:
The sole remedy for breach of this limited warranty shall consist entirely of replacement of the defective disc. IN NO EVENT SHALL PRIMA OR THE AUTHORS BE LIABLE FOR ANY other damages, including loss or corruption of data, changes in the functional characteristics of the hardware or operating system, deleterious interaction with other software, or any other special, incidental, or consequential DAMAGES that may arise, even if Prima and/or the author have previously been notified that the possibility of such damages exists.

Disclaimer of Warranties:
Prima and the authors specifically disclaim any and all other warranties, either express or implied, including warranties of merchantability, suitability to a particular task or purpose, or freedom from errors. Some states do not allow for EXCLUSION of implied warranties or limitation of incidental or consequential damages, so these limitations may not apply to you.

Other:
This Agreement is governed by the laws of the State of California without regard to choice of law principles. The United Convention of Contracts for the International Sale of Goods is specifically disclaimed. This Agreement constitutes the entire agreement

LICENSE AGREEMENT/NOTICE OF LIMITED WARRANTY

By opening the sealed disc container in this book, you agree to the following terms and conditions. If, upon reading the following license agreement and notice of limited warranty, you cannot agree to the terms and conditions set forth, return the unused book with unopened disc to the place where you purchased it for a refund.

License:
The enclosed software is copyrighted by the copyright holder(s) indicated on the software disc. You are licensed to copy the software onto a single computer for use by a single concurrent user and to a backup disk. You may not reproduce, make copies, or distribute copies or rent or lease the software in whole or in part, except with written permission of the copyright holder(s). You may transfer the enclosed disc only together with this license, and only if you destroy all other copies of the software and the transferee agrees to the terms of the license. You may not decompile, reverse assemble, or reverse engineer the software.

Notice of Limited Warranty:
The enclosed disc is warranted by Prima Publishing to be free of physical defects in materials and workmanship for a period of sixty (60) days from end user's purchase of the book/disc combination. During the sixty-day term of the limited warranty, Prima will provide a replacement disc upon the return of a defective disc.

Limited Liability:
The sole remedy for breach of this limited warranty shall consist entirely of replacement of the defective disc. IN NO EVENT SHALL PRIMA OR THE AUTHORS BE LIABLE FOR ANY other damages, including loss or corruption of data, changes in the functional characteristics of the hardware or operating system, deleterious interaction with other software, or any other special, incidental, or consequential DAMAGES that may arise, even if Prima and/or the author have previously been notified that the possibility of such damages exists.

Disclaimer of Warranties:
Prima and the authors specifically disclaim any and all other warranties, either express or implied, including warranties of merchantability, suitability to a particular task or purpose, or freedom from errors. Some states do not allow for EXCLUSION of implied warranties or limitation of incidental or consequential damages, so these limitations may not apply to you.

Other:
This Agreement is governed by the laws of the State of California without regard to choice of law principles. The United Convention of Contracts for the International Sale of Goods is specifically disclaimed. This Agreement constitutes the entire agreement